For Cicci and Bibi, with all my love – always.

SKYE McALPINE

THE CHRISTMAS COMPANION

BLOOMSBURY PUBLISHING
LONDON · OXFORD · NEW YORK · NEW DELHI · SYDNEY

Contents

This bow indicates a recipe or a homemade festive decoration that makes an excellent gift.

Making Merry

Your Christmas

If Only It Could Be Christmas Every Day

The chance to write this book is, in so many ways, a dream come true for me. I love Christmas. I have always loved Christmas. I love the bonhomie and the conviviality and the excess of it all: the food, the sweets, the brandy-laden puddings, the rustle of tissue paper on Christmas morning, the jolliness of sing-along carols. I love that sweet, outdoorsy smell of a real fir tree and the twinkling lights in the street at night. I even love how bustling and busy the shops get in that last mad rush before the day itself. I love it all. So, to have the excuse to lose myself here in the unadulterated joy of egg nog-fuelled holiday baking, to conjure up festive menu upon festive menu for family and friends, this is truly my happiest place.

Before we really get started, I should say that the holidays should never feel like work: there's plenty to do and plenty more to be getting on with in the pages that follow, but it's important to me that none of it reads like it's a 'to-do' or 'should-do' list. If we're going to think in terms of 'shoulds' (and I am loath to do so, because it is 'shoulds' and 'musts' that suck all the joy out of the holidays): cosy, relaxed, perfect and memorable in its utterly human imperfection is exactly how Christmas 'should' be. And that's the kind of Christmas you'll find here.

I wrote this book imagining that you would dip in and out of each chapter, taking from here and there what is most useful to you and ignoring all the rest, with no pressure to 'do Christmas' in any one 'right' or 'wrong' way. Maybe you want to host a big holiday party this year or maybe you don't; maybe you've taken it upon yourself to run the school bake sale and need festive recipes you can churn out on a semi-industrial scale; maybe you're cooking Christmas lunch (so many options here), or maybe that's someone else's responsibility, and what you're looking for is a thoughtful edible or decorative gift for your host. I don't claim to have all the answers, but, if you too love the fanfare of Christmas, I trust you'll find lots here by way of inspiration and ideas. Equally, if the thought of the holidays fills you with a looming sense of dread, I hope you'll find solace in these pages, along with the support to get you through – even come to enjoy – this festive season. Above all, I hope you'll find recipes here for your own happy Christmas.

In this book, you will discover menu suggestions for Christmas lunch, whether you're feeding two or twenty. You'll also find ideas for what to cook in the days leading up to, as well as in the languorous wake of, 25 December, stretching from Thanksgiving in late November to the quiet, happy-tired aftermath of New Year.

There are pages of inspiration for decorating your home, your table, your tree; recipes for edible gifts; and instructions on everything from making an advent calendar to crafting your own crackers (far easier than it sounds, trust me). And because, for all my love of Christmas, I too sometimes (often) find the busy-ness and the weight of expectation of it all overwhelming, you'll see I've also made plenty of suggestions for ways to make life easier. I've given you a few thoughts on how to plan the holiday season so it comes together more effortlessly; tips on what you can prepare in advance (if you're that kind of organised); quick fixes for the moment when you realise you weren't that kind of organised, but rather wish you might have been; instructions for cooking all sorts of different birds, using up leftovers, accommodating various dietary requirements and quick ways to decorate a Christmas cake; and lots of useful lists. This book is full of lists.

It will come as no surprise that what I love most about Christmas is the food. I, greedily, just love to eat, so I look forward, year round, to the excuse to do so: panettone, fruit cake laden with marzipan, gingerbread, turkey sandwiches dripping with cranberry sauce and chestnut-laced stuffing... For all the festive frippery and wreath-making and table-dressing in these pages (because I love that, too), food is at the centre of this book, just as it is at the heart of my holiday season, whether I'm celebrating with friends in the build-up to Christmas proper or sitting down to a feast on the day itself.

Cooking for Christmas – when we get the balance right and don't overstretch ourselves (I emphasise this caveat, because it's an important one) – is infinitely more fun than cooking over the rest of the year. There is a treat-like quality about what we eat at Christmas, a unique mix of the celebratory and the deeply comforting, which makes Christmas food very gratifying to eat, of course, but also hugely rewarding to prepare and to share. Even those who don't cook much often relish being in the kitchen at Christmas: the one moment in the year when we have the time (or more time, anyhow) and the excuse; when we have the people we love most gathered around us to share our meal with. Even in the absence of those we love, the food we eat over the holidays is often so laced with tradition and nostalgia that it becomes a way of bringing those poignantly absent that little bit closer, of evoking their presence. I'm a firm believer that food on a plate is rarely just the sum of its ingredients. It has meaning and emotion and conjures feelings as well as taste, and at Christmas this is most especially the case.

I've painted an idyllic picture of what it means to cook at Christmas, but I know things don't always quite pan out as we hope. Life is messy and complicated, and it doesn't stop being so because of the holidays; but Christmas cooking is nothing to fear. It might be perhaps a little chaotic – many of the best Christmases are – but there is nothing innately tricky about roasting a bird or baking a fruit cake, trust me: I can show you how. A turkey is effectively just a big chicken, while Christmas cake is the most forgiving of all cakes to bake. And if, indeed, that really doesn't sit comfortably, then there is so much else that is

good which we can happily cook, enjoy and call 'Christmas'. I find that the real difficulty is resisting the temptation to be a perfectionist, remembering that the holidays are just that: a time for your favourite things and your favourite people, not for perfection or for performance. Though this is a book about all that we can do to celebrate at this time of year, all the recipes we can bake and the dishes we can feast upon, I have come to understand that enjoying Christmas, ironically, is as much about what we choose not to do, the things we let go, as it is about all that we *do* do. Holding on to this belief, I find, can be helpful in those moments (and they come for us all) when our plans are not going to plan.

෴

As with all my cookbooks, there is an Italian flavour to many of these recipes. I was born British, but grew up in Italy. One of the privileges of being from one place and growing up in another is that you're blessed with the luxury of picking and choosing traditions from across both cultures. When I was a child, we would always celebrate Christmas twice: on Christmas Eve with fish and seafood, panettone and pandoro, as the Italians do, with Italian friends; and then again, for a second time, on Christmas Day, with stockings, crackers, turkey and all the trimmings, as my mother does it, and in the British way. Still now, there is so much about what and how we as a family eat, cook and celebrate at Christmastime that is an idiosyncratic Anglo-Italian mix, now with an added Antipodean flourish introduced by my Australian husband, who was brought up eating ice cream on the beach on Christmas Day. There is such magic in Christmas traditions, but as I grow older, I recognise that it's a very special thing to make new traditions too: our own family Christmas is ever-evolving, ever-growing and ever-changing, and I wouldn't have it any other way.

Lastly, I feel it's important to acknowledge that, in this book, I paint a picture of lightness: I list all the things I love most about Christmas and revel in them unabashedly. This is because Christmas is, for me, overwhelmingly a happy time: all the food and decorations and jolly bits I so love make my days and my world feel lighter. But I know the holidays carry very different meaning for each of us, just as they can carry a different meaning at different stages in our lives.

Some of us grow up with a wealth, or perhaps a weight, of Christmas traditions, others learn to forge our own precious traditions later in life. Like a magnifying glass, Christmas has a way of amplifying our feelings, sometimes for the better, but at other times also for the worse. For all the excitement and joy that the festivities bring, they can also shine a searingly bright light on what we don't have, but very much wish we did. The year after my father died, for example, was a difficult Christmas; no amount of holiday baking or spoiling gifts could change that, though it did nourish me in some way with a feeling of hope.

The perfect Christmas is a chimera: there is no such thing; just as, in truth, there is no one recipe for a happy Christmas. However, there are things that you can do to make your Christmas happier, perhaps even a little magical, and that's what you will find here. My greatest hope for this book is that it inspires you to create the Christmas you wish for: that it prompts you to step away from the everyday grind of real life, to shine a light at this darkest point of the year. To revel in the childish excitement for which the holidays provide such a happy excuse... if only for a moment. And because I forever hold tightly on to the wish that it could be Christmas every day, I hope you'll carry some of that joyful holiday spirit, much of the fun and the food and the magic, beyond the strict seasonal confines defined by convention and into your everyday life.

Magic Making

....

In those last few weeks before Christmas, I like to wake up before everyone else in the house. I creep out of bed while it's still dark, slip my feet into warm slippers, shuffle quietly into the kitchen (taking care not to wake the others) and make myself a mug of tea. Then I go and admire the Christmas tree. I'll sit on the sofa, with my tea, gazing at the tree for a good chunk of time, wallowing in its sweet, I-can't-wait-until-it's-Christmas scent and shimmering lights, soaking up the magic. Because it is magic. One of the things I love most about Christmas is the excuse to make magic and to live amid it, if only for those few weeks.

You'll see that this book comes in three parts. The middle part is a collection of recipes and needs little by way of explanation or introduction. The third part is formed of ideas about how to throw a happy Christmas, whether you're hosting the masses or hunkering down with just your nearest. But this first part is a tangle of those other bits and bobs – decorating, planning and so on – that go a long way to making Christmas feel like Christmas. And so I've called it 'magic making', because that's what you are doing when you decorate the tree or hang a wreath from the front door or find someone that perfect present. In each of these little things, you make magic.

Just as there is no expectation for you to cook every single recipe listed in this book, the intention here is to offer inspiration and how-tos for you to pick and choose from as you like. You'll find everything from ideas for edible ornaments to hang from the tree, to instructions for fashioning a festive wreath for the front door. I'm conscious that taking on any sort of crafting project, most especially at this busy time of year, might feel daunting. That's why you'll see that the ideas and recipes here are all easy for even the most cack-handed of people, like me, to recreate: simple tricks for beautiful things you can make out of little or nothing.

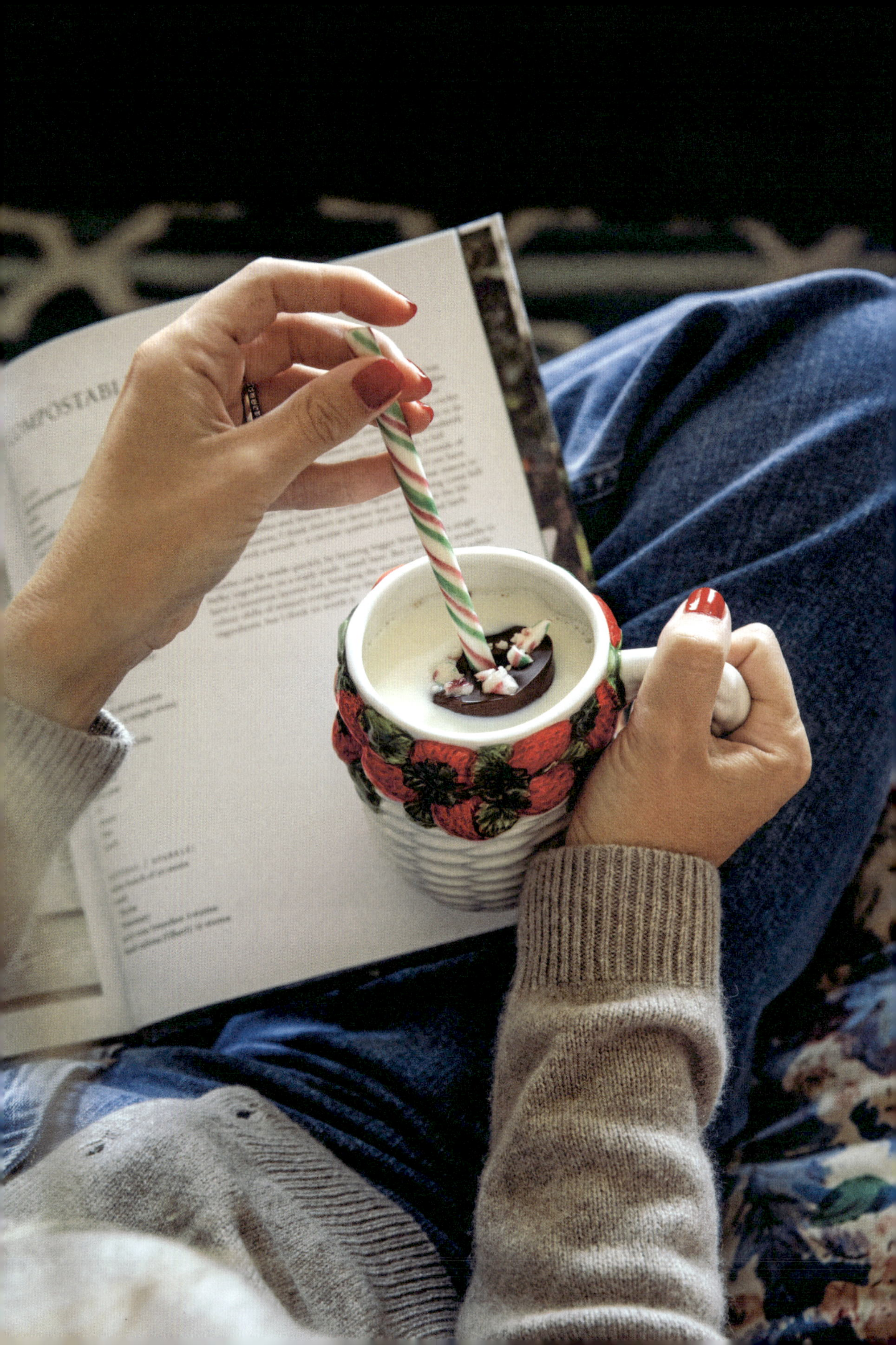

Start with a Plan

So many of the best things in life begin with a list: a packing list for a holiday, a wish list for your birthday, a guest list for a party, even a humble to-do list has a certain pleasingly hopeful quality about it. Christmas is no exception: the very best Christmases all start with a list. You can start your own on page 349.

This is largely for practical reasons: a solid plan will help you breeze through the season. But there's also an innate magic to the ritual of planning for the holidays: I love that moment when I sit down with a cup of tea, or a mug of hot chocolate, and start making Christmas happen. When I was younger, I used to take disproportionate pleasure in reading Christmas cookbooks; in fact, I still do. But back then, I read not because I planned on cooking from any of those books, but simply because I enjoyed their familiar, pleasingly formulaic structure, like reading a storybook when I already knew the ending. My favourite bit was those pages at the very beginning, those in which the author draws out a timeline for Christmas and tells you – in delicious, punctilious detail – exactly what you need to do and when you need to do it. In part, this appealed to the child in me who sought comfort and stability, who relished organising her pencils and books by colour (which I still do, by the way); but mostly, I think, I enjoyed these festive calendars because they seemed to bring Christmas closer. That's the magic of planning for the holidays: it draws Christmas out, it makes it start earlier, last longer and feel better.

The truth is there is always more to do over Christmas than there is time to do it, so the secret to setting yourself up to really enjoy the holidays, not just muster your way through, is to plan well and do as much of the prep as far ahead as you can. And while it might feel as though I'm just adding to everything you already have to do with all this talk of lists and timetables, trust me when I say that, conversely – and, I'll admit, somewhat counter-intuitively – taking the time to work things through properly before wading into the celebrations will make life so very much easier in the long run. I promise.

My best advice is to start by thinking about everything that needs doing and jot it down. I scribble this in my rather dog-eared notebook, but you could just as well make a note on your phone, or on the back of an envelope, just somewhere easy to keep to hand. Make one big, long list; the bigger, the better.

Then – and this is key – go over that list again. Separate out those bits you're happy to do, everything that to you says 'Christmas' and 'fun' and makes you feel an excitable tingle of joy, then put those firmly at the top of the list. These are non-negotiable. Now, think about those bits you don't enjoy so much, the tasks that feel like chores: either drop these from the plan completely or – to a degree that is possible – ask for help, outsource or delegate them to someone else.

It's essential to be both a little brutal and completely honest with yourself in this process, because this is the way to do Christmas as you want, rather than as you feel you should.

Once you have your definitive to-do list(s), filled with happy tasks, take one last moment to block out time in your calendar for everything you want and need to do: I always want to do all-the-things and wear myself out in the process, so I find that pencilling everything into my diary helps me to maintain an honest perspective on what's feasible for me to achieve, and what's not. This doesn't have to be an exact science – indeed it rarely is – nor does marking something in your diary mean it's set in stone and that plans can't change (they almost certainly will), but it's an excellent starting point.

You'll find at the back of this book a few pages in which you can make your own festive notes and lists, and create your own to-do lists to refer back to and play around with as you go, year on year. And to get you in holiday-planning mode, here is a list of things to think about as you start work on your own Christmas calendar:

ADVENT CALENDAR

You need your advent calendar ready for 1 December, so you want to get started on this relatively early. If you are making your own (see page 34 for a few ideas on how to do this), allow time to source supplies and, of course, to make the calendar itself; remember that once you've made the body of the calendar, as it were, you can use it again year on year and simply replenish the gifts. If you're filling your advent calendar with small gifts, then you might want to take your time buying these. My mother, for example, used to make an advent calendar for me every year and would start as early as January by sourcing little gifts for it: whenever she saw something suitable, she would buy it, wrap it and have it ready to go. I'm not that organised: I make time for a shopping session (usually a mix of online and a mad dash to the pound shop and/or toy shop), then block out an evening to wrap the little gifts and tie them to the calendar. Typically I do this at the last minute, right at the end of November.

CARDS

I'll be honest: I don't usually get round to sending Christmas cards, though each December I promise myself that next year I will. And I certainly love receiving them! You can obviously send your cards out right up until the week before Christmas, but it's preferable to send them sooner, ideally round about the beginning of December, so the recipients can enjoy them through the month. Fanny Cradock recommended buying cards in January in the winter sales, and, if you're an organised kind of person, there is no reason not to. Though nowadays, with online retailers and frequent special offers, there are bargains to be found throughout the year.

TREE AND DECORATIONS FOR THE HOUSE

I buy our tree online and find that, to get a good, early December delivery slot, the order needs to be placed in early November, or certainly in the first half of the month. It's worth signing up with a supplier if you're getting your tree delivered, as then you'll get a reminder email notifying you when delivery slots are open for booking. If you're going to pick up your tree in person instead, you'll want to pencil a date in the diary to make that trip, then allow time to decorate the tree afterwards, too. Typically, the earlier you go, the more variety and better trees there are to choose from. But you'll also want to consider how long the tree is likely to last once it's set up inside a warm house, as you don't want it to be looking sad and dried out by the time you get to Christmas Day. (For tips on how to help keep your tree happy and healthy, see page 45.) I tend to think that the second week of December is a good time to set up the tree and any decorations around the house; equally, if I'm hosting a Christmas party of some kind, I take that as the start date for festivities and want to have the tree set up before then.

CHRISTMAS HOSTING

I've added this category to the list, because if you're planning on holding a party or doing much by way of entertaining in the build-up to Christmas Day, it's one more thing to think about. As a rule of thumb, everyone tends to get extra-busy and booked up in December, so it's worth getting your invitations out sooner rather than later. Once you've settled on a date, you might as well go ahead and decide on the menu, then place any online orders for ingredients and/or decorations at the same time, for ease and peace of mind. Lastly, pencil in time to allow you to cook and, if applicable, decorate.

PRESENTS

You can start on this as early as you like, in fact there's nothing stopping you from drawing up your lists over the summer and getting everything wrapped and ready to go well ahead of time. One of my dearest (and most organised) friends, Alex, has all her shopping done and wrapped by October. Personally, I like to do my Christmas shopping once things begin to feel festive, even if this does make things a little busier and more manic in the build-up to the holidays. I draw up a list of names in late October, then take the month of November to buy or make most of my gifts (such as baking Christmas cakes); then December is just finishing off those last few bits. Allow time for gift-wrapping everything, too: I find it's helpful to block out a couple of evenings or afternoons to do this.

FOOD SHOPPING

This is a big one. I do most of my food shopping online for ease, then make a separate list of things that I can't or don't want to buy that way (such as order turkey from the butcher, buy special chocolates from the Italian delicatessen, or what have you). Delivery slots with supermarkets are especially competitive to pin down in this period, so it's worth booking a couple with a preliminary order (you can then add to it closer to the date) as soon as they're released. Think about fridge space when you make your order and, if that is at a premium, consider staggering deliveries accordingly, so food and ingredients arrive in a couple of drops, as they are needed. If you prefer not to shop online, you can do everything more last minute: this is more time-consuming, so just make sure to allow room for it in your calendar.

CHRISTMAS BAKING

If you're making your own Christmas pudding or cake, you can bake these months ahead and store them, wrapped tightly in foil, until needed. Equally, there is nothing stopping you from baking the cakes and puddings close to Christmas, as long as you allow a couple of days for the fruits to soak in brandy and time for the cakes to cool before you decorate them. You'll see that the recipe for fruit cake here (see page 202) calls for baking with a lot more alcohol than you might expect; this might seem extravagant, but in practice it means you can bake yourself a rich, moist Christmas cake pretty much immediately without the rigmarole of feeding it over the course of months, as you traditionally would. It's a nifty shortcut for those of us who are time-poor or of an impatient sort of a disposition. I've written a list for you of other recipes that work well as edible gifts too (see page 304), with guidelines on how far in advance each can be prepared, so you have plenty of options to choose from, whether you're planning ahead or improvising something at the last minute. As you choose what you would like to make, create a time slot or note for each batch in your Christmas calendar. And in the spirit of being super-organised, place an online order for the ingredients now.

To: Nonna
with love
always xx

Tips and Tricks
for Gift Wrapping

The world divides between those who enjoy wrapping presents and those who find the whole business to be a bit of a chore: I'll admit, I love it! I enjoy choosing my colour schemes each year, then playing around with ribbon and paper and tags. But I say this with a caveat: as with everything in life, it's about pacing yourself and having time to do it; wrapping isn't fun when you're in a rush.

I typically like to allocate wrapping evenings or afternoons, when I lock myself away in a room, put on an old movie, podcast or audiobook that I really enjoy, then give it a good solid few hours of wrapping until everything is done. I usually pencil in time for two of these sessions each year. The first is in November or very early December for the first wave of gifts (school teachers, work colleagues, friends who I won't see at Christmas...). The second is just before the holidays, when I tackle our stockings, those gifts that Father Christmas might need assistance wrapping, and any presents for family and friends who we will be seeing. If I were a more organised person, I would concentrate these two waves together earlier in the year and have everything ready to go well in advance. But in practice and in truth, I enjoy my wrapping sessions and it gets me in the Christmas mood. I also find that, inevitably, I end up buying little things here and there during December, so it works best to put them aside and wrap them all in one go.

THE SET-UP
There are a couple of tricks that make wrapping easier.

Firstly, set yourself up properly on a table. The ideal height is something like a workbench and if you have one of those at home in some capacity (or trestles that will adjust to that height), I feel that it's worth clearing it and conscripting it for the festive period. I wrap on our kitchen island. If you don't have a table at workbench height, then work from the dining table or a desk; do not wrap gifts on the floor (as tempting as this might seem, and, of course, all rules are there to be broken), like I used to do, and did for the photo on the previous page, as it will kill your back. In order to do nice, long, productive and efficient sessions (and find them enjoyable) you need to be well set up.

Next, get out everything that you'll need: paper and ribbon, of course, but also sticky tape, cards, tags, pens, scissors and any other decorative bits and bobs that you might like to use. You also want a wastepaper basket (or bin bag) to throw away any scraps directly as you create them, to minimise mess. If, like me, you're working on a surface that is usually in regular use (when it hasn't been colonised as a wrapping area), it's helpful to have a tray, box or basket to put all your materials back into when you've finished for that day. This way, you keep everything together and it's easy enough to unpack and set up again when you tackle your next lot of wrapping.

YOU WILL NEED
Wrapping paper

A good pair of sharp scissors

Sticky tape in a stand
  (so it's easy to cut to the right
  length with one hand)

Ribbon

Tags

A good pen to write on the tags

Any decorative elements you
  might want to use

A rubbish bin or bag for scraps

Sticky notes for scribbling any
  notes-to-self (such as addresses,
  reminders and so forth)

PAPER
The easiest, most budget- and user-friendly option is tissue paper: I love it. It both looks pretty and is very forgiving when wrapping even the most un-accommodating of shapes. You can dress the tissue up, if you like, with extravagant and colourful ribbons, but you don't need to: it has a rather joyful and playful quality all on its own. If in doubt, white tissue always looks nice (you could stick or draw golden stars on it, if you wanted to jazz it up), but, for my part, I love colour. Don't feel that you have to choose red or green because they're 'Christmas' colours, there are plenty of ways to make unexpected colours feel festive. You might add a bright red ribbon to a dusty rose-pink tissue for a candy cane-themed colour scheme, or a gold ribbon to a soft pistachio green. Choose colours you like and work from there.

Beyond tissue, there is a world of printed papers at different price points to choose from. A little time spent in a nice stationery shop, or browsing online (Etsy I typically find to be particularly helpful for this), will give you lots of options. I'm always quite partial to plain brown or coloured Kraft wrapping paper, which you can dress up with ribbons, twine, decorations, stickers or by drawing or writing directly on the paper. Quite a nice trick for making printed papers go that little bit further – they can be quite expensive – is to wrap a present in brown paper, then cut a wide strip of printed paper to wrap round it, much like a belly band on a book. You could then leave the wrapped gift as is, or tie a single strand of ribbon around the middle of that strip.

RIBBON
There are so many wonderful ribbons in haberdashery shops, flower markets or online. I avoid buying ribbon from stationers, as it usually comes in small quantities and feels overpriced, certainly more expensive than buying ribbon in bulk elsewhere. I also save ribbons from presents received each year to recycle

the next. Satin ribbon is the easiest to tie and it comes in all different colours and widths. I find both grosgrain ribbon and velvet to be very elegant, though they can be a little more fiddly to tie and are, typically, a little more expensive than satin. If you want to create a stiff, sculpted bow, you will need a wired ribbon, which allows you to shape the bow as you like it and for it to hold that shape nicely. Twine is a nice, rustic-looking and inexpensive alternative to the finer ribbons: I like plain, natural twine, but you can find coloured or even candy cane-striped twines online. If you're buying ribbons in bulk, remember to get different widths to allow for the varying sizes and shapes of gifts: in some instances, it can be nice to layer a narrow ribbon in a contrasting colour over a wider ribbon and then tie the two together into a bow.

So as to keep things looking neat, when you tie the bow, you always want to thread both ends of the ribbon under the central strand first, so it holds its place and doesn't slip around. Be creative as to where you tie the bow: central always looks nice, but depending on what shape a present is, it can be quite effective to position the bow in a corner, or weighted to the top or bottom. You can also not tie a bow at all: sometimes it's nice to have long strands of ribbon, perhaps in different colours, tied in a simple knot and flowing, or even just a little decorative ribbon loop with both ends crossed over each other, stuck with a candy cane or sprig of berries on to a corner of the gift.

OTHER DECORATIONS

Especially if you haven't gone wild with paper or ribbon, slipping a little decorative element on top of each gift can be a very nice way of zhuzh-ing it up. For this, I especially like candy canes (which I usually bulk-buy from the pound shop), just slipped under the ribbon and on top of the gift, or tied into the bow. Other nice decorative touches are a sprig of holly or other greenery (from a florist, or foraged if you have access to a garden), or a small Christmas tree ornament, bought or homemade, such as perhaps a candy cane heart or festive wreath-shaped biscuit (see pages 270–271).

GIFT TAGS

My go-to is a brown or white paper luggage tag: these allow plenty of space to write a little note on and they have a pared-back, utilitarian quality which I like and which works well with all kinds of wrapping paper. You can also write directly on to the paper: this doesn't work well with tissue, but is good with brown or other plain papers (do a couple of trial runs with different pens on a scrap of the paper before writing on the wrapped gift itself). You can obviously buy gift tags, either to match or complement printed paper, or perhaps if the wrapping is on the plainer side you might want to do something quite 'statement' with the tag. But you can also make your own, by folding a rectangular piece of printed paper in two, like a little booklet, then punching a hole in the top left corner (with a hole-puncher, or scissors), through which you can tie a little ribbon or string. Also quite nice are sticker tags: you can buy these online or from good stationers. If you buy plain white stickers, you can embellish them yourself by drawing on them, or create a design on a laptop and have them printed by one of the many online suppliers.

... AND IF YOU REALLY DON'T LIKE WRAPPING

For those who truly loathe the idea of all this, there are a couple of shortcuts that might make life easier. You could try to buy presents from shops that offer an in-house gift-wrapping service, or at least packaging that could pass – even if only loosely – as wrapping. You can buy paper envelope bags (from some stationers and online), slip in the gift and seal, then either stick on a pretty tag, or tie with a little ribbon. For larger, bulkier presents, you can always buy a gift bag, slip the gift in and stuff tissue paper over the top to conceal it and also to create a festive effect. If gift bags feel too extravagant, you can buy good sturdy brown paper bags and either leave them plain, or embellish with ribbon, or write on them (or all of the above). If the worst comes to the worst, sometimes just tying a ribbon around the gift feels enough to be special.

Advent Calendars

Displaying your advent calendar in pride of place can be an effective way to build excitement from the start of the festive season.

ADVENT CALENDARS

There are so many different advent calendars in the shops to choose from, with different themes. Some are filled with chocolates or sweets, others contain small gifts and others still – the old-fashioned kind – are large paper cards, with each painted window depicting a different festive scene. In my family, we all choose our own advent calendar every year, then set them up all together in a corner of the kitchen.

You can also make your own advent calendar and there are various ways of doing this. Growing up, I had a calendar that resembled a wall hanging, with twenty-four small rings on it. My mother would wrap twenty-four small gifts and tie one to each ring, then every night before bed through the month of December I would open a present. You can buy advent calendars of this kind online (Etsy, for example, offers a great selection), or for someone confident with needle and thread it would be easy enough to make.

Following the same principle, you could wrap twenty-four small gifts and put them in a sack, basket or bag (decorated, if you want), then every day lucky-dip a small gift. Or add a little tag numbered 1–24 on each gift and hang it from the Christmas tree, or from a collection of branches arranged in a large vase.

The gifts needn't be extravagant. I buy small items: rubbers, pens, pencils, keyrings and so forth, for my boys, then alternate gifts with sweets or chocolates, such as a candy cane, a small bar of chocolate or a bundle of marshmallows or sugared almonds. You could even write little 'promise' cards with a note each day, offering a hot chocolate, a special bedtime story or a trip to the cinema.

HOW TO MAKE AN ADVENT CALENDAR

The simplest way to make this kind of advent calendar is out of felt, which you can easily glue together and which requires the minimum amount of sewing and crafting. You will need a hot glue gun for this, but if you don't have one already, trust me when I say that it's the most gratifying piece of kit and infinitely less intimidating to use than its name suggests. You can readily buy a glue gun, along with everything else that you need, online or from a craft shop.

If you would prefer to make the calendar in fabric rather than cosy, more homemade-looking felt, the same principles apply, only instead of largely glue-ing the calendar together, you will need to stitch it, and you'll want a heavier fabric for the backing.

YOU WILL NEED

2 large pieces of felt, roughly 75 × 45cm, plus extra felt in different colours (optional), for decoration

A hot glue gun

24 small brass rings, roughly 3cm in diameter

Needle and thread (or 24 safety pins)

A long stick or dowel, roughly 2cm in diameter and 45cm long

80–100cm length of 1–2cm ribbon

If you want to decorate the calendar, cut out shapes in felt in contrasting colours (stars, or a Christmas tree, or personalise with a name) and glue them on to the first large felt rectangle, using a hot glue gun: apply the glue to the edge of the reverse side of each shape, place it on the felt and hold firmly for 30 seconds until the glue has dried. Make sure to leave a 10cm empty margin at the top of the calendar; you will later fold this bit of fabric over to create a hanger.

Now, sew twenty-four small brass rings on to the calendar, in a pattern or at random, just allow enough space between each, and at the margins, for the gifts. If you want to avoid using needle and thread, you could attach each ring with a small safety pin, so the body of the pin sits on the reverse side.

Next, back your calendar so that it feels sturdy and hangs nicely: turn the calendar face-side down and lay the second felt rectangle over the top, lining the sides up, but laying the top edge of the second felt rectangle at 9-10cm lower than the top edge of the front. One you've got your two sheets of felt lined up neatly, apply the hot glue carefully to stick them together. Do this in stages, as the glue hardens quickly: glue the first edge, hold in place firmly for 30 seconds, then move on to the next section. Neatly trim any messy or crooked edges.

Now, tie the ends of the ribbon to the extremities of the dowel, 3–4cm from each end. You want this to hold firmly, so tie the ribbon in a tight double knot, then, if needed, use a little hot glue to stick each knot in place. Set the dowel at the top of the calendar, parallel to the shorter edge and in line with the point where the two sheets of felt are stuck together. Make sure that the ribbon is looped over the very top of the calendar, so when you fold the top edge down to cover the dowel, you have created a loop to hang the calendar up with. Apply two lines of hot glue on to the felt, at 3–4cm under the dowel and all the way across, then fold the top flap of felt down over the dowel to seal it in. Hold firmly in place for 30 seconds to allow the glue to dry completely.

Lastly, tie a small gift to each brass ring to complete the calendar, and hang it up for everyone to enjoy.

Stockings

My friend Sarah, who is queen of all things Christmas, hangs stockings for each member of the family on her mantelpiece on the first day of December: it sets a festive mood that signals the start of the season.

My mother embroidered stockings for me and each of my boys and I treasure them: every year they come out of storage and hang proudly on our mantelpiece. They are beautiful, but also feel characterful and deeply personal: everything that a stocking should be. You can buy kits to needlepoint your own stocking and, if it's something you think you might enjoy, I cannot urge you to do so strongly enough: it might take a while, but it will give you something precious to treasure for a lifetime.

However, there are other ways to personalise stockings that offer a little more by way of fast – if not instant – gratification. You'll find a wide selection of stockings which can be personalised with initials or names to buy online (again Etsy offers rich pickings, but so do countless other websites and retailers), so that is a good place to start. If you would like something a little more DIY, you can buy a pattern online to download, then sew your own stocking in your choice of fabric. Or you can buy a felt stocking (also online) very affordably and then use marker pens or glitter-glue pens to embellish it with initials, names or nicknames, or just add a personalised luggage tag (paper or otherwise) with a name.

The great quandary with stockings is always what to fill them with.

A few ideas for stocking fillers include: **WHOLE WALNUTS** and **SATSUMAS** aplenty (these are essential); **PAPERBACK BOOKS** (ideally on the smaller side) you've enjoyed reading that year and think others will enjoy too; anything bought and edible that feels special and personal to that person, be it a jar of personalised **MARMITE**, a couple of sachets of their favoured **TEA**, a bar of their favourite **CHOCOLATE** and/or **CHOCOLATE COINS** and so on... You can customise **JARS OF PRESERVES** or packets of preferred foods by **PERSONALISING STICKERS** by hand (such as 'this belongs to the world's best Papa') and then using the stickers to embellish the packaging. Or you can also make your own little edible gifts to include.

In my experience, the following all work well as stocking fillers:

EDIBLE STOCKING FILLERS

A small paper bag with a Candy Cane Hot Chocolate Stick (see page 66) and a note with the promise of breakfast in bed

A small bundle of Christmas Brownies (see page 283)

A cellophane bag with a couple of Candy Cane Hearts (see page 271)

A single Miniature Marzipan Pear (or other marzipan fruit of your choosing), or a bundle or small tin with a few marzipan fruits (see page 272)

A Chocolate Salami wrapped in baking paper and tied with twine (see page 275)

A small bundle of Gilded Gingerbread Tree Ornaments (see page 266)

A gingerbread man or two, made using the recipe for gingerbread (see page 266)

A small bundle of Christmas Wreath Biscuits (see page 270)

A paper bag, or small tin, filled with a few Cocoa and Panettone Truffles (see page 280)

NON-EDIBLE STOCKING FILLERS

A nice bar of soap or any other spoiling beauty bits and bobs

A pack of playing cards, perhaps with a nice note with the rules for some suggested games to play

A box of personalised notecards. You could even make these yourself, by decorating a set of plain notecards with handwritten initials and/or stickers, or a stamp of some kind, then tie together with ribbon

Wool or cashmere socks; there is something always quietly pleasing to me about a sock inside a sock!

Bubbles (children always love bubbles)

Stickers

A pencil case filled with special pencils and crayons (the surprise element of a present inside a present inside a present never ceases to delight)

A special photo in a small frame

Bake Sales

It is in the nature of bake sales that they always seem to have been in the diary forever, yet then crop up out of nowhere, with immense pressure to whip something up at the last minute and in bulk. Certain recipes work better for these sorts of events than others, and, as is so often the case with cooking, you can spare yourself a huge amount of angst by choosing the right item to bake. In my experience, bake sales are either about volume and scale, or they are about 'specialness': you either want a recipe that you can easily churn out in vast quantities, or you want a single beautiful cake (or a couple of them) that the stall can sell for a relatively high price, because they look and feel special. Whatever you choose, make sure it's a recipe that keeps well for a few days, so it doesn't need to be baked at the very last minute, or will already be stale when you come to selling it.

The following are all great for bake sales, though be sure to clearly label anything that contains nuts:

Candy Cane Hot Chocolate Sticks (see page 66), sold individually, or as bundles of four or six in paper or cellophane bags

Cinnamon and Cranberry Bundt (see page 196) by the slice, either iced or plain

Pistachio Cream Croissants (see page 70)

Sticky Marzipan Breakfast Buns (see page 72)

Gingery Christmas Cake (see page 202)

Pistachio, Almond and Parmesan Cantucci (see page 91), sold as bundles in paper or cellophane bags

Cocoa and Panettone Truffles (see page 280), sold as bundles in paper or cellophane bags

Candy Cane Hearts (see page 271), sold as bundles of four or six in paper or cellophane bags

Chocolate Salami (see page 275), perhaps made smaller and sold individually

Peppermint Meringues (see page 279)

Maxim's Mince Pies (see page 228), sold individually, or as batches of four or six in paper or cellophane bags

Nutty Chocolate Torrone (see page 238), sold by the slice, each piece in a paper or cellophane bag

Gilded Gingerbread Tree Ornaments (see page 266), sold individually, or as batches of four or six in paper or cellophane bags

Christmas Wreath Biscuits (see page 270), sold individually, or as batches of four or six in paper or cellophane bags

Christmas Brownies (see page 283)

The Tree

REAL VS ARTIFICIAL

I'm a big fan of a real fir tree, because I do so love the scent and I can never quite resist its magical allure. However, there are of course practical advantages to an artificial tree, not least the fact that you can re-use it year after year. It's low maintenance, as you don't need to water it, nor worry about the branches drying out or dropping needles. And, while an artificial tree might be more costly upfront, over time it works out as a distinctly more affordable option.

CHOOSING AND CARING FOR A REAL TREE

Make sure to measure the space where it's going to go before committing to a tree. There are all sorts of different varieties of pine to choose from, but try to make sure that the tree is healthy before you take it home. If you run your hand along the branches, its needles should hold fast and feel flexible; if they feel stiff or brittle, they are more likely to dry out and drop. Once you get your tree home, trim the bottom of the trunk with a saw (or ask the seller to do it for you) before you set it in its stand, then fill the stand with cool, clean water. Make sure to keep the stand topped up regularly, so it doesn't dry out. Trees don't like excess heat, so set it up somewhere cool, away from direct sunlight, and try not to have the central heating up too high if you want it to last as long as possible.

DECORATIONS

A beautifully decorated tree is all about layers: start with the lights. My personal preference is for a warm glow and static rather than twinkly lights, which I find a little distracting. Take your time getting their position right, because once the other decorations go on, they will be fiddly to adjust. Start at the bottom of the tree and drape the lights in and out of the branches, working your way up in a slalom of sorts. Take care that the tree doesn't look like it's been wrapped in a string of lights, rather that they're peeking out and giving light in patches. Keep adjusting until you've got them right.

Next, I like to layer on my garlands or tinsel, anything 'drape-y', distributing them evenly and swinging them across the tree; then bows and/or ribbons tied straight on to the branches. Lastly I hang the ornaments, filling in any holes or gaps as I go, using a mix of edible ornaments and vintage baubles that I've collected over the years.

Homemade Decorations

If you have the time, or can find a way to make a little time, I urge you to try making some of your own decorations. And not just because it's a practical and sustainable way of swathing the house in Christmas, nor even because it's more economical (though, let's be honest: it is). Mostly I insist on this idea because the ritual, the actual practice of making them, is something I've come to really enjoy, and I think you'll enjoy it, too. Part of the magic of DIY decorations, you see, is that the very making of them brings as much joy, if not more, as the decorations themselves: that's where the memories – and a lot of the magic – reside. So here are a few favourite and simple ideas for decorations which even someone as un-crafty as me can happily make and to great, dramatic effect.

PAPER CHAINS

Child's play to make, but surprisingly effective-looking, both draped over the Christmas tree and also arranged in swags around the house, perhaps hooked over the mantelpiece, shelves, or even hanging from the ceiling.

To make the chains, you cut rectangular strips of paper (I make mine about 25cm long and 5–7.5cm wide). Take the first strip and fold it into a loop, so the ends overlap by 0.5–1cm, then seal the ends together on both sides of the join with a strip of clear sticky tape. (I've also tried glue-ing the ends, which is neat, but to be honest tape is by far the easiest and most effective way to close the loop and will hold well.) Then repeat this process with a second strip of paper, but threading it through the first loop before sealing the ends together. Keep going in this way to make a long chain.

It goes without saying that you can make the chains in whatever colour combinations you like: two-tone can look pretty, alternating pink and red loops, or light and dark green, for example. You don't need special paper, though weightier papers tend to work best. It's also a great way to use up scraps of wrapping paper to make patchwork-style chains with all sorts of different colours, prints and textures. I also have a particularly soft spot for marbled prints: I've made chains in a single continuous print and others that juxtapose contrasting colours and patterns. Both look wonderfully effective.

POPCORN GARLANDS

A classic for a reason: it's easy and cost-effective to make and looks utterly charming. Start by making a big batch of popcorn (or buy ready-made, if you prefer), then thread a needle with a long strand of thread, fishing line or floss, tying a double knot at the end. Thread the popcorn kernels on to the string, by firmly pushing the needle through the middle of each kernel and nudging them together like beads on a necklace. You can alternate popcorn kernels with cranberries or dried slices of apple or orange (see below), if you would like to mix things up. You can also play around with different varieties of corn, to create different colours on the garland. Once assembled, they can be draped on the Christmas tree, but also look very nice nestled among festive greenery.

FRUITY DECORATIONS

You can make these rustic little ornaments with oranges, lemons or even slices of apple: I quite like a mix of fruits, to add more texture and colours to my decorations. Heat the oven to 140°C / 120°C fan / Gas 1. Slice your fruit into rounds as thinly as you can: a mandolin is useful here, if you have one, otherwise a sharp knife is good. Set them on a baking tray lined with baking paper or a silicone liner and bake for 45–60 minutes, until completely dried out, turning the slices over halfway through, so they bake evenly. Once the fruit has cooled, thread ribbon, twine or string through the centre of the slices (use the tip of a sharp knife to make a hole, if needed), then tie in a loop and hang to decorate. It also looks quite good to make double layers here: you might want to put a slice of lemon or apple on top of a slice of orange and then tie the two together; you could also try layering a slice of dried apple or citrus with a cinnamon stick and tying those together. Once assembled, these look charming hanging from the Christmas tree, but are also a nice little touch attached to a gift or a wreath, or dotted here and there around the house.

EDIBLE ORNAMENTS

There is something about hanging sweets from the Christmas tree as decorations that has a very special charm. You'll find recipes in this book for gingerbread and shortbread ornaments, which you can bake and decorate, then hang from the tree to great effect (see pages 266 and 270). You'll also find a method for moulding candy canes into heart-shaped sugar ornaments (see page 271), which is one of my favourite hacks. But even just candy canes alone, dangling from the branches by their crooks, look wonderfully effective. You could tie a little bow, in narrow satin ribbon with flowing tails, to each sugar-striped cane if you really wanted to gild the lily, but it's certainly not needed: there is a rather nostalgic magic to a lone unembellished candy cane twirling gently on the tree.

FESTIVE BOWS

One year, I decorated our tree with a thousand and one floppy bows: maybe it wasn't strictly quite that many, but it was a lot. Just bows, lots of bows: it looked glorious. I went for ribbons in a broad mix of widths, lengths, colours and textures and tied them to the branches. The best way to do this is to tie a bow with your ribbon (I make two loops, like bunny ears, with the single length of ribbon, then tie the two together in a knot and leave the ends hanging long).

Once you have your bow, thread a piece of fine florist's wire (from your local florist, or online) through the back of the bow to attach it to the tree (or garland, or wherever it's going). The bows look especially effective with their ends cut to different lengths, some long and flowing and others shorter and neater: don't be afraid to mix and match. Otherwise, you can use wired ribbon to make bows for the tree: the wire will allow you to shape the body of the bow and arrange its ends as you like. Because wired ribbon is a little more forgiving, you can simply tie these straight to the branches of the tree, though I still find that it works best to make the bow and then tie it on to the tree by means of another fine wire threaded through the back.

QUICK DECORATION HACKS

If making decorations isn't your thing, these are plenty of small, low-effort touches with which you can magic up the feeling of Christmas.

I'm a big fan of **POINSETTIAS**, for example. A few of these, ideally potted in a nice planter or terracotta pot, or even just in the pot they come in, instantly look like Christmas with their cartoon-like, merry red flowers and dark green leaves. Everyone loves **MISTLETOE** hanging over the doorway, though beware that the berries are poisonous, if you have small children or pets who might eat them. Similarly, potted **AMARYLLIS** in a rich dark shade of red have a certain festive quality about them. If you have access to a garden (or even to a park), gather a little **GREENERY** (or buy a few fir branches from your local florist or supermarket), and dot it about on the mantelpiece here and there, for flashes of festive mood. Bowls of **WHOLE POMEGRANATES**, or even individual fruits, dotted here, there and everywhere, look instantly Christmassy, in large part because of their rich reddish colour (and if you wanted to literally gild the pomegranate, you could embellish some of the fruits with gold leaf, see page 316). **CANDLES** and **CANDLELIGHT** are a great way of creating a cosy yet celebratory mood: if you can use gold candles or set tea lights in little gold holders, even better, as few things say Christmas quite like a bit of gold and sparkle. Similarly, draping **FAIRY LIGHTS** in places beyond your tree goes a long way to creating a festive atmosphere, as does **HANGING YOUR STOCKINGS UP** on the mantelpiece early (more on stockings at page 38). And, by the same principle, piling **PRESENTS** under the tree as you wrap them gets everyone in the holiday mood well before Christmas Day. Personally, I find this also allows me to enjoy them, all decked out in their pretty wrapping, before I give them away.

How to Make Christmas Crackers

I find it tricky to find Christmas crackers which I both like and which don't cost the Earth, so I've often resorted to making my own. It's one of those things that sounds infinitely more complicated than it actually is. It's also – incidentally – a great way to make happy use of leftover scraps and used wrapping paper that feels too beautiful to throw away but doesn't really have any other obvious use.

MAKING CRACKERS FROM SCRATCH

YOU WILL NEED

A large sheet (or two) of heavy card

Good-quality wrapping paper

Cracker snaps (buy these online or from a craft shop)

Clear tape (or, even better, double-sided sticky tape)

Nice ribbon

Gifts, paper hats and whatever else you would like to go inside

Begin by making the cylindrical body for the cracker(s). You could use leftover loo rolls, but I find the shape a little too squat for a handsome-looking cracker. Cut the card into three 20 × 13cm rectangles, then roll each into a cylinder with a 1–2cm overlap and seal with tape. Don't worry if it's a bit messy (no one will see it), but tape the roll well, folding tape over the edges and all along the seam. Double up the tape and stick some pieces crossways too, if needed. Now place the three cardboard rolls in a line on the plain side of your wrapping paper, taking care that you have enough paper to cover and overlap the rolls. Put a snap through the tube and secure to the middle roll with tape. Now, cut your paper so it's the same width as the three cardboard rolls. Roll the wrapping paper over the cardboard rolls to cover, then overlap the paper by 2–3cm and seal with a piece of tape in line with each cardboard roll. Don't tape all the way along or in between the rolls, or the crackers won't 'crack' when you pull them. If you're using double-sided tape (which looks marginally neater), press down to stick the tape firmly to the paper and place three pieces of double-sided tape along one end of the wrapping paper, each in line with each cardboard roll (on the side that sticks to the paper not to the roll). Roll the wrapping paper over the rolls to cover, then overlap the paper and press down to stick the tape to the paper.

Now, gently pull the two cardboard rolls on either end slightly away from the middle. Between one end roll and the middle roll, tie a loose knot with your ribbon and gently tighten to create the cracker end. Very gently pinch the gap between the rolls to help bunch the paper together neatly and make it easier to tie the ribbon. Now tie into a bow, remove the end roll that you were using as a guide, and cut any excess ribbon. Fill the cracker, then repeat the process on the second side. Save the spare two rolls to use again as guides for your next cracker.

ZHUZH-ING UP BOUGHT CRACKERS

For a lower-effort cracker which still feels luxurious and somewhat bespoke, buy crackers that you broadly like and aren't overly expensive, then just dress them up. When choosing the crackers, focus on their size, shape and the paper they're made from: either something matching the aesthetic of your festive table, or something neutral. Now, carefully cut the bows off and replace with big bows in a fabric and colour you like. If you want a stylised 'perfect' cracker, attach the bows with wire (see pages 47–49). Either way, the trick is length: you want a generous bow with floppy, oversized ears and long flowing ribbons to give that luxurious touch. You also want a nice fabric: velvet always looks grand; grosgrain is unusual and chic; silk ties easily and nicely. You can then customise your crackers by writing guests' names on them in gold pen, or sticking a decoration on to the front with a glue gun.

CRACKER GIFTS

If you're going to the effort of making your own crackers, you want to fill each one with something thoughtful and personal. A few ideas:

Sample-sized packages of perfume, bath oil or face cream that they might especially enjoy

A nice lip gloss, lipstick or lip salve

Coloured pencils tied together with a ribbon, or a nice pen

Seeds to plant in the garden

A friendship bracelet

A personalised keyring

Hair scrunchie or bow

A small toy such as Lego, joke sweets, tiny car, or figurine

... or, if in doubt, sweets and nice chocolates always go down a treat.

Christmas Wreaths

Making your own festive wreath is a wonderfully rewarding business and one of those things that sounds infinitely more intimidating to do than it is in actual practice. There are three simple methods for making a wreath your own, all involving varying degrees of commitment: which one is right for you depends largely on how much time you have to dedicate to the project, and how creative you want to get.

ZHUZH-ING UP A BASIC WREATH

You can buy a plain, simple wreath from a florist or garden centre very affordably and then add your own decorations to give it that opulent touch. When it comes to decorating the wreath, it really is very simple: you will need florist's wire (which is both inexpensive and easy to buy online) and then an assortment of decorations, which can really be whatever you want them to be. Good options include: **CINNAMON STICKS; DRIED SLICES OF ORANGE AND APPLE** (which you can buy, or make your own from fresh fruit, see page 47); extra bits of greenery such as **MISTLETOE** and/or **HOLLY WITH BERRIES; CANDY CANES; RIBBONS** to tie in bows (see page 47), or tie simply in a knot and leave the ends flowing; **DRIED FLOWERS** for a more rustic look; **PINE CONES** of all shapes and sizes; small bunches of **DRIED RED BERRIES; MANDARINS STUDDED WITH CLOVES; WHOLE DRIED CHILLIES;** maybe even **BAUBLES** if you like. The list goes on...

STARTING A WREATH FROM SCRATCH

If you live in the countryside, have a garden, or easy access to foraged foliage, you might want to make your own wreath from scratch. Equally, if you live in a city centre, you should be able to readily source foliage from a garden centre or from a wholesale flower market. To make the wreath, you will need **A WIRE WREATH RING**, which you can buy online, from a wholesale flower market or from a craft shop. You'll also need: **MOSS; GREEN TWINE**; a selection of **DIFFERENT TEXTURED FOLIAGE**, such as spruce, ivy, evergreen herbs or evergreen oak; and **FLORIST'S WIRE** (for attaching your decorations). Start by covering the wreath ring with green moss, so you have a green base to work with: secure generous handfuls of the moss to the wreath ring, tying it on tightly with green twine to make a compact and sturdy base. Now, gather the branches together in small bunches, tying each little bundle together firmly with twine. Use a mix of lengths and textures in each bunch, then attach them to the green moss base by tying firmly in place with the twine: you might need to tie each bundle in two or three places, to be extra sure it stays where you want it to be. Layer the bundles of branches over each other, so that gradually you cover the whole ring, trying to avoid any gaps. Once all your moss is covered, go back over the wreath, filling in any gaps as needed by sticking in the odd branch here and there; then decorate as you would if you were zhuzh-ing up a basic wreath (see opposite).

DECORATING A WOVEN WICKER WREATH

It was my friend and brilliant florist, Charlotte D'Arcy, who first showed me how to decorate a wreath this way, and I love her method both for its intuitive simplicity to execute, and also for the charmingly higgledy-piggledy, slightly rustic character of the finished piece. You will need to invest in a woven wicker (or willow) wreath ring; these aren't especially extravagantly priced and you can re-use it year on year, so I feel that it's worth buying a big, good-quality one. You can buy these rings online, or, as December approaches, at garden centres or wholesale flower markets.

Once you have your ring, you simply thread your greenery through it with no need for any binding, string or wires to attach it: it's delightfully easy and intuitive to do. What kind of greenery you use is entirely up to you, though ideally you want something relatively pliable, so you can weave it in and out of the ring's nooks and crannies. Work in small-to-medium-sized bunches of branches, then mould them to the wreath, tucking in the ends to hold them in place: some sprigs will pop out here and there, which gives the wreath a nice, unaffected shape and a little movement. Similarly, if little bits of wicker show through, it rather adds to the charm of the wreath, so don't worry about doing it all too perfectly; if anything it looks better if you don't.

While you could do the whole wreath with just the one kind of foliage, having a bit of variety and laying different shades of green and textures over each other is what tends to look most effective: think of using different kinds of **PINE**, **BILBERRY**, **SPINELESS BUTCHER'S BROOM**, thick branches of **ROSEMARY** or **BAY LEAVES**, and so on... Once you have your wreath assembled, you can then either decorate as opposite, or just leave as is.

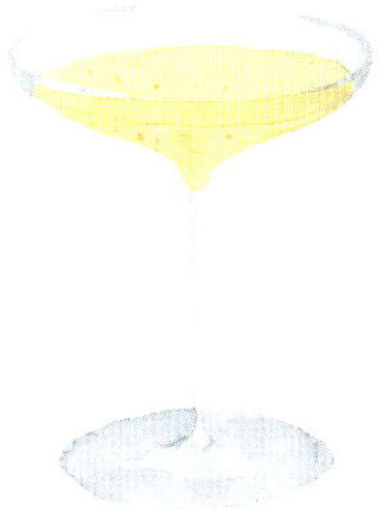

Feasing

This chapter is the heart and soul of the book: it's the food. You'll find, in the pages that follow, recipes for what to cook on Christmas Day, yes, but also dishes for throughout the festive season. There are a multitude of ideas for celebratory breakfasts, there are canapés and cocktails, extravagant centrepieces, more simple main dishes, warm vegetable sides, colour and freshness in the form of winter-y salads – which tend to be overlooked at Christmas but are so often what we truly want – as well as for cakes, biscuits, puddings, sauces and so on and so forth… it's all the good things!

What to cook at Christmas is a delicate balancing act: on the one hand, we crave comfort, tradition and a meal that isn't so much gourmet, perhaps, as it is happily familiar: it's 'Christmas' because it's always been that way at Christmas. On the other hand, we also want to celebrate with something that feels special to us: we want to eat all our most-desired foods. In my experience, a mix of these – new as well as old favourites – makes for the best Christmas feasts. So that is what you'll find here: some recipes are festive because they're canonical and others, quite simply, because they're delicious.

Importantly for the cook, there are also logistical considerations when planning a Christmas menu. For that reason, you'll see notes in each of the recipes on how to prepare things in advance, so you don't end up feeling overwhelmed or over-stretched on the day. And if there's one piece of advice I can share, it's this: when planning what to cook, do give some thought to the layout of your kitchen, then work with it and play to its strengths. A traditional classic Christmas roast with all the trimmings relies heavily on an oven, for example, so if oven space is at a particular premium, do tweak your menu to include more of those dishes that you can serve at room temperature, cook on the hob, or prepare well in advance, to go with your turkey or goose or pie or what have you. It may seem like a little thing, but it will ease the stress of festive cooking immeasurably, I promise.

Recipe List

BREAKFAST AND BRUNCH
❀ Candy Cane Hot Chocolate Sticks
Nutella Christmas Wreath
Pistachio Cream Croissants
❀ Sticky Marzipan Breakfast Buns
Red Berry Breakfast Panzanella
Panettone Perduto
Panettone Grilled Cheese Sandwich
Cheesy Ham and Croissant Bake

COCKTAILS AND NIBBLES
Holiday Mood Egg Nog
Olga's Sticky Sausages
Mulled Wine
❀ Pistachio, Almond and Parmesan Cantucci
Amarena Amaretto Sour
Gorgonzola-Walnut Panettone Crostini
Saffron Popcorn
Spiced Hot Apple Juice
Christmas Mocktail
Chestnut Martini
A Few Ideas for Canapés

STARTERS
Mushroom Tortellini in Brodo
Creamy Chestnut Soup with Pomegranate
Seafood and Saffron Cocktail
Gilded Miniature Baked Potatoes with Crème
    Fraîche and Caviar
Potted Salmon with Preserved Lemon
Walnut and Gorgonzola Stuffed Pears

MAIN COURSES
Pomegranate-Glazed Turkey
Rolled Turkey Breast with Chestnut and
    Sage Stuffing
Ginger and Apricot Glazed Ham
Roast Poussins with Crisp Prosciutto
    and Sage
Roast Goose with Caramelised Clementines
Pork Tenderloin with Persimmons and
    Pomegranate
Cotechino and Spinach Roll

VEGETARIAN MAIN COURSES
Nut and Cranberry Terrine
Camembert and Cranberry Pithivier
Beetroot and Horseradish Galette
Black Truffle, Mascarpone and Quail's
    Egg Pasta Pie
Gnocchi and Pumpkin Gratin
Stuffed Pumpkin with Wild Rice, Cranberries
    and Chestnuts

WARM SIDE DISHES
The Best Roast Potatoes
Cheesy Fondue Roast Potato Bake
'Hedgehog' Potatoes
Panettone, Chestnut and Sage Stuffing
Nonna's Stuffing
Sticky Roast Sprouts with Dates
    and Pistachios
Martin's Ruby Red Cabbage
Especially Good Maple-Roast Parsnips
Wilted Kale with Marmite Butter
Roast Savoy Cabbage with Pancetta,
    Chestnuts and Gorgonzola

WINTER SALADS

Wild Rice, Lentil, Chestnut and
    Pomegranate Salad
Red Chicory and Candied Pecan Salad
Christmas Salad
Orange, Carrot and Pistachio Salad
Red Cabbage Panzanella
Red Cabbage, Feta, Hazelnut and
    Mint Salad
Shaved Fennel, Grapefruit and
    Pomegranate Salad
Shaved Brussels Sprouts with Pecorino,
    Cranberries and Pecans
Good Luck Salad

CAKES

❀ Cinnamon and Cranberry Bundt
Panettone Woodland Cake
❀ Gingery Christmas Cake
❀ Black and Gold Cake
Pandoro Tower
Flourless Chocolate Orange Cake
Chocolate and Chestnut Yule Log
Black Cherry and Ricotta Cheesecake
❀ Christmas Cupcakes with Brandy
    Buttercream

SWEET PIES, TARTS
AND PUDDINGS

❀ Maxim's Mince Pies
Puff Pastry Mince Pies
Salted Caramel Pecan Pie
Pistachio Cream and Ginger Pie
Egg Nog Cream Pie
❀ Nutty Chocolate Torrone
❀ Hidden Orange Christmas Pudding

Salted Caramel Zuccotto
Pomegranate Campari Jelly
Gingerbread, Cranberry and Zabaione Trifle
Gorgonzola, Fig and Hazelnut Terrine
Saffron Poached Pears with Chocolate
    Caramel Sauce
Sugar Plum Sorbet
Christmas Cake Ice Cream
Christmas Pavlova

BISCUITS AND SWEETS

❀ Gilded Gingerbread Tree Ornaments
❀ Christmas Wreath Biscuits
❀ Candy Cane Hearts
❀ Miniature Marzipan Pears
❀ Chocolate Salami
Crispie Christmas Trees
❀ Peppermint Meringues
❀ Cocoa and Panettone Truffles
❀ Christmas Brownies

SAUCES

❀ Homemade Mincemeat
   (and Why it's Worth it)
Brioche Bread Sauce
❀ Cranberry and Marsala Sauce
Make-Ahead Gravy
❀ Boozy Amaretto Butter
Easy Peasy Hot Brandy Custard
Making Good Use of Leftovers

Candy Cane Hot Chocolate Sticks

There is a Willy Wonka-esque quality about these: especially at that moment when you swizzle the stick in a mug of warmed milk and, as if by magic, the liquid turns to hot chocolate, infused with heady peppermint and tasting unmistakably like Christmas. The fact that they are so simple to make that family members of all ages (and culinary skill sets) can easily (and happily) help, is just the proverbial cherry on the cake. The method I've given below calls for melting chocolate in a bain-marie: I prefer this as it's failsafe. But, if you prefer, you can melt it in the microwave. Chop it finely, then microwave in thirty-second blasts in a microwaveable bowl, taking the bowl out each time and giving the chocolate a good stir (just take care, as it can catch and burn in a moment).

You can make these with any chocolate you like: dark, milk, praline, white, you name it. Or even use a combination of melted white and milk or dark, then use a toothpick to twirl a marbled pattern in each little pool of chocolate before sticking the candy canes in. But while that might look fancier, I have a soft spot for the unadulterated After Eight-like quality of dark, almost bitter chocolate with a shot of intense peppermint, topped with shards of chewy candy cane shimmering like broken stained glass against its darkness.

Once assembled, these will keep happily in an airtight container somewhere cool (but not in the fridge) for up to one week.

HANDS ON TIME
15 minutes
HANDS OFF TIME
10 minutes cooling,
    plus 2 hours setting
MAKES 12

≈≈≈≈

12 candy canes, each ideally
    about 10cm tall
200g dark chocolate (or see
    recipe introduction),
    broken into pieces

Use a sharp knife to trim off the curved crooks of the candy canes, then finely chop the trimmings. Set a 12-hole silicone mini-muffin tray on a rigid baking tray: this makes it much easier to move, without spilling, once you've filled the holes.

Bring a pan of water, roughly one-third full, to a gentle boil. Place the chocolate in a heatproof bowl and set over the pan, taking care the bowl doesn't touch the bubbling water. Stir until melted, then take off the heat. Divide it between the holes of the mini-muffin tray. Sprinkle the chopped candy canes over, then chill for 10–12 minutes, until they start to harden. Take out of the fridge and stick a candy cane stick upright in each pool of chocolate. If they won't stand up straight, chill the chocolate for a bit longer, then try again.

Once the candy cane sticks are standing upright like little soldiers, return to the fridge to set completely for 1–2 hours (or 30 minutes in the freezer, if you're in a hurry).

≈≈≈≈

To use, heat a mug of milk, then swizzle the stick in the warm liquid until the chocolate melts.

e sledge dived
into the snow.
137

Nutella Christmas Wreath

This is wonderful: super-easy but with great impact! It is de facto a giant, chocolate-laced breakfast pastry, a sort of gargantuan pain au chocolat of dreams. The fact that its shape loosely resembles that of a festive wreath gives it a holiday feel that I particularly enjoy for Christmas morning. That said, there is of course nothing stopping you from baking and eating this on any other day. Indeed, so delightfully simple is it to throw together that I often make it for those mellow, indulgent days between Christmas and New Year.

I have assumed you don't want to have to think about this on Christmas morning, so the instructions here are for assembling the wreath the night before. Then all you need to do the next day is brush it with egg glaze, sprinkle with sugar and pop it into a hot oven.

HANDS ON TIME

15 minutes

HANDS OFF TIME

30 minutes

SERVES 8–10

≈≈≈≈≈≈

2 × 320g sheets of
   ready-rolled all-butter
   puff pastry (ideally,
   rectangular sheets)

280g Nutella

1 egg yolk

1 heaped tablespoon
   caster sugar

The day before you want this, line a large baking sheet with baking paper. Take the first sheet of puff pastry out of the fridge and unroll it on a work surface, leaving it on its paper, with a long side closest to you. Spoon half the Nutella on to the pastry and spread it out evenly, leaving a 0.5–1cm margin at the edges. Moving quickly, so the pastry doesn't melt in your hands, fold a long edge of the pastry over itself so you have a double layer, encasing the Nutella, then roll it up tightly, so you have a Nutella-laced pastry roll.

Carefully lift on to the lined baking tray and shape it into a half-circle, with the seam lying underneath.

Now, repeat with the remaining pastry and Nutella and set this on the mirror side of the first one. Gently press the ends together to make a single, wreath-like circle.

Use kitchen scissors to cut 'leaves' of pastry at a 45-degree angle, every 3–4cm or so: cut right up to 1.5cm from the centre of the circle. Lift each leaf of pastry and gently pull to alternating sides. Cover and chill overnight.

≈≈≈≈≈≈

The next day, heat the oven to 180°C / 160°C fan / Gas 4. Set an upturned dark baking tray (or pizza stone) in the middle of the oven.

Lightly beat the yolk with a fork in a small bowl, then use a pastry brush to glaze the pastry all over. Sprinkle the sugar over, then set in the oven and bake for 25–30 minutes until lightly golden. Leave to cool for 10 minutes before serving, as the melting Nutella inside the pastry will be very hot.

Pistachio Cream Croissants

These are 'cheat's croissants': you twist scraps of ready-made puff pastry into little horns that bear a sweet, if rather naïf, resemblance to a croissant, then fill with pistachio cream. It's the kind of mindless, instantly gratifying baking that I'm happy doing last minute, but you can make these a day ahead and gently reheat for five to ten minutes to warm them through. Or you can freeze them, before baking when needed (just adjust the baking time accordingly). The trick is to set a dark baking tray (or pizza stone) in the oven when you switch it on: this absorbs a lot of the heat, so when you set your tray of croissants on top, the bottoms bake through to a lovely crisp texture, rather than turning soggy.

You can fill these with whatever you like, from Nutella to jam, and they are great for bake sales filled with a chunk of dark chocolate for a nut-free alternative. But my all-time favourite is ambrosial pistachio cream, which I will happily eat by the spoonful. You can buy it from Italian delicatessens or online, or make your own by blitzing pistachios with white chocolate and a little caster sugar until you have a smooth, spreadable, gloriously verdant cream.

HANDS ON TIME

10–15 minutes

HANDS OFF TIME

25 minutes

MAKES 10

Butter, for the tin

2 × 320g sheets of ready-rolled all-butter puff pastry

150g pistachio cream

1 egg yolk, lightly beaten

20g pistachios, finely chopped

Icing sugar, to dust

Heat the oven to 200°C / 180°C fan / Gas 6. Grease a large roasting tin and line it with baking paper. Set a large dark baking tray upside down on the lowest shelf to heat up.

Place the sheets of pastry on a work surface and, using a sharp knife, cut 5 triangles, roughly 12–14cm at the base and 24cm long on the sides.

Spoon a heaped teaspoon of pistachio cream on the centre base of each triangle, roughly 2 fingers' width from the edge. Fold the bottom edge over the filling and roll up as snugly as you can. Pinch the tips to seal the pastry tight, so no filling spills out while they bake, then fold them to make little horns that loosely, at least, look like a croissant. At this point, they can be frozen. Place in the prepared tin

Use a pastry brush to glaze each with the egg yolk, then sprinkle the pistachios over. Cover with foil and bake in the oven on the hot baking tray for 15 minutes. Uncover and bake for another 5–10 minutes, until golden and puffed up. Let cool for a few minutes, then dust with icing sugar.

To reheat cooked croissants, cover with foil and warm up in an oven preheated to 180°C / 160°C fan / Gas 4 for 5 minutes. To cook the croissants from frozen, cover with foil and bake for 25 minutes, then remove the foil for a final 5 minutes.

Sticky Marzipan Breakfast Buns

It was my friend Cleo who first introduced me to the notion of warm, sweet buns on Christmas morning, and while a more labour-intensive choice than most of the other recipes in this chapter, they are undoubtedly above and beyond worth it: they are truly scrumptious and always a hit with everyone. For the longest time, I tried making a version of these that didn't involve any proving or yeast, before accepting that it's just not possible to get the ambrosial fluffy dough that you crave from a good sticky bun without a little help from some raising agent. The compromise, you'll see, is the recipe below, in which you only need to prove the dough once and which uses instant yeast, infinitely less temperamental than its fresh counterpart. In fact, it's not temperamental at all: you just want to make sure that the warmed milk and melted butter in which you dissolve the yeast aren't so hot that they kill it. Test the liquid on the back of your wrist, much as you would a baby's bottle, and it should feel warm but not uncomfortably hot. Another trick is to allow the buns plenty of time to rise before baking: they must double in size (at least) before you put them in the oven, even if that means allowing them a little more time to prove before baking.

As much as I love the idea of warm sticky buns straight from the oven on Christmas morning, the notion of baking them from scratch that same day feels a little too much like hard work for me, so the instructions here assume you want to make and prove them the day before. Alternatively, if you would really like to get ahead, you can follow the recipe and bake the rolls for just 10 minutes, then let cool completely, cover tightly and freeze for up to three months. To serve, let the frozen rolls defrost in the fridge for a few hours or overnight (still in their pan), then bake in a 190°C / 170°C fan / Gas 5 oven for fifteen to twenty minutes and glaze with the hot golden syrup (do not skip this step), as per the instructions below. Swap the marzipan out for chocolate chips for a nut-free alternative.

HANDS ON TIME
30–35 minutes to make
  the dough, then
  10 minutes to make
  the glaze after baking
HANDS OFF TIME
Overnight (or at least
  90 minutes) proving,
  then 30 minutes baking
MAKES 10–12

The day before you want to eat these, lightly grease a 23cm springform tin. Combine the flour, caster sugar and salt together in a large mixing bowl and set aside.

In a small pan, gently warm the milk and half the butter together over a medium heat until the butter is completely melted, then take the pan off the heat to cool a little. When the melted butter is warm to the touch (not hot), whisk in the dried yeast until dissolved. Pour the liquid into the bowl of flour mixture, crack in the egg and stir with a wooden spoon to bring the dough together.

Turn the dough out on to a work surface and knead for 5 minutes or so, until it feels soft and elastic. The dough will feel sticky and you can add a little flour to the surface to make things easier as you knead, but try to add as little as

80g salted butter, plus more for the tin

340g plain flour, plus more to dust

50g caster sugar, plus 1 heaped tablespoon for the filling

½ teaspoon fine sea salt

180ml whole milk

7g sachet of instant dried yeast

1 egg

110g soft light brown sugar

3 heaped teaspoons ground cinnamon

60g currants

40g mixed peel

70g marzipan, coarsely chopped

100ml golden syrup

possible, as too much extra flour will cause the buns to be heavy and solid rather than light and fluffy. Once kneaded, set the ball of dough back into a clean mixing bowl, cover with a clean tea towel and set aside to rest for 10 minutes.

Meanwhile, in a small pan, gently melt the remaining 40g butter over a gentle heat, then leave to cool. Combine the brown sugar, cinnamon, dried fruit and chopped marzipan in a small bowl and toss together.

Roll the dough out into a large rectangle about 36 x 20cm.

Use a pastry brush to brush roughly two-thirds of the melted and cooled butter over the rectangle of dough, then sprinkle over the spiced filling, leaving a 2–3cm bare margin around all the edges. Starting on a long side, roll the dough up tightly away from you, as you would a Swiss roll, then brush all over with the last of the melted butter.

With a sharp knife, cut the long, filled roll into 10–12 smaller rolls and snugly arrange them cut sides up in the prepared tin. Cover with foil and set in the fridge to prove overnight. Or, if you want to bake them immediately, put them somewhere warm to prove for 90 minutes.

The next morning, the rolls should have visibly doubled in size. Bring them to room temperature while you heat the oven to 190°C / 170°C fan / Gas 5. Remove the foil, set the tin in the oven and bake for 25–30 minutes until puffed up and lightly golden. If the rolls are browning too fast, cover them once more with foil. If you're uncertain as to whether they're cooked through, you can insert a thermometer into the middle of the bake: when it reads 91–93°C, they're done.

During the last 5 minutes of cooking time, warm the golden syrup in a small saucepan over a gentle heat until hot and liquid, but not boiling. Take off the heat. When the rolls are done, take them out of the oven, and, while still in their baking tin, use a pastry brush to generously brush the hot syrup all over. Serve warm or at room temperature.

Red Berry Breakfast Panzanella

A tumble of sticky, jammy red fruits – raspberries, blackberries, redcurrants, sweet cherries and glassy pomegranate seeds – a deconstructed and low-effort summer pudding of sorts, this recipe should by rights only work in summer, when the berries are in season. But, if you use frozen fruits, you'll find that it still tastes wonderfully vibrant, that perfect balance of sweet and sharp, even in the very depths of winter. Plus, I can't resist the very redness of it on Christmas morning. I like the sweetness of brioche here, but it also works well with toasted panettone or pandoro, if you have either on hand and they need using up, or even stale croissants.

This fruit and sweet bread salad is wonderful on its own, but you could serve it with a generous dollop of creamy Greek yogurt or crème fraîche, as well. And while, delighted by the ease and simplicity of this recipe, I most often make it for breakfast, there is absolutely no reason why you can't serve it for pudding at any other time of the day.

HANDS ON TIME
5–10 minutes
HANDS OFF TIME
1–2 hours, to defrost the fruit,
    plus 8 minutes baking
SERVES 6
෴
330g mixed frozen berries
100g frozen cherries
50g caster sugar
Juice of ½ lemon
150g brioche
60g pomegranate seeds
Greek yogurt or crème
    fraîche, to serve (optional)

Toss the frozen berries and cherries into a large salad or fruit bowl, sprinkle over the sugar, squeeze over the lemon juice, toss together so all the fruit is coated, then set aside to defrost. You can do this overnight in the fridge, if you prefer.

Heat the oven to 200°C / 180°C fan / Gas 6.

Tear the brioche into bite-sized pieces and spread out on a baking tray. Set in the oven for 6–8 minutes, until toasted and lightly golden, then set aside to cool. Once toasted, you can store the chunks of dried bread in an airtight container for up to 2 weeks.

෴

Once the fruit is defrosted and you have a jammy mess of berries swimming in red wine-hued syrup, then tumble in the toasted sweet bread and add the pomegranate seeds. Toss together so the bread is coated in sweet juices and serve immediately, with a dollop of thick Greek yogurt or crème fraîche, if you like.

Panettone Perduto

Panettone makes for an excellent *perduto* (the Italian version of French toast): soft and pillowy, almost headily spiced from that hint of cinnamon in the eggy batter and the scented candied orange peel that peppers its fluffy, bready dough. This is an excellent way to make good use of scraps of leftover, even dried-out, panettone – in fact it works best with stale bread – but is also a spoiling breakfast for Christmas morning. If you wanted to make an extra-indulgent pudding of it instead, you might want to serve it with a dollop of Boozy Amaretto Butter (see page 293) on top, so the sweet butter melts into the rich, cinnamon-scented, golden-toasted, raisin-studded bread. I can't tell you how good it is.

Getting French toast right, as with pancakes, is about managing the heat on the pan: too cool and you'll end up with soggy bread; too hot and it will burn. Once you've got the hang of it, I'm confident you'll find yourself *perduto*-ing all manner of baked goods with zeal. Heat the pan before adding the butter, then wait for it to melt completely and for the pan to be hot before adding the custard-dipped slices. If it feels that the toast is burning, take it off the heat for a few moments; if the butter is burning, use kitchen paper to wipe the pan and start again. If you only have a small pan, set your oven to a very low heat (110°C/ 90°C fan / Gas ¼, or the lowest setting), then, as you go, pile golden slices in there to keep warm while you cook the rest. This must be eaten just-cooked, so last-minute cooking is inevitable, but you can slice the panettone and make the custard the night before, then all you need do at breakfast is dip and fry.

HANDS ON TIME
20–25 minutes

HANDS OFF TIME
None

SERVES 4–6

500g panettone, ideally a
   little stale
120ml double cream
2 eggs
20g caster sugar
1 teaspoon vanilla extract
¼ teaspoon ground
   cinnamon
Salted butter, to fry
Icing sugar, to dust
   (optional)
Sea salt flakes, to serve
   (optional)

Slice the panettone into pieces roughly 2 fingers thick.

In a large mixing bowl, whisk the cream, eggs, sugar, vanilla and cinnamon together until well combined.

Dip each panettone slice into the mixture, holding it in there for at least 20 seconds, so it can soak up the custard. Carefully lift the panettone out of the custard and allow any excess liquid to drain off.

Melt a little butter in a large nonstick frying pan and fry half the panettone slices gently over a medium-low heat for 3–5 minutes, until lightly golden, then flip over and cook for a further 3–5 minutes on the second side, until warm all the way though. To check if they're done, gently press the centre of a slice: if it feels firm, it's ready; if it feels a little jiggly, keep cooking on a low heat a little longer. Repeat this process with the second half of the slices.

Dust with icing sugar and a sprinkling of salt flakes, if you like, and serve immediately.

Panettone Grilled Cheese Sandwich

There is so much that is seemingly wrong about this combination of melted, rich cheese with golden toasted sweet bread, yet – by some kind of alchemy – the two work exceptionally well together. Trust me on the addition of mustard: you need a slick of something sharp and peppery to cut through the glorious greasy, buttery richness of the whole affair (indeed, by the same principle, this would be good with a few cornichons or pickled onions on the side). Trust me also on the mayonnaise: I know it seems egregious to slather mayo over something as delicately flavoured as a slice of panettone, but you won't taste it. I promise. The mayonnaise seemingly evaporates into nothingness, but the combination of its constituent parts – eggs and olive oil – paves the way for a perfectly golden exterior on the sandwich.

This makes for a gloriously rich and indulgent breakfast, especially for those who like to start the day with something savoury, but I am also quite partial to a grilled cheese sandwich for supper, with nothing more than a little crisp green salad on the side.

HANDS ON TIME
10 minutes

HANDS OFF TIME
None

MAKES 1 perfectly sized
toasted sandwich

❧❧❧❧❧

80–90g panettone

10g salted butter

2 heaped teaspoons
mayonnaise

1 teaspoon Dijon mustard

2 heaped tablespoons grated
mild Cheddar

Slice the panettone into 2 evenly (and roughly equal) sized pieces. If it's a round, crossways section, I like to cut it on the diagonal, so that when sandwiched together you have a rounded triangular sandwich.

Set a nonstick pan over a medium heat and melt the butter. Spread the mayonnaise over 1 side of each of the pieces of panettone. Now turn a slice over so its mayonnaise-coated side is facing downwards and spread with a thin layer of mustard, then top with the grated cheese. Sandwich together with the second slice of panettone, mayonnaise-coated side facing upwards this time, then set in the pan.

Fry gently over a medium heat for 2–3 minutes, until the bread turns golden, then carefully flip the sandwich on to the other side and fry for a further 2–3 minutes, until golden on both sides and the cheese has melted. Serve immediately.

Cheesy Ham and Croissant Bake

This is halfway between a croque monsieur and a puddingy, cheesy bread-and-butter pudding. You can make it from scratch on Christmas morning without much hassle; or prepare the tray of filled croissants the night before, all snugly fitted into their dish, and whisk the eggs, milk and cheese together in a jug and store in the fridge. When you're ready for breakfast, drench the croissants with the milk mixture, top with a last grating of cheese and pop in the oven to bake.

This is a great option if you find yourself cooking breakfast or brunch for a crowd, as it's one of those recipes which you can happily scale up or down depending on numbers. I typically allow one croissant and a few slices of ham and cheese per person.

HANDS ON TIME

15 minutes

HANDS OFF TIME

25 minutes

SERVES 6

~~~~~

6 croissants

240g Taleggio, sliced

120g sliced ham

6 sage leaves

5 eggs

90ml whole milk

50g finely grated Parmesan

30g Gruyère, grated

Sea salt flakes and freshly
  ground black pepper

Heat the oven to 220°C / 200°C fan / Gas 7.

Cut the croissants open and fill each with slices of Taleggio and ham and a sage leaf, then sandwich back together. I always leave the rind on the Taleggio, but you can cut it off if you prefer. Arrange the filled croissants snugly in an ovenproof dish.

In a mixing bowl, combine the eggs, milk and Parmesan, whisk with a fork, then season the mixture generously with salt and pepper.

~~~~~

Pour the eggy mixture over the croissants, sprinkle over the grated Gruyère and bake in the oven for 25 minutes, until the cheese is melted and golden.

Holiday Mood Egg Nog

A glass or two of egg nog + Christmas music + cookies or biscuits = instant holiday mood.

I make this in copious quantities over the festive season. I enjoy having a bottle of egg nog on hand in the fridge to serve to friends when they pop by, or for after dinner with a dish of chocolates or a plate of Miniature Marzipan Pears (see page 272) in place of a full dessert, or quite simply whenever I want to conjure up that holiday feeling.

The great debate when making egg nog is what proportions and quantities of alcohol to mix into the milkshake-like custard that forms its base. The conclusion I have come to, after some trial and error, is that there is no wrong answer, it is just a matter of taste. That said, my friend Davin – somewhat of an egg nog aficionado – insists that you need equal parts of rum, brandy and whisky to achieve the perfect balance of flavours. That is now the ratio I strictly abide by when mixing this gloriously custardy cocktail and which is the recipe I've given you below. If I'm making a batch to enjoy with children, then I leave the alcohol out, or I'll make half the batch plain and spike the rest. Equally, if I'm out of one of the three kinds of liquor, I simply make up the difference with whatever I have on hand.

Some people like to whisk the egg whites to a cloud-like consistency, then fold them into the drink just before serving, but I like the richer texture of egg nog made only using the yolks. I also appreciate that you can make this yolk-only version up to a week in advance, chill it in the fridge, then just give it a quick stir and a (entirely optional but very much appreciated) grating of nutmeg, before serving. That makes it the kind of drink I feel very happy and relaxed about serving to a large crowd, which, in my view, is exactly how egg nog should be enjoyed. Don't waste the egg whites, though: you can use them to make a Christmas Pavlova (see page 262).

HANDS ON TIME
10 minutes

HANDS OFF TIME
About 2 hours chilling

SERVES 10–12

❧❧❧❧❧

6 egg yolks
200g caster sugar
500ml whole milk
120ml double cream
80ml rum
80ml brandy
80ml whisky
Whole nutmeg, to serve
  (optional)

Combine the yolks and sugar together in a large mixing bowl, then whisk with electric beaters until well-blended, creamy and voluminous; this will take 3–5 minutes. Pour in the milk and cream, whisking all the while, until you have a thick, creamy drink rather like a milkshake. Lastly, whisk in all 3 liquors: the rum, brandy and whisky.

❧❧❧❧❧

Cover and chill in the fridge, then finely grate the nutmeg (if you're adding it) over the egg nog before serving. If storing for a longer time, keep in a sealed jar or bottle for up to 1 week.

Olga's Sticky Sausages

Whenever my godmother Olga throws a party, she serves trays of these sticky, mustardy sausages and everyone goes wild for them: there is nothing better to enjoy with cocktails, after all, than a good cocktail sausage. You'll see the quantities here err on the generous side, as somehow, however many of these you roast, it's never quite enough.

HANDS ON TIME

10 minutes

HANDS OFF TIME

30 minutes

SERVES 8–12

❧

2 tablespoons olive oil

48 cocktail sausages,
    separated from each other,
    if strung

3 tablespoons runny honey

2 tablespoons wholegrain
    mustard

1 tablespoon English
    mustard

Heat the oven to 200°C / 180°C fan / Gas 6.

Pour the oil into a large roasting tin and heat in the oven for 3–4 minutes, then take the tin out of the oven and toss in the sausages. Toss to coat lightly in oil, then roast the sausages for 20–25 minutes until browned on the exterior and cooked through. You can slice into a sausage to see if it's cooked: the middle should feel hot to touch.

Drain the sausages and pat them down with kitchen paper. At this point, you can keep them in an airtight container in the fridge for up to 2 days.

❧

In a small bowl, lightly whisk the honey and both kinds of mustard together with a fork. Tip the sausages into a clean roasting tray lined with foil, then drizzle the mixture over them and toss so that they're all evenly covered in sauce.

If glazing these straight from the oven, then roast them for just another 5 minutes until slightly burnished and irresistibly sticky. If glazing cold from the fridge, roast for 10–12 minutes until warmed all the way through. Either way, serve immediately.

See previous page for a photograph.

Mulled Wine

....

Mulled wine is ambrosial: you can taste its delectable warmth, so richly spiced, right down into the hollow of your belly with each sip. But the very best thing about mulled wine, I can't help but feel, is the inimitable scent of Christmas that permeates the house as it bubbles away on the hob. There are few things that taste, feel and smell more deliciously festive.

The quantities below are for a single bottle of red wine, which broadly should make enough for six cups or servings. Of all the drinks in this chapter, however, mulled wine is easiest to make for a crowd. You can prepare it in advance – indeed there is a strong argument to be made that preparing it ahead allows the flavours more time to develop and intensify – then reheat gently as needed. All you need is a large saucepan for the wine to simmer away in.

HANDS ON TIME

5 minutes

HANDS OFF TIME

10 minutes

SERVES 6

❧

1 bottle of fruity red wine

30ml brandy

50g caster sugar

4 cloves

2 long cinnamon sticks

¼ teaspoon mixed spice

1 orange

1 lemon

Pour the wine and brandy into a large saucepan, then add the sugar and spices.

Use a sharp knife to slice off the peel and pith of the orange and lemon in thick strips and toss into the pan with everything else. (You only need the peel here, so you can use the fruit itself for something else, such as Orange, Carrot and Pistachio Salad, see page 185.) Otherwise, just halve the fruit and chuck it in.

Set the pan over a medium heat and bring to the boil. Once the wine begins to bubble, reduce the heat and let simmer for 5 minutes to infuse the flavours. If making this in advance, turn off the heat and cover with a lid; it will be fine like this for up to 24 hours in a cool kitchen.

❧

Reheat gently over a medium heat. Serve warm and straight from the pan.

See overleaf for a photograph.

Pistachio, Almond and Parmesan Cantucci

A playful, cheesy twist on a classic Italian sweet biscuit, these are delightfully simple to make. No rolling or chilling of pastry required: you basically bung all the ingredients into a food processor, blitz, then loosely shape the dough into a long sausage; bake, slice into pieces and bake again. Even more joyfully, cantucci last for (seemingly) ever when stored in an airtight container (you can also freeze the dough in logs, then defrost in the fridge and bake off as needed), which means you can make them well in advance.

I like to have a couple of jars of these on hand through the festive period, to wheel out as needed, usually just piled high and as is, in a dish, for guests to nibble on with drinks before Christmas lunch or dinner; but there is absolutely nothing stopping you from topping each crumbly biscuit with a dollop of blue cheese, a wafer-thin sliver of ham, or a little smear of mascarpone and half a dried fig. They're also a lovely addition to any cheese board.

Leave out the pistachios and almonds and swap for a handful of dried cranberries, if you want them to be without nuts.

HANDS ON TIME
10 minutes to make, plus 5 minutes to slice mid-bake

HANDS OFF TIME
30 minutes baking, plus 3 hours cooling

MAKES 26–28

100g salted butter, chilled, plus more for the tray
250g self-raising flour
80g Parmesan, finely grated
50g almonds, coarsely chopped
50g pistachios, coarsely chopped
2 eggs, lightly beaten
Sea salt flakes

Heat the oven to 180°C / 160°C fan / Gas 4. Grease a baking tray and line it with baking paper.

Chop the butter into pieces and combine in a food processor with the flour and a generous pinch of salt, then blitz until you have something that resembles the consistency of flour. Add the Parmesan and blitz again to combine. Now, add both types of nuts and blitz once more to combine. Lastly, add the eggs and blitz to make a dough.

Divide the dough into 2 large sausages (roughly 5cm thick) and set on the prepared tray. Bake in the oven for 18 minutes, until the rolls of dough are puffed up and lightly golden.

Take the tray out of the oven and let the rolls of dough rest for a few minutes, until cool enough to handle. Now, with a serrated knife, slice into pieces roughly 1cm thick and arrange the biscuits, cut sides up, on the baking tray.

Set back in the oven to bake for a further 9–10 minutes, until lightly golden and crisp. Cool for at least 3 hours, then store in an airtight container for up to 2 weeks.

Amarena Amaretto Sour

This recipe comes from my dear friend Delilah, unparalleled in her gift for glamorous cocktails: intensely sour cherries, almond liqueur and sharp lemon juice. I mix it in my high-powered blender, somewhat less elegant than shaking, but so quick and low-effort that I can't bring myself to do it any other way. These are best made last minute: put the ingredients in the blender cup in the fridge, adding the lemon and egg white to serve.

HANDS ON TIME
5 minutes

HANDS OFF TIME
6 hours, for the ice cubes to freeze (optional)

SERVES 6

≈≈≈≈

12 amarena cherries
150ml Amaretto
80ml amarena syrup
120ml lemon juice
1 egg white

Make the extra-large ice cubes in advance, if you like: drop 2 amarena cherries in each mould, fill with cold water and set in the freezer to freeze completely. You can skip this step if you're happy to go with plain ice; just drop a cherry or two into the finished cocktail.

≈≈≈≈

Combine all the ingredients – the Amaretto, amarena syrup, lemon juice and egg white – together in a blender, then blitz until pale pink and frothy. Pour over the ice cubes to serve.

Gorgonzola-Walnut Panettone Crostini

I especially like this combination of sweet, dry, bready panettone with creamy, rich blue cheese and topped with a crisp walnut, but try wafer-thin, salty prosciutto crudo, or a dollop of pâté, either chicken liver or perhaps porcini or truffle.

HANDS ON TIME
5–10 minutes

HANDS OFF TIME
8 minutes

MAKES ABOUT 16

≈≈≈≈

280g panettone
160g Gorgonzola
16 walnut halves

Heat the oven to 200°C / 180°C fan / Gas 6.

Slice the panettone 1.5–2cm thick. I like to cut it across to make big round slices, then into smaller, bite-sized pieces. Arrange them on a baking tray.

Bake for 6–8 minutes, until lightly golden and crisp, then let cool. Once toasted, you can store them in an airtight container for up 1 month.

≈≈≈≈

To make the crostini, top each piece with a generous smear of Gorgonzola and a walnut.

Saffron Popcorn

The idea to season buttery kernels of popcorn with finely ground, intensely flavoured saffron comes from my husband, Anthony, and I can't help but feel that it's a stroke of genius. The saffron is a simple touch, but it adds a warmth of flavour to the plain corn that makes it feel both special and irresistibly moreish.

HANDS ON TIME
10 minutes
HANDS OFF TIME
None
SERVES 6–8

2 teaspoons saffron strands
1 teaspoon sea salt flakes,
    plus more if needed
3–4 tablespoons olive oil
200g popcorn kernels

Grind the saffron and salt flakes together with a mortar and pestle to make a fine powder. Set aside.

Heat the oil in a large, deep saucepan over a medium heat. Add 3–4 popcorn kernels and wait for them to pop. Once they have popped, add the remaining kernels in a single layer. Cover the pan immediately, then remove it from the heat and pause for 30 seconds; then set the pan back over the heat, still covered, and listen to the kernels pop.

Every now and then, give the pan a good shake to move the kernels around and stop them burning. Once the popping slows to several seconds between explosions, remove the pan from the heat. Add the powdered saffron and toss together, then taste and season with more salt, if needed. If you like, serve warm straight away.

Or serve a little later, at room temperature!

Spiced Hot Apple Juice

An excellent, non-alcoholic alternative to mulled wine, with the same heady combination of aromatic and sweet scented spices, but made with a base of apple juice. Typically, if I'm hosting a holiday party for more than a few people, I'll get a batch of both going, as I find that, warming and soothing with each sip, children and grown-ups alike love this. My preference is for cloudy apple juice, the very best that I can get my hands on, as I find the sharper, rougher-round-the-edges and not quite so sickly sweet flavour lends itself better to the concoction of spices. But if you prefer something sweeter and more syrupy to drink, then apple juice made from concentrate is what you're looking for. Like Mulled Wine (see page 89), this is an excellent recipe for scaling up or down to cater for anything from four to one hundred.

HANDS ON TIME

5 minutes

HANDS OFF TIME

10 minutes

SERVES 4–6

❧❧❧

1 litre apple juice, ideally
   cloudy (or see recipe
   introduction)

1 orange

10–12 cloves

1 long cinnamon stick

5cm piece of root ginger,
   sliced, if you like

4 star anise

Combine all the ingredients together in a large saucepan. Set over a medium heat and bring to the boil: when the juice is bubbling away in the pan, reduce the heat and let simmer for 5 minutes or so to allow the flavours to infuse. If making in advance, leave to cool, then decant into a container you can cover and store in the fridge to chill for up to 24 hours.

❧❧❧

Reheat gently over a medium heat. Serve warm, straight from the saucepan.

See previous page for a photograph.

Christmas Mocktail

Coming up with a good non-alcoholic drink to serve at Christmas, something that doesn't taste overly sweet and that holds the same intangible glamour as a martini, is always a bit of a challenge. When in Italy, I love drinking Sanbitter, which sits somewhere in the faux negroni family. It feels innately festive, because of its bright red colour, and, these days, you can easily buy it in the UK too (either online or from good Italian delicatessens). Otherwise, you can always dress up posh elderflower pressé for the holidays, by serving it in Champagne coupes or flutes, then tumbling a few ruby-red pomegranate seeds into each glass.

For something a little more exciting, though, I very much like this combination of pomegranate and ginger, with its scarlet hue and hint of peppery spice, which both looks and tastes wonderfully festive.

HANDS ON TIME
5 minutes
HANDS OFF TIME
None
SERVES 6

1 litre pomegranate juice
1 litre ginger beer
Ice
Pomegranate seeds, to serve

Combine the pomegranate juice and ginger beer over ice in a large jug, then serve chilled with a sprinkle of pomegranate seeds in each glass.

See overleaf for a photograph.

Chestnut Martini

These martinis come out the most exquisite shade of pale, ambrosial gold, like very light honey: the syrup adds a shot of sugary sweetness to the fiery vodka, but with an unmistakable hint of the distinct flouriness of chestnut.

Chestnut syrup is easy enough to buy online and I would happily invest in a bottle for the pleasure of these martinis alone, but once you have a ready supply of the syrup on tap, you should try adding a shot to coffee or hot chocolate: both are delectable (and innately festive-feeling) combinations.

If you're mixing your chestnut martinis for a small group, you might want to shake the vodka and syrup together with ice in a cocktail shaker, mostly for effect; but I'll admit that if I'm making these for a crowd, I simply combine the two together in a jug and stir vigorously. If catering for larger numbers still, you can mix the martinis in extravagant quantities, then store in a bottle in the freezer until ready to serve. My only insistence is that, if the martinis are not already freezer-cold, you serve them over ice, because this really is a cocktail best enjoyed chilled.

HANDS ON TIME
5 minutes

HANDS OFF TIME
None

SERVES 4

200ml chilled vodka
120ml chestnut syrup
Ice (optional)
Marrons glacés, to serve
   (optional)

Combine the vodka and syrup together and stir. Store in a bottle in the freezer until ready to serve.

To serve, pour over ice, if required, and top the glass with a single marron glacé on a cocktail stick, if you like.

A Few Ideas for Canapés

Laying out a generous selection of nibbles is a wonderfully welcoming way to greet hungry guests, most especially if you don't want to bother with a formal starter. People find it relaxing, I think, to help themselves to a little bit of this and a little bit of that before lunch or dinner, often while I potter in the kitchen finishing off the preparations for the meal. And even if you are offering a starter – which on a special occasion you might – it's still a good idea to have something to pick at beforehand: however much you might meticulously plan the timings for a meal, sometimes (often) things don't work out quite how you planned. Knowing that everyone has plenty to snack on in the meantime eases the time pressure and any associated anxiety! Plus, the nibbles often end up being my favourite bit. So as well as the simple recipes you've just read, here are a few more ideas.

POTATO CRISPS WITH CAVIAR

I fill a large salad bowl or dish with good-quality salted crisps, then place a pot of lumpfish caviar at its centre for everyone to scoop up on to their crisps. I can't tell you how delicious this is, nor how indulgent it feels. Furthermore, it's almost no effort to throw together and looks wonderfully chic.

GINGERNUT BISCUITS TOPPED WITH BLUE CHEESE

A Swedish friend brought this delectable flavour combination into my life, and I'm so grateful she did: the sweet, fiery nuttiness of the biscuit together with the creamy, pungent cheese is utterly glorious. You can make these with Gorgonzola or Stilton and you might also want to add a little dollop of cranberry sauce – a blob of ruby red atop each canapé – which looks delightfully festive, but is also an excellent complement to the richness of the cheese.

DATES STUFFED WITH MASCARPONE AND A WALNUT

These can be assembled days beforehand and kept in the fridge. The combination of fudgy, sweet date with creamy mascarpone and crunchy walnut is unexpectedly good. You can also swap the walnuts for almonds.

SAFFRON MAYONNAISE WITH RED CHICORY LEAVES AND/OR RAINBOW CARROTS

You'll find the recipe for saffron mayonnaise on page 109, or you could simply whisk a small amount of saffron-infused cooled water into a bowl of good, shop-bought mayonnaise. Then set a dish of this golden, creamy goodness at the centre of a larger dish and surround it with crisp red chicory leaves or spindly rainbow carrots (or both) for dipping. It looks wonderfully effective and tastes exceptionally good.

BOWLS OF CANDIED PECANS

You'll find the recipe for these at page 181. They're quick and simple, can easily be prepared both in advance and in large batches and everyone always loves them. If pushed, bowls of salted nuts generally are a great idea, but these are so good and so moreish that they're worth the extra effort to make, particularly on a special occasion.

Mushroom Tortellini in Brodo

In many households across Italy (including ours), it is traditional to eat tortellini *in brodo* – stuffed pasta swimming in a piping hot chicken or capon broth – on Christmas Eve. I've given recipes for chicken broth in *A Table Full of Love* and for tortellini *in brodo* in *A Table in Venice*, but this recipe is a nourishing vegetable broth peppered with mushroom-filled pasta: a vegetarian twist on a classic. You can of course make pasta from scratch, but for ease at a time when there is already so much going on, I buy it from a good delicatessen, or the supermarket. Beyond the precious fact that it is one of those dishes that everyone, of all ages, enjoys, I'm especially fond of it on Christmas Eve, as you can make the broth ahead, then it takes mere minutes (and just one pan) to reheat it and cook the pasta. It's the kind of low-effort, intuitive cooking – a metaphorical scrambled-eggs-and-toast kind of dish – that I crave the night before the celebrations (and associated cooking) get going.

As it's a meal in itself, I happily serve a piping hot dish of this before a good pudding, perhaps Egg Nog Cream Pie, Christmas Pavlova or just a plate of gingerbread biscuits or a Chocolate Salami (see pages 236, 262, 266 and 275). Or, if Christmas Eve is for you the main event, you can serve this to open a feast of many courses.

HANDS ON TIME
20 minutes
HANDS OFF TIME
3 hours
SERVES 6

FOR THE BROTH
2 celery stalks
1 leek
1 red onion
2 carrots
½ butternut squash
2–3 litres cold water
Small bunch of sage
Parmesan rind
Sea salt flakes and freshly
   ground black pepper

TO SERVE
500g mushroom tortellini
Parmesan shavings
   (optional)

Cut the celery stalks, leek, onion, carrots and butternut squash in half, toss into a large saucepan and cover with the measured cold water. Add the sage and the Parmesan rind, salt generously, then set over a medium heat and bring to the boil.

Once the water begins to gallop, reduce the heat, cover the pan and let simmer over a gentle heat for 2–3 hours. Scoop out and discard all the cooked vegetables, then season the broth to taste with salt and pepper.

You can store the broth in a sealed container in the fridge for 3–4 days or, if you prefer, freeze it for up to 3 months.

When you're ready to serve, bring the broth to a gentle boil in a large saucepan, then add the pasta. Cook until al dente according to the packet instructions, then serve the broth in warmed bowls with the tortellini swimming in it and, if you like, Parmesan shavings melting on top.

Creamy Chestnut Soup
with Pomegranate

I've never been one to get hugely excited about soup. And yet, this cream of chestnuts – buttery and almost sweet to taste – is a concoction of such utter exquisiteness that I find myself waxing lyrical about it to anyone who will listen. Both the dollop of crème fraîche, a puddle of snowy whiteness against honeyed brown, and the glistening red pomegranate seeds, are entirely optional, you could happily leave them out, and sometimes I do. But I quite enjoy the intense sourness of the cream and the fresh sharpness of the seeds against the rich, soft background of the chestnut.

This is a pretty simple dish to make, but if you would like to spare yourself extra hassle on the day, you can easily cook it ahead of time. Either keep in its pan, ready to reheat on the hob when required, for up to two days, or store in the fridge for up to a week (I like to use empty plastic water bottles to save on fridge space). Alternatively, you can freeze the soup in a ziplock bag for up to three months, then just defrost and reheat as needed.

HANDS ON TIME

20 minutes

HANDS OFF TIME

None

SERVES 6 as a starter

2 tablespoons extra virgin
   olive oil

1 onion, chopped

500g cooked chestnuts

1.5 litres vegetable stock

120g crème fraîche

60g pomegranate seeds

Sea salt flakes and freshly
   ground black pepper

Heat the oil in a medium-sized saucepan over a medium heat. Add the chopped onion together with a generous pinch of salt and fry gently for 3–5 minutes until soft and translucent. Now add the chestnuts and cover with the vegetable stock.

Bring to the boil, then reduce the heat and simmer gently for 10–15 minutes.

Take the soup off the heat and, using either a handheld blender or a food processor, blitz until creamy and smooth. Taste, then adjust the seasoning.

Gently warm the soup before serving, then top each bowl with a dollop of crème fraîche and a smattering of pomegranate seeds.

Seafood and Saffron Cocktail

There is something gloriously retro, but also utterly perfect, about a seafood cocktail on Christmas Day. I serve mine in glass coupes with crisp green lettuce leaves cradling a dollop of mixed, juicy seafood doused in a rich mayonnaise.

I've waxed lyrical before about the virtues of homemade mayonnaise: it is one of those recipes that can feel intimidating to execute, but in practice, after you've made it once, you'll wonder what you were ever doing with shop-bought. It takes only a few minutes to whisk up the mayonnaise and you can store it, covered, in the fridge for up to three days, then bring it out for your seafood cocktail, or to zhuzh up a good leftovers sandwich, or serve with crisp red chicory leaves and carrots for wintry crudités of sorts.

Equally, if making your own mayonnaise feels like too much of a stretch at a time when there is so much else going on, you can cheat. Whisk shop-bought mayonnaise (I urge you to buy the best quality you can get your hands on, it really is worth it) with the saffron-infused water here to give the warmth of flavour and gloriously radiant, almost golden, colour which really makes this dish.

HANDS ON TIME
30 minutes, depending
   on how quickly you
   can make mayo!

HANDS OFF TIME
None

SERVES 6
❧❧❧❧❧

FOR THE SAFFRON MAYONNAISE
1 teaspoon saffron strands
1 tablespoon boiling water
2 egg yolks
Juice of ½ lemon
200ml sunflower oil

FOR THE REST
¾ large fennel bulb, thinly
   sliced, fronds reserved
250g white crab meat
300g large cooked and
   peeled prawns
2 Baby Gem lettuces
Sea salt flakes

Set the saffron in a small dish or cup, then cover with the measured boiling water and set aside for at least 5 minutes.

Put the egg yolks in a bowl with the lemon juice and a very generous pinch of salt and whisk vigorously until the yolks thicken a little. Slowly add the oil, a few drops at a time to begin with, whisking all the while. As it becomes well blended, add a little more oil. You'll see the mayonnaise grow in volume, at which point, pour in the remaining oil in a steady trickle, whisking all the while. Lastly, whisk in the cooled saffron water. To speed things up when assembling the dish, you can make the mayonnaise in advance, then store in the fridge, covered with clingfilm, for up to 3 days.

Combine the fennel and crab in a large mixing bowl. Chop the prawns into small pieces, reserving a handful of whole prawns for each portion. Add the chopped prawns and saffron-scented mayonnaise to the bowl and toss together. You can do this up to 4 hours in advance, then give it all a good stir before finishing and serving the dish.

❧❧❧❧❧

Arrange 3–4 Baby Gem leaves in each dish, then spoon in the seafood cocktail and decorate with whole prawns. Serve immediately, or at least within an hour or so.

Gilded Miniature Baked Potatoes with Crème Fraîche and Caviar

The idea to gild buttery baked potatoes with edible gold leaf comes from my ever-glamorous friend, Charlotte, who served a version of this recipe at her Halloween party last year. I became instantly obsessed. Everyone loves a baked potato, of course, but laced with crème fraîche and intensely salted, jet-black caviar, then dressed in a gold-flecked jacket, the humble, comforting and cosy potato becomes something gloriously luxurious that spells out 'party'.

While you likely don't need a recipe for how to bake a potato, the trick here is to add the gold leaf once the spuds are already cooked. This is very simple to do: the gold leaves come inside a small paper booklet, you open it up carefully to expose one side of the square of gold, then very gently press the gold side on to the potato (wherever you like, but I usually aim for the top half), then gently lift off the paper. You might find that some of the gold leaf peels away or drifts to another part of the potato: I don't mind this, I think the gold looks best when it has imperfect, slightly worn edges to it. If you like, you can use a paintbrush (or pastry brush) to brush out the edges further. Once you've got the hang of it, this is quick to do: have all your components ready and on hand, so you can easily gild the potatoes as they come out of the oven and plate them up for each guest.

HANDS ON TIME
5–10 minutes
HANDS OFF TIME
40 minutes
SERVES 6

6 small baking potatoes
6 sheets of edible gold leaf
120g crème fraîche
120g lumpfish caviar
Sea salt flakes

Heat the oven to 200°C / 180°C fan / Gas 6.

Use a fork to pierce the potatoes all over, then arrange on a baking tray. Sprinkle generously with salt flakes and set in the oven for 40 minutes, until the skins are lightly golden and you can insert a knife and feel no resistance.

To serve, while still piping hot, slice each potato open across its longest point, then gently press 1 gold leaf on to the skin. If the gold isn't sticking, then brush the tiniest amount of water on to the potato skin and the leaf will stick perfectly. Spoon a dollop of crème fraîche into the middle of each potato, then top with a smaller dollop of glossy black caviar. Serve immediately.

Potted Salmon with Preserved Lemon

I've taken this recipe, barely adapted, from Claire Macdonald's glorious book *Seasonal Cooking*, which, while sadly now out of print, remains for me an endless source of joy and inspiration year round. It is, though, most especially so over the festive season, when the nostalgic, delightfully almost-old-fashioned quality of the beautiful recipes really comes into its own. This, in particular – a creamy-pink salmon pâté of sorts, intensely salty, laced with preserved lemon and crunchy, buttery chunks of walnut – I'm especially partial to, not least when smeared on sweet toasted brioche or a chunk of crunchy white baguette, or just regular toast.

Because I love a shortcut, I buy fillets of hot-smoked salmon from the supermarket, so then the making of this is really just a matter of throwing everything together and blitzing in a food processor. You can prepare it well in advance and the individual ramekins make it easy to portion up as a starter. If catering for a crowd, you could also make it in a single large dish, then plonk it in the middle of the table with a loaf of warm bread (either homemade soda bread or a couple of those baguettes which you buy half-baked then finish off in the oven), for everyone to dig in and help themselves.

HANDS ON TIME
10 minutes
HANDS OFF TIME
5 minutes, plus chilling
SERVES 6

⋐⋐⋐⋟

160g salted butter
80g walnuts, coarsely
  chopped
360g hot-smoked salmon
2 preserved lemons
Sea salt flakes

Melt the butter in a frying pan over a gentle heat. Once melted, pour off 120g of the butter into a small bowl and leave to cool. Add a generous pinch of salt and the chopped walnuts to the remaining butter in the pan, then fry over a gentle heat for 5 minutes until lightly browned, shaking from time to time to stop them from catching. Set aside to cool.

Remove the skin from the salmon, then toss the flaked pink flesh into a food processor. Slice the lemons in half, remove and discard the pips, then toss into the processor with the fish. Blitz to combine.

Once you have a chunky paste and you can see that the lemons have been blitzed into fine pieces, slowly add the cooled, melted butter and blitz again until you have a thick, creamy pink paste. Mix in the toasted walnuts, then divide between 6 ramekins and chill in the fridge until ready to serve, covered with clingfilm that rests on the surface of each pot. The potted salmon will keep up to the use-by date that the hot-smoked salmon has printed on its packaging.

⋐⋐⋐⋟

Serve the potted salmon straight from the fridge with slices of toasted sourdough or brioche or regular bread, warm soda bread, or crunchy baguettes.

Walnut and Gorgonzola Stuffed Pears

There is so much to love about these baked pears: the buttery crisp pastry, the tender sweet fruit – its flavours mellowed from gently roasting in the oven – and the dollop of rich blue cheese and nuts, creamy and pungent, at its centre. I quite like a single pear, enrobed in golden puff pastry, as a starter, but it could also double as a savoury, in place of cheese or pudding, after a meal.

This recipe works best with fruit that is on the under-ripe side, as it holds its shape better and gives a superior texture once roasted than over-ripe fruit. You can wrap the pears in puff pastry, glaze them with egg, then store in the fridge for up to twenty-four hours, before popping them straight in the oven to bake.

HANDS ON TIME

20–25 minutes

HANDS OFF TIME

20 minutes

SERVES 6

✿✿✿✿✿

180g Gorgonzola

60g walnuts, coarsely chopped

6 pears, no need to peel

Juice of 1 lemon

3 × 320g sheets of ready-rolled all-butter puff pastry

1 egg

Heat the oven to 200°C / 180°C fan / Gas 6.

Combine the Gorgonzola and chopped walnuts together in a small bowl and mix well. Now, slice a pear in half, straight down the middle top to tail, then use a teaspoon to scoop out the core and make a small hollow in the centre of each half. Use a pastry brush to coat the cut sides in lemon juice. Spoon a generous dollop of the cheese and nut mixture into each hollow and then press the 2 halves back together. Repeat to fill and reassemble each pear.

Cut 2 rounds out of each sheet of pastry, then place a pear at the centre of each pastry round and carefully fold the pastry up around it, trimming away excess as needed and leaving the pear's stalk poking out. Set them on a baking tray. Gather the pastry offcuts and cut into leaf shapes, then use to decorate each of the pears. At this point, you can store the pears in the fridge, ready to go on their baking tray, for up to 24 hours.

✿✿✿✿✿

In a small bowl, lightly whisk the egg with a fork, then use a pastry brush to glaze the pastry-enrobed pears. Set in the oven and bake for 20 minutes, until lightly golden all over, then serve immediately.

Pomegranate-Glazed Turkey

There are two elements which contribute to making this my favourite way to roast a turkey. First, you brine the bird, so the meat stays succulent, however you roast it. Second, the pomegranate molasses glaze turns the skin a seductive burnished colour and gives a sticky, salty tartness that is nigh-on irresistible. I don't stuff my turkey, but if you do, simply fill the cavity after brining, increasing the roasting time accordingly to allow for the heavier weight.

For guidance on roasting times according to weight, see page 139.

HANDS ON TIME
1 hour
HANDS OFF TIME
12 hours brining, 2½ hours
   roasting and resting
SERVES 6

3.5kg free-range turkey

FOR THE BRINE
1.4 litres pomegranate juice
70ml maple syrup
150g fine sea salt
1 tablespoon peppercorns
4 bay leaves
5–6 rosemary sprigs
1 orange, quartered
Juice of ½ lemon

FOR THE TURKEY
220ml pomegranate juice
100ml pomegranate
   molasses
1 tablespoon maple syrup
6 tablespoons olive oil
1 teaspoon crushed
   peppercorns
1 tablespoon sea salt flakes,
   plus more to sprinkle
600–800ml chicken stock

Place the turkey in a large, deep pan, add the brine ingredients and top with cold water to cover (4–5 litres, depending on the pan). Cover and set somewhere cold for 10–12 hours. (I know some recipes require you to boil the brine first, but I never bother and it's still amazing.)

When ready to roast the turkey, lift it out of the brine, discard the liquid and put the bird on a rack in a roasting dish. Leave it for 1 hour to come to room temperature.

Heat the oven to 220°C / 200°C fan / Gas 7.

Combine the 220ml pomegranate juice, molasses, maple syrup, 2 tablespoons of the oil, the crushed peppercorns and salt flakes in a small bowl and whisk with a fork, then use a pastry brush to brush some of this glaze on the turkey, sprinkling more salt flakes over, to help it crisp in the oven. Now, pour 300–400ml of the stock into the roasting dish.

Reduce the oven temperature to 180°C / 160°C fan / Gas 4 and immediately set the turkey in the bottom half of the oven. After 30 minutes, pour half the remaining glaze over the breast with 2 tablespoons more of the olive oil and top up the roasting dish with a little more stock. Repeat again after a further 30 minutes. If the skin looks browned, cover the turkey with foil before placing back in the oven, though it will inevitably blacken a bit with its sticky dark glaze.

Roast until it has cooked for 1 hour 40 minutes in total (or 2 hours 10 minutes for a not free-range bird). Start checking the temperature halfway through cooking by inserting a meat thermometer in 3 places – the breast, the outer thigh and the inside thigh – to get an accurate reading. When the thermometer reads 72°C, it's done. Remove the turkey from the oven and rest on a carving board, covered with foil, for 20–30 minutes, before carving and serving.

Rolled Turkey Breast with Chestnut and Sage Stuffing

A lovely alternative to roasting a whole bird. I would even go so far as saying that I prefer rolled turkey breast, my favourite part of the bird to eat. But also – and crucially – it allows for an excellent stuffing-to-meat ratio, in this case with a pleasing chestnut-and-sage-scented bread stuffing running through the middle of the roast, infused with its delicious juices. On an entirely practical note, this is a far easier joint to carve than wrestling with a whole turkey, as you simply slice it into thick rounds much as you would slice a loaf of bread. And without the bones the meat will cook faster, which can make life easier, most especially on Christmas morning, when it can feel frustrating to have the rhythm of the day dictated entirely by the tyranny of oven timings for a big bird.

Ask your butcher to prepare the breast for you: they should roll it, leaving the skin still on the top, so it turns golden and salty-crisp in the oven. If you can, ask them also to create a hole through the middle of the roll, using a boning knife. Otherwise, you can do this yourself at home. I don't own a boning knife, but use the longest, skinniest knife I do have to poke holes from either end of the meaty roll, then get in there with my hands to prise the hole a bit wider before packing the meat tightly with stuffing. This is about as elegant a process as it sounds, but somehow even though every time it feels like I'm doing it wrong, it always works out just so. I can't help but draw a little frisson of happy satisfaction when I slice into the meat to reveal a pleasingly round centre of delectable stuffing at the heart of each slice.

As with the Pomegranate-Glazed Turkey on the previous page, I strongly recommend using a meat thermometer to confirm if the meat is cooked. You can of course do it by eye and check the juices run clear, but, most especially at Christmas, I enjoy the reassurance that comes from a number telling me that everything is cooked and good to go. That said, make sure to allocate time for the turkey to rest before carving: given its size and mass, it will go on cooking as it does so and it allows time for the juices to permeate the meat with more flavour.

HANDS ON TIME
20 minutes
HANDS OFF TIME
1 hour to bring to room
   temperature, 2½–3 hours
   cooking, 30 minutes
   resting
SERVES 12–14

On Christmas Eve, heat 1 tablespoon of the olive oil and the butter together in a saucepan over a medium heat. Once it is melted, add the onion and sage with a generous pinch of salt, then fry gently together for 3–5 minutes until the onion becomes soft and translucent. Take off the heat and set aside to cool.

Add the breadcrumbs to the cooled, cooked onion and give everything a good stir to combine. Crumble in the chestnuts, then season to taste with salt and pepper. Now,

4 tablespoons olive oil

1 tablespoon salted butter

1 onion, chopped

Small bunch of sage, coarsely chopped

180g fresh breadcrumbs

100g cooked chestnuts

1 egg, lightly beaten

3–3.2kg skin-on, rolled boneless turkey breast

Sea salt flakes and freshly ground black pepper

add the egg and use a wooden spoon to bring the stuffing together. Leave to cool completely.

Use a long, sharp knife to make a hole through the middle of the rolled turkey breast, if your butcher hasn't already done this for you. I do this by poking the knife in at one end, as far as I can get it, then repeat the same process from the other side and use my hands to prise the hole open a bit wider. Use your hands to stuff the cold chestnut stuffing into the hole, packing it in as tightly as you can: it might seem like there is too much stuffing for the hole, but keep pressing it down in there – try using the handle of a wooden spoon to help get it into the nooks and crannies, if you're struggling – and you'll see it all comes together in the end. Cover and refrigerate overnight. Any leftover stuffing you didn't manage to get in the bird can be baked separately for about 30 minutes alongside the vegetables. The joint will keep like this happily for up to 24 hours in the fridge.

Bring the rolled turkey breast to room temperature: take it out of the fridge at least an hour or so before roasting.

Heat the oven to 220°C / 200°C fan / Gas 7.

Set the turkey joint in a roasting tray, skin side up, then drizzle the remaining 3 tablespoons of olive oil over the skin and sprinkle very generously with salt flakes.

Set in the hot oven and roast for 20 minutes to crisp up the skin, then reduce the oven temperature to 180°C / 160°C fan / Gas 4 and roast for a further 1 hour 45 minutes (or roughly 35 minutes per kilo, depending on the size of the joint). Check the roast after it has cooked at the reduced oven temperature for 90 minutes: if the internal temperature in the thickest part of the breast registers at 70–72°C and the juices run clear, then it's done; if not, return it to the oven to roast for a little longer.

Cover with foil and let rest for at least 20–30 minutes before slicing to serve.

Ginger and Apricot Glazed Ham

There is something wonderfully picturesque about a whole sticky glazed and studded ham: it looks the part, like something out of a Georgian feast, as much as it tastes like celebration and Christmas. The ginger and apricot are subtle here: the ham tastes delectably sticky without being overly spiced or peppery, just gently flavoured. And whereas timings for roasting a turkey can be a delicate matter, a good ham is every bit as wonderful served warm, straight from the oven, as it is at room temperature, which makes this a lower-stress – yet still traditional and resplendent – alternative for Christmas Day.

HANDS ON TIME
30–40 minutes

HANDS OFF TIME
3 hours simmering, plus
    40 minutes glazing

SERVES 8–10

3kg gammon joint
1 red onion, peeled
    and halved
2 litres ginger beer
Handful of cloves
2 heaped tablespoons
    apricot jam
4 teaspoons water
1 teaspoon ground ginger
4 teaspoons light
    muscovado sugar

Put the gammon joint and the onion halves in a deep saucepan, then cover with the ginger beer. Set the pan over a high heat, bring to the boil, then reduce the heat and let simmer for 3 hours. Check on the ham every now and then and top up the pan with boiling water, as needed, to keep the meat completely covered.

When the ham is cooked, drain and discard the cooking liquid, then set the joint, skin-side up, in a roasting tray. Let it cool a little so it's comfortable to touch, then use a sharp knife to remove the skin, leaving a thin layer of fat. Score the fat to make a diamond pattern and stud each diamond with a clove.

Heat the oven to 240°C / 220°C fan / Gas 9 and line a roasting tray with foil.

In a small saucepan, combine the jam, measured water and ginger and set over a medium heat. Heat for a couple of minutes, stirring regularly, to make a thick syrup. Carefully spoon the hot, sticky syrup over the scored fat, taking care to glaze it all, then sprinkle over the sugar, patting it down gently so that it sticks to the glaze. Set in the oven to roast for 10–15 minutes, until burnished.

If you want to make the ham in advance, cool it completely after cooking in the ginger beer, then skin it, score the fat, stud with cloves, glaze, loosely tent in foil and store in the fridge for up to 1 week. When you're ready, bring it to room temperature and then bake in an oven heated to 180°C / 160°C fan / Gas 4 for 30–40 minutes to serve warm.

Roast Poussins with Crisp Prosciutto and Sage

There is so much to recommend poussins as an alternative to the more traditional Christmas poultry, such as turkey or goose. They are much quicker to roast than a larger, single bird, and, because poussins are so small, the meat always comes out succulent and tender, never dry. You can squeeze a number of small birds into a roasting tray, so it's a practical and low-stress recipe to cook in larger quantities, and if you allocate a single small bird for each guest, you don't have to worry about carving. I've given quantities below for six, allowing for one poussin each, though at a push (and with plenty of trimmings) you could happily double that number and cater for twelve with just the six birds. If you would like to scale the quantities up, however, it's easy enough to do so by allowing for roughly ½ tablespoon of olive oil, a couple of sage leaves and two or three slices of prosciutto per poussin: the cooking time remains the same.

You can prepare the birds ahead of time in their trays and keep them in the fridge, then when you're ready to go, pop them in the oven to cook for just under an hour. You could of course also roast the birds more simply, by dousing the skin in olive oil and seasoning them with a generous showering of salt and freshly ground black pepper and a nice squeeze of lemon juice, but I love the delectable contrast between the tender, succulent poussin and the gloriously salty, crisp, thin slices of prosciutto.

HANDS ON TIME
5–10 minutes

HANDS OFF TIME
60 minutes

SERVES 6

꙳꙳꙳꙳

6 poussins
3–4 tablespoons extra virgin olive oil
Small bunch of sage
12–18 slices of prosciutto crudo
Sea salt flakes

Heat the oven to 200°C / 180°C fan / Gas 6.

Nestle the birds into a large roasting tray, sitting them snugly so they're nestling up against each other. Drizzle the olive oil over the birds, sprinkle generously with salt, then rest 2–4 sage leaves on top of each breast and drape over 2–3 slices of prosciutto so each little bird is enrobed in a blanket of thinly sliced cured ham. You can store in the fridge like this, all ready to go, for up to 1 day, then return to room temperature before roasting.

꙳꙳꙳꙳

Roast for 45–60 minutes until the prosciutto and any exposed skin is crisp and the juices run clear when you stick a knife into the thickest part of the body. After 30 minutes you may need to cover the birds with foil, if it looks like the prosciutto is crisping too much.

Roast Goose with Caramelised Clementines

There is something Dickensian (in a good way) about a roast goose; many, my husband included, very much prefer it to turkey. The sticky, sweet roasted clementines, with their golden, burnished hues, just add to the delectable extravagance of it all.

When you cook the bird, you want the meat buttery-rich and tender, but the skin salty crisp; that same delectable texture as Peking duck. The best way to achieve this is with the cooking method below, where you pour boiling water over the bird, then pat dry.

A brief note on timings: for a larger (or smaller) bird, roast for 10 minutes at 240°C / 220°C fan / Gas 9. Reduce the heat to 190°C / 170°C fan / Gas 5 and cook for 32 minutes per kg. When calculating cooking time, include the weight of the citrus inside the bird.

HANDS ON TIME

20 minutes

HANDS OFF TIME

2 hours to dry in the fridge,
  3 hours to cook,
  30 minutes to rest

SERVES 6

4.5–5kg goose

3 lemons, plus the finely
  grated zest and juice of
  1 lemon

12 clementines

Small bunch of bay leaves

Small bunch of rosemary

2–3 tablespoons olive oil

3 tablespoons clear honey

Sea salt flakes and freshly
  ground black pepper

Bring a kettle of water to the boil. Pierce the skin of the goose all over with a fork. Set it on a wire rack in the sink, then pour boiling water over it. Pat dry with kitchen paper, then settle the bird, on its wire rack, in a roasting tray. Slice 3 lemons, cut 6 clementines in half and stuff them inside the cavity with most of the bay leaves and the rosemary sprigs. Sprinkle the skin generously with salt and set in the fridge to dry for at least 2 hours (or, better still, overnight).

An hour before you're ready to roast the goose, take it out of the fridge and heat the oven to 240°C / 220°C fan / gas 9. Halve the remaining 6 clementines, slicing them across their bodies, and arrange them snugly in a roasting tray; then season generously with salt and pepper, throw in a few more bay leaves and drizzle over the olive oil. Set aside.

In a small bowl, combine the honey with the lemon zest and juice, add a generous pinch of salt and smother all over the skin of the bird. Cover with foil and set in the oven; after 10 minutes, reduce the oven temperature to 190°C / 170°C fan / Gas 5 for 2½–3 hours. For the last 30 minutes of cooking, remove the foil so the skin can crisp up. To test if the goose is done, insert a sharp knife into the thickest part and check the juices run clear; or use a probe thermometer: it is cooked at 70°C. Take out of the oven, cover with foil and a couple of clean tea towels, then rest it for 30 minutes.

Meanwhile, set the tray of clementines in the oven to roast for 30-40 minutes, until tender and caramelised. Serve the goose with the roasted sweet fruit.

Pork Tenderloin with Persimmons and Pomegranate

Roast pork isn't a canonical choice for Christmas lunch, yet this way of serving the tender meat together with buttery, sweet persimmons and a cascade of sharp, shimmering red pomegranate seeds feels and looks innately festive. It looks like Christmas.

There is some last-minute frying and slicing involved, so it's not a dish I would relish cooking for a large crowd, but for a more intimate group of up to six, even, at a push, eight people, I can't think of anything more spoiling. And unlike a large bird or roast, which takes time to roast and rest, this is a dish you can throw together with ease and in haste.

HANDS ON TIME
10–15 minutes
HANDS OFF TIME
25 minutes
SERVES 6

2 pork tenderloins
    (500–700g each)
1 tablespoon extra virgin
    olive oil
3 persimmons
30g salted butter
Handful of pomegranate
    seeds
Sea salt flakes and freshly
    ground black pepper

Heat the oven to 220°C / 200°C fan / Gas 7. (If you don't have a large ovenproof frying pan, put a roasting tin in the oven to heat up.)

Pat the pork dry with kitchen paper and rub it all over with the oil and salt and pepper. Place a large (ideally ovenproof) frying pan over a medium heat, add the tenderloins and cook until browned all over, about 2 minutes on each side.

Set the pork in the oven (ideally in the same pan, or change to the preheated roasting tin if your pan isn't ovenproof) and roast for 10–15 minutes, until the thickest part of the meat registers 62–65°C on a meat thermometer. Take the pork out of the oven, remove from the pan and wrap in foil. Rest for 10 minutes.

While the pork rests, slice the persimmons into crescents 5mm thick. Melt the butter in the pan with the pork's cooking juices, then add the persimmon slices and a generous pinch of salt. Gently fry for 3–4 minutes, until the fruit softens and begins to caramelise slightly at the edges.

Unwrap the pork and, moving as quickly as you can, slice it into small pieces (1–2cm thick). Arrange the pork and the caramelised persimmons on a serving dish, pour over the juices from the rested meat and sprinkle with the ruby pomegranate seeds. Serve while still warm.

Cotechino and Spinach Roll

It is traditional in Italy to eat cotechino – that oversized, fatty and utterly delectable Italian sausage – on a bed of braised lentils on New Year's Eve (or Day). The lentils to bring you wealth and prosperity in the coming year (a custom that dates back to Roman times); the pork to bring abundance and fertility. Beyond the happy talismanic significance, it also happens to make for an excellent culinary pairing.

You can pre-order cotechino from a good butcher or Italian delicatessen. It comes in two varieties: the first you boil for two or three hours; the second more widely sold pre-cooked kind comes in a sealed silver bag and only needs twenty minutes in simmering hot water before it's perfectly cooked and melt-in-your-mouth, buttery tender. The latter option is both my preference and my go-to.

Traditionally, you serve your cotechino as is, sliced into thick rounds, over a bed of soupy braised lentils. But I've recently started cooking it this way, in something that resembles a rather Italianate sausage roll with a thick layer of buttery spinach, encased in golden shortcrust pastry. For ease, and if you prefer, you can prepare your roll in advance and keep it in the fridge for up to twenty-four hours, then just pop in the oven as needed, because this really is a dish that is best served warm and straight from the oven. You can make the roll with either shortcrust or puff pastry, but given how rich the sausage in the middle is, my personal preference is for shortcrust, which offers a good crisp complement to the indulgent fattiness of the meat. Mostarda di Cremona, with its glowing mustardy fruits, is a good sharp condiment to serve alongside.

You must then serve this with lentils: you could make braised lentils by starting with a base of softened onion, then simmering the dried pulses in stock until soupy and tender. But I most like to serve this with a lentil salad, the Good Luck Salad at page 192 to be specific, and – un-canonically but joyfully – also with a generous dollop of creamy mashed potatoes.

HANDS ON TIME

35 minutes

HANDS OFF TIME

20 minutes cooling, plus

   30 minutes baking

SERVES 6

Cook the cotechino in its silver wrapper in a large pan of boiling water for 20 minutes, then lift it out of the water. Carefully open the sachet and discard the fatty liquid surrounding the sausage (take care not to scald yourself here, as the cooking liquid will be hot and has a tendency to come pouring out when you open the bag). Set aside to cool to room temperature.

Heat the oil in a large pan over a medium heat, then add the spinach and cook for 8–10 minutes until completely defrosted. Take the pan off the heat and let the spinach cool, then carefully squeeze out all the water while the spinach is cool enough to touch but still warm. Return it to the dry pan

1 pre-cooked cotechino (or
    see recipe introduction)
2 tablespoons olive oil
600g frozen spinach
30g salted butter
320g sheet of shortcrust
    pastry
1 egg, lightly beaten

away from the heat, add the butter to the spinach and stir to melt. Leave to cool for another 5 minutes.

Unroll the sheet of pastry and slice one-third off. Lay this smaller piece on a baking tray lined with baking paper. Spoon just under half of the spinach in the middle of the sheet of pastry to cover a surface area roughly the size and shape of the cotechino. Carefully remove the skin from the sausage (it should come away easily in your fingers), then lay the cotechino over the heap of spinach. Use your hands to press the rest of the spinach over its top and to its sides as best you can, so the whole sausage is hidden under a blanket of buttery spinach.

Now, drape the larger piece of pastry over the spinach-enrobed cotechino and use your fingers to gently press down at its base to seal the 2 sheets of pastry together. Trim away any excess pastry and use these offcuts to decorate the roll, sticking them on with a little egg, then use a fork to press a ridged pattern round the edges. (I like to do this partly because it looks pretty and partly to ensure the roll is well sealed.) Lastly, cut a few small slits in the top of the roll to allow the steam to escape as it bakes, then, using a pastry brush, glaze all over with some more of the egg. At this point the roll will keep, covered on its baking tray and ready to go, in the fridge for up to 24 hours.

Heat the oven to 180°C / 160°C fan / Gas 4. Set an upturned baking tray (or pizza stone, if you have one) on the middle shelf of the oven.

Glaze the roll once more with the remaining egg, then set it in the oven, on top of the upturned hot baking tray, to ensure the bottom crisps as nicely as the top. Bake for 30 minutes (or 40 minutes if baking straight from the fridge), until lightly golden all over. Serve immediately.

Rules for Roasting

It's not often that we have an occasion to roast a whole turkey, and, perhaps because of that element of unfamiliarity, it can feel like an especially intimidating business, not least as turkeys can be big beasts (quite literally) to wrangle. But trust me when I say that it's just that: it's big, but it's not actually tricky to cook.

CHOOSING AND WELCOMING YOUR TURKEY

As soon as you get your bird home, check that it fits in the oven. Choose a roasting tray for it and adjust the shelves in your oven (or your 'oven furniture', as my husband calls it) to make room for it. Then you can assess where you stand in terms of oven space and what else you might be able to fit in there alongside the bird on Christmas Day. If it doesn't fit, then this gives you a little time at least to come up with a plan B and beg, borrow or steal a larger oven.

If you're roasting a frozen turkey, at this point take it out of the freezer, set it on a tray and put it somewhere cool to allow it to defrost. Bear in mind that a large turkey to serve fourteen-odd people (9kg or so) will take up to 48 hours to defrost, so allow plenty of time and aim to have your turkey fully thawed by Christmas Eve. Lastly: make a note of the bird's weight. You think you're going to remember, but if you're like me, you won't. As to what size bird to buy, there's a chart overleaf which recommends rough serving quantities by weight.

BRINING (AND HOW TO ENSURE THE MEAT IS NOT DRY)

I like to brine my turkey: this basically means soaking the bird in a salty solution of water, sugar and spices. This way, the meat soaks up extra liquid (and flavour), which stops it from drying out in the oven. This will all but guarantee you wonderfully succulent meat that never tastes dry, even if the turkey is cooked for a little longer than it should: a culinary insurance policy.

Depending on the size of the turkey, you'll need a large pot or bucket that will snugly fit the whole bird with enough headroom to cover it with brine. If you don't have a vessel large enough, you can buy handy plastic 'brining bags' online. You'll find at page 118 a recipe for brining and roasting turkey with spices and pomegranate juice. But even if you would like to go in a different direction, I urge you to nonetheless make a basic brine of 4 scant litres of water to 170g salt flakes, 100g sugar and 5 heaped tablespoons honey. To this you can add whatever seasoning you like: sage, bay, rosemary, citrus (orange and/or lemon and/or clementines), peppercorns, juniper berries, star anise, cinnamon sticks, chunks of onion or fennel and so on. Pretty much whatever you've got to hand, toss it in!

Cover the bird completely with the brining liquid, topping up with more water and/or salt and sugar as required, seal with a lid and set in the fridge (or outside) overnight, or for up to 24 hours, to soak up the juices. (If you're going to put it outside, make certain your vessel is secured from the attentions of wildlife.) Once brined, discard the liquid, pat the bird dry with kitchen paper, set it in a roasting tray and cover with foil. If you're using a frozen turkey, you can start brining from partially frozen, as it will continue to defrost in the liquid.

If brining the turkey in liquid feels like a logistical bridge too far, you can also dry-brine your bird: rub it down with salt, then let it rest in the fridge. The salt changes the protein structure of the meat, so it releases moisture which the bird then re-absorbs, resulting in tender, juicy turkey once roasted. Crucially, you want to use sea salt flakes and not table salt, as fine salt is too pungently flavoured. Use roughly ½ tablespoon sea salt flakes per 1kg of turkey weight, then mix it to a paste with olive oil and citrus (finely grated zest and juice). Rub this all over the bird and set it, uncovered, in the fridge, to brine for 24–48 hours.

ALLOW TIME TO BRING YOUR TURKEY TO ROOM TEMPERATURE

It's very important that the turkey is at room temperature before roasting, so make sure to take it out of the fridge and set it somewhere cool for a couple of hours at least before you put it in the oven. Half an hour beforehand, heat your oven.

COOKING TIMES

Cooking times for turkeys are in no way an exact science. They can vary significantly based on all sorts of factors, including the weight of the bird and how it was raised, so please take the below guidance on timings as exactly that: a guide rather than an absolute. The best (and easiest) way to get the timings right for your turkey is to regularly test it with a meat thermometer: when it reaches 72°C, it's comfortably done (though some cooks even recommend that it's done at 60°C). Take it out of the oven and let the bird rest.

As a guide, allow 25–30 minutes in the oven per kilo of turkey weight, then 35–40 minutes additional roasting time, for a standard bird. I've included a table, opposite, for your reference, of suggested timings, based on both weight and this formula.

A couple of things that are worth bearing in mind when calculating your cooking time: first, a free-range turkey from a good butcher will cook roughly 30 per cent faster than a mass-produced turkey. This is because free-range birds are typically raised for longer and therefore have more intramuscular fat, which conducts the heat faster as they roast in the oven; it's also why the meat tends to be more succulent. Similarly, a brined turkey, where the proteins of the meat have already been partially broken down by a saline solution, will also roast faster than one which hasn't been brined. So do check with your meat thermometer regularly, and before the end of the suggested cooking time, to avoid overcooking it.

WEIGHT / SERVES / COOK (FREE-RANGE) / COOK (NOT FREE-RANGE)

3.5kg / 6 / 1 hour 40 minutes / 2 hours 10 minutes
4.5kg / 6–8 / 2 hours / 2 hours 45 minutes
5.5kg / 8–10 / 2 hours 30 minutes / 3 hours 20 minutes
6.75kg / 10–12 / 3 hours / 4 hours 10 minutes
7.5kg / 12–14 / 3 hours 20 minutes / 4 hours 40 minutes
9kg / 14–16 / 4 hours / 5 hours 15 minutes
10kg / 18–20 / 4 hours 30 minutes / 5 hours 50 minutes
11kg / 22 people plus / 5 hours / 6 hours 30 minutes

CHECKING THE BIRD IS DONE

While I'm typically not an advocate of kitchen gadgetry, this is one instance in which I would say that a meat thermometer is both incredibly helpful and a worthwhile investment. If you don't already own one, do consider buying a thermometer when you order or purchase your next turkey. Many butchers sell them, as do supermarkets, and you can, of course, easily order them online as well. You can also buy leave-in meat thermometers that stay in the roast while it cooks, so you can easily see the internal temperature at any point.

If you don't have a thermometer, you can test to see if the turkey is cooked by inserting a knife into the thickest part of the bird (the thigh): if the juices run clear, then it's done. To be on the safe side, test the bird in multiple places.

STUFFING

All the cooking times above assume the turkey is not stuffed; plus it's better not to stuff a brined turkey. If you stuff your bird, make sure to factor in the additional weight and calculate cooking time accordingly. I prefer to cook stuffing separately from the bird (I've given two stuffing recipes at pages 166–167). Frankly, cooking stuffing separately is a less messy business than squeezing it into the cavity; it speeds up the roasting time, but also – crucially – means you get lots of nice crispy bits, as it browns nicely on top. If you're worried the stuffing will miss out on flavour from the turkey's roasting juices, or that it will be dry, an excellent tip from my friend, Maxim, is to drizzle warm gravy over it just before serving. (Again, don't use the juices from a brined turkey for making gravy, as they are too salty.)

RESTING

Once cooked, it's essential to allow plenty of time for the turkey to rest before serving. Carefully lift the bird out of its roasting tray and on to a carving board, cover loosely with foil, then lay a couple of tea towels over that to keep the warmth in, and set it aside to rest. A roast turkey can happily rest for up to half the time it took to cook it; allow at least an hour for smaller and 1½–2 hours for larger birds.

Nut and Cranberry Terrine

It seems a great culinary injustice that the nut loaf is often maligned as a lesser vegan alternative to turkey. There is certainly and absolutely nothing lesser about *this* terrine. Each bite is wonderfully crunchy, buttery and rich, with pops of sour-sweetness from the glossy layer of cranberries swimming in glossy red syrup atop the tumble of grains and nuts at its heart, encased in crisp golden pastry. It looks every bit as spectacular sitting at the centre of the table as poultry; arguably, even more spectacular... and it happens also to be vegan.

For ease, I use both ready-rolled pastry and those bags of pre-cooked long-grain rice: two shortcuts that make this quite a speedy dish to assemble and pop in the oven. Although it goes without saying that you could of course make your pastry from scratch, if you prefer, and you can cook the rice – long grain or wild, as you like – from dried grains according to the packet instructions.

To avoid the anxiety of lifting the whole thing out of a metal loaf tin, I like to make this in the same disposable foil loaf tins that I use to make Nutty Chocolate Torrone (see page 238). I buy them in bulk online and use them for baking and for storing leftovers; they're just a useful sort of thing to have kicking around in the kitchen. That way, if I'm taking the terrine to a friend's house, it can travel nicely in its foil container; when I want to serve it, I simply strip away the foil and it's ready to go. Otherwise, make sure to leave a generous overhang of baking paper when you line your loaf tin: then, to remove the terrine, gently tug on the paper overhang and it should raise up the terrine, so you can then lift it out fully.

HANDS ON TIME
30 minutes
HANDS OFF TIME
50 minutes baking, plus
   3 hours cooling
SERVES 6–8

Heat the oven to 220°C / 200°C fan / Gas 7.

Heat the oil in a large frying pan over a medium heat, add the onion, leek and fennel, then fry gently for 5–7 minutes until soft and translucent. Set aside to cool a little.

In a large mixing bowl, combine the cooked rice with the cooked onion, leek and fennel. Add the parsley, chestnuts and walnuts and toss everything together. Spoon in the almond butter and give the mix a good stir to combine well.

Drape the pastry over a 1.2-litre disposable loaf tin and press it down gently into the corners and up against the sides, then trim away the overhanging pastry. Spoon the rice and nut mixture into the pastry case and smooth out the surface with the back of the spoon. Roll the pasty offcuts into thin sausages and press gently around the rim to make a raised border.

Use a pastry brush to glaze the pastry border with the egg or non-dairy milk, then set it in the oven to bake for

2 tablespoons olive oil

1 onion, chopped

1 leek, trimmed and
   finely sliced

½ fennel bulb, finely
   chopped

350g cooked long-grain rice

Small bunch of parsley
   leaves, coarsely chopped

100g chestnuts, coarsely
   chopped

50g walnuts, coarsely
   chopped

80g almond butter

320g sheet of ready-rolled
   shortcrust pastry (check
   it's vegan if it needs to be)

1 egg, lightly beaten, or
   non-dairy milk

190g cranberry sauce

160g fresh cranberries

45–50 minutes, until the pastry is lightly golden and a skewer comes out piping hot when inserted into the middle. Leave to cool completely in its tin.

Combine the cranberry sauce and the fresh berries together in a small saucepan and set over a medium heat; let simmer for 3–5 minutes, until the sauce is syrupy and the fruit starts to pop. Remove the foil container and set the terrine on a serving board, open side up, then spoon the cranberry topping over the nutty filling, staying within the pastry border. Leave to cool before serving.

❧

Once assembled, and before baking, the terrine will keep happily in the fridge for up to 2 days; just bring to room temperature before baking and serving.

Camembert and Cranberry Pithivier

A dish so exquisitely rich and so utterly indulgent, with its golden, crisp, buttery pastry and oozing melted pungent cheese – and the sweet, bubbling red cranberry jelly hidden inside – that it really comes into its own at Christmastime, that moment for joyful excess and all things good.

It's delightfully simple to make: more a matter of assembling ingredients than cooking in any strict sense of the word. Moreover, once assembled, the pie will happily sit in the fridge, on its baking tray and ready to go, for one or two days. When you're ready to bake it, just pop in the oven until golden brown all over. My only caveat is to make sure to seal the edges of the pie well, by firmly crimping the top and bottom layers of pastry together, or sealing the join with the prongs of a fork. If it's not properly sealed, the filling will ooze out of any cracks as it melts and bakes in the oven; this matters little for the taste, but might take away from the pie's appearance when you bring it to the table for all to enjoy.

HANDS ON TIME

10 minutes

HANDS OFF TIME

20 minutes chilling, plus
    25 minutes baking

SERVES 6

€€€€

2 × 320g sheets of
    ready-rolled all-butter
    puff pastry (ideally,
    circular sheets)
250g Camembert cheese
    (a whole small cheese)
260g cranberry jelly
Leaves from a small bunch
    of thyme
1 egg yolk, lightly beaten

Line a baking tray with baking paper.

Unroll the first sheet of puff pastry and, if it's rectangular, cut a large circle (as big a circle as possible) out of its centre. Set the circle on the prepared baking tray and place the Camembert in the centre, then spoon the cranberry jelly around it, leaving a small margin (about 2cm) around the edge. Scatter the thyme leaves over the cheese and jelly, discarding the stalks.

Lightly brush the pastry margin with the egg, then unroll the second sheet of pastry and, if it's rectangular, cut a large circle (again, as big as you can) out of its centre. Lay this second disc on top of the first, then seal or crimp the edges with a fork or your fingers. Use a sharp knife to mark 4–6 long scored lines in the top of the pie, in a pinwheel design. Brush all over with egg, then trim the offcuts to make holly leaves and berries (or whatever you like) and gently stick them to the top, glazing them, too, with egg. Set the pie in the fridge to chill for 20 minutes, or up to 2 days.

€€€€

Heat the oven to 220°C / 200°C fan / Gas 7. Set a dark baking tray (or a pizza stone) upside down in the middle of the oven.

Set the pithivier in the hot oven, on top of the heated, upturned baking tray, and bake for 20–25 minutes until golden and crisp. Gently lift on to a serving dish or board and serve immediately, while still warm.

Beetroot and Horseradish Galette

If you're hungry or feeling especially greedy (which most often is the case for me), might I humbly suggest that you consider making two of these tarts, if only so you can enjoy a leftover slice, cold and with a little salad on the side, for lunch the next day.

I use ready-rolled puff pastry for this, with a mild preference for the kind that comes in a large circle (and looks rather like a pizza base) so I can easily fold the edges over into a pleasingly round galette, though you can just as well go for a rectangle. I also use ready-cooked vacuum-packed beetroot (though there is nothing to stop you roasting your own).

The trick for getting the tart just right is to heat a dark baking tray in the oven when you switch it on (I lay mine upside down so it's an easy surface to rest upon) and then to set the tart on top. The heat from the tray underneath helps cook the bottom of the tart through, so it's crisp and deliciously flaky, rather than soggy. If you don't have a baking tray to spare, then set the tart on the bottom of the oven instead.

This is such a simple dish to prepare that I feel quite comfortable doing it last minute. If you want to get ahead, you could slice the beetroot and leave it in a covered dish in the fridge, or somewhere cool, ahead of time, then just assemble at the very last minute. Or you can par-bake the tart and simply warm it in the oven as your guests arrive, or assemble and store uncooked in the fridge for up to 24 hours. If really pressed for time, there is absolutely no reason not to eat it at room temperature.

HANDS ON TIME
10 minutes

HANDS OFF TIME
35 minutes

SERVES 6

❧❧❧

320g sheet of ready-rolled
    puff pastry

100g creamed horseradish
    sauce

500g cooked beetroot, thinly
    sliced into rounds

1 tablespoon extra virgin
    olive oil

1 egg, lightly beaten

Sea salt flakes

Unroll the pastry and lay it, still on the paper it came in, on a baking tray. Spoon the horseradish over the middle, leaving a roughly 5cm margin round the edges. Arrange the sliced beetroot over the horseradish: there's no need to do this in an especially fancy way, I just try and make sure the entire surface is covered as evenly as possible.

Fold the edges of the pastry over all the way round so it's overlapping the edge of the beetroot layer. Drizzle the olive oil over the beetroot and season generously with salt. At this point, you can store the tart in the fridge for up to 24 hours.

❧❧❧

Heat the oven to 190°C / 170°C fan / Gas 5. Set a dark baking tray upside down in the middle of the oven.

Brush the pastry with egg, then set the galette in the oven on the upturned baking tray to bake for 30–35 minutes, until the pastry is golden and puffed up. Lift the tart gently and tap underneath to check that the bottom is cooked through and crisp. Once cooked, slide the tart on to a serving dish or board, then serve warm or at room temperature.

Black Truffle, Mascarpone and Quail's Egg Pasta Pie

Carb on exquisite, glorious carb in one indulgent, festive-looking pie: wonderfully creamy and rich, filled with pasta, cheese, slivers of musky black truffle and jammy-yolked quail's eggs. I buy the black truffle, already sliced and in a jar, online. I find it's quite a useful, albeit spoiling, ingredient to have in the house at Christmastime, to add to, and instantly elevate, anything from scrambled eggs on toast to a plain risotto.

You'll see that the quantities below allow for a cheesy pasta filling that is heavy on the truffle, but taste the pasta as you go and see how truffley you like it; you can always add more or less to taste. Strictly speaking, you need neither the truffle nor the miniature eggs in this pie, as the three kinds of cheese together with the pasta and the buttery, flaky pastry are plenty flavourful enough, but given that it's Christmas, a little excess feels *de rigueur*. Plus, there is something about both quail's eggs and truffle that feels like a special treat, so I couldn't quite resist.

HANDS ON TIME
30–40 minutes
HANDS OFF TIME
40 minutes baking, plus 10
   minutes resting
SERVES 6

Roll out the first sheet of puff pastry into a circle large enough to line a 23cm springform cake tin with a little overhang. Using the rolling pin, drape it into the tin, pressing it into the bottom. Prick it all over the base with a fork (this stops the pastry from puffing up too much), cover with baking paper, fill with baking beans and blind bake for 15–20 minutes, until the edges are very lightly coloured. Remove the baking paper and the beans from the tin and set back in the oven for a further 5 minutes, until the pastry is dry to the touch but still only very lightly coloured.

Meanwhile, bring a large pan of generously salted water to the boil. When the water begins to gallop, add the pasta and cook it very al dente: you want the pasta to be slightly undercooked, as it will continue cooking when it's wrapped in pastry in the oven. Drain it well.

Heat the olive oil in a pan over a medium heat, add the onion and fry gently for 3–5 minutes until soft and translucent, then take off the heat. Combine the cooked pasta and cooked onion together with the mascarpone, cream, Parmesan and Gouda and give everything a good stir (I do this in the saucepan I cooked the pasta in, to save on washing up). Now add the sliced black truffle and stir again to combine well.

2 × 320g sheets of
   ready-rolled all-butter
   puff pastry
250g short pasta, such
   as penne, rigatoni
   or macaroni
2 tablespoons olive oil
1 onion, chopped
250g mascarpone
190ml double cream
80g Parmesan, finely grated
50g Gouda, grated
20–25g sliced black truffle
   from a jar
6 quail's eggs
1 regular hen's egg,
   lightly beaten
Sea salt flakes

Spoon roughly half the cheesy, truffled pasta into the baked pastry shell and spread it out evenly over the bottom. Make 6 small indentations in the layer of pasta, then crack each of the quail's eggs into the little holes, so they're neatly nestled in there. Spoon the remaining cheesy pasta over the top to cover them in an even layer.

Take the second sheet of pastry and drape it over the pie, trim away any excess and press the edges together to seal. Use a knife to cut 4 slits into the top of the pie, to allow any steam to escape, then collect any spare pieces of excess pastry and use them to make decorations for the top, attaching them with a little of the egg. Lastly, using a pastry brush, glaze the top of the pie with the egg. Set the pasta pie in the fridge for up to 24 hours, until you're ready to bake.

When you're nearing time to eat, heat the oven to 190°C / 170°C fan / Gas 5 and set an upturned baking tray (or pizza stone) in the middle.

Set the pasta pie in the hot oven on top of the upturned baking tray (the heat of the tray will ensure the pie has a crisp pastry bottom as well as top). Bake for 30 minutes (or 40 minutes if you're taking it straight from the fridge), until lightly golden on top and the filling is completely heated through. (You can slide a knife, through a steam hole, into the middle of the pie: when it comes out, it should feel hot to touch.) Let the pie rest for 10 minutes in its tin, then take it out and set on a dish to serve while still warm.

Gnocchi and Pumpkin Gratin

This is pure comfort in a pool of melty, cheesy, potato-y deliciousness. I don't doubt that many Italians would shudder at the use of Cheddar here and I wholeheartedly accept that it's not canonical, but in my defence, Cheddar does melt beautifully and gives this dish the deeply comforting character of a macaroni cheese. If grated Cheddar – the kind you buy in bags in supermarkets all ready to go – feels like a bridge of unsophistication too far for you, then feel free to swap it out for some provolone (or similarly mild, melty cheese). And while we're talking about shortcuts and the virtues thereof, I'll admit that I typically make this with those bags of ready-diced butternut squash.

I love the moreish sweet crunch which you get from the crumbled toasted panettone scattered on top here: for me, it's the perfect complement to the rich stodginess of the rest of this dish. Round about Christmas, I typically have leftover panettone croutons kicking around, perhaps from making the crostini to serve before dinner (see page 92), but I've included a method here for whipping up the toasted panettone gratin nonetheless. And if you don't have any leftover panettone to hand (or are reluctant to crack into a whole cake just for this), you can either buy a miniature panettone, or substitute with toasted brioche, or even regular breadcrumbs.

HANDS ON TIME

40 minutes

HANDS OFF TIME

30 minutes

SERVES 6

❧❧❧❧❧

80g panettone (or see recipe introduction)

2 tablespoons olive oil

1 red onion, thinly sliced

350g prepared chopped pumpkin or squash

Small bunch of sage

10g salted butter

500g gnocchi

100ml single cream

200g mild Cheddar, grated

40g Parmesan, finely grated

Heat the oven to 180°C / 160° fan / Gas 4. Tear the panettone into small pieces, spread out on a roasting dish, then toast in the hot oven for 6–8 minutes until lightly golden. Set aside.

Heat the oil in a large, ideally ovenproof, pan. Add the onion and fry gently for 3–5 minutes, until translucent and soft. Now add the pumpkin or squash, sage and butter, frying gently over a medium heat for 5–10 minutes until the pumpkin starts to colour. Now reduce the heat a little, cover the pan and cook for a further 10–15 minutes until the pumpkin has softened (if you insert a knife, you should feel little by way of resistance).

Take off the heat, add the gnocchi, cream and Cheddar, then toss together. (If your pan wasn't ovenproof, transfer everything to an oven dish at this point.) Crumble over the panettone and sprinkle over the Parmesan. Cover with foil. At this point, you can cool to room temperature, then cover and store in the fridge for up to 2 days before baking.

❧❧❧❧❧

Heat the oven to 180°C / 160° fan / Gas 4. Set the gratin in the oven for 20 minutes, then uncover and bake for a further 10 minutes until the cheese is all melted and lightly golden on top. Serve immediately, while still piping hot.

Stuffed Pumpkin with Wild Rice, Cranberries and Chestnuts

I love this way of cooking pumpkin: roasted whole, still holding its imperfectly spheric shape and a mess of wild rice, crumbled chestnuts and whole dried cranberries spilling extravagantly out of its hollowed-out middle. It's one of those dishes that undoubtedly is a showstopper: it brings a touch of drama to the table, and the combination of sweet, buttery pumpkin flesh with crunchy grains is nothing but pure joy to eat. It's a dish that deserves to be a centrepiece, and can therefore very much hold its own as an excellent (even preferable) alternative to turkey on feast days, be they Christmas or Thanksgiving.

That said, I enjoy this tangle of flavours so much that I've also been known to serve it as a side dish. The searingly orange buttery flesh and rice can be scooped out together and served alongside Pork Tenderloin with Persimmons and Pomegranate, or Roast Goose with Caramelised Clementines (see pages 131 and 128), or any roast poultry.

It's worth knowing that you can happily prepare this recipe in advance: hollow out and roast the whole pumpkin; cook the rice, dress it and pack it into the squash; then store in the fridge for up to two days. Then all you need to do is bring it to room temperature and put in the oven for twenty to thirty minutes until warm all the way through to its core.

HANDS ON TIME
20 minutes

HANDS OFF TIME
40 minutes baking
  pre-stuffing, then
  30 minutes baking
  with stuffing

SERVES 4 as a main,
  8 as a side dish

~~~

1 medium Delica pumpkin
  (about 1.5kg)
4 tablespoons extra virgin
  olive oil
200g wild rice
850ml boiling water
60g dried cranberries
100g cooked whole
  chestnuts, roughly
  broken up
Sea salt flakes

Heat the oven to 200°C / 180°C fan / Gas 6.

Cut the top off the pumpkin and scoop out and discard the seeds. Put the pumpkin on a baking tray, rub the inside with 2 tablespoons of the olive oil and season with salt. Roast the body and lid separately for 40 minutes, until the flesh is tender and the skin begins to burnish.

For the filling, put the rice in a large saucepan, add a generous pinch of salt and cover with the measured boiling water. Cover and simmer for 40 minutes, until the grains have popped. Drain any excess liquid, then dress the rice with the remaining 2 tablespoons of olive oil. Add the cranberries and chestnuts and toss together, then pack the rice into the pumpkin. At this point, you can store the stuffed pumpkin in the fridge for up to 2 days.

~~~

Heat the oven to 200°C / 180°C fan / Gas 6.

Pop its little lid on the pumpkin and set back in the oven for 10–15 minutes (or 20–30 minutes if coming from the fridge), until piping hot. On serving, scoop out the flesh to eat with the rice.

The Best Roast Potatoes

The secret to a really good roast potato is to roast it for a long time, swimming in more olive oil than could ever seem sensible (or healthy). I also like to parboil the potatoes first: this step isn't essential, you can roast a very decent potato without it; and indeed on days when feeling lazy, or happy enough with a good roast potato rather than the very best (i.e. not at Christmas), this is exactly what I do. But to get a really fluffy middle and a golden crisp outside, the best way is to parboil until soft and tender, rough the potatoes up a little in the colander when you drain them, then lastly douse in flour before roasting. This is what gives that golden, irresistibly crunchy hardened exterior, which is almost everyone's favourite bit of the meal (it most certainly is mine). The other trick is not to peel the potatoes: this is a habit I fell into out of sheer laziness because, of all the kitchen chores, I loathe peeling potatoes. But I have found that the skins are what give the potatoes their structure and texture, and they crisp up so magnificently that it would be a shame and a waste to roast the spuds without them.

To ease things up on Christmas Day, you can parboil the potatoes up to two days ahead of time, arrange in their roasting trays, leave to cool, then cover and keep somewhere dark(ish) and cool (but not the fridge). When you're ready to go, toss the potatoes in flour, douse with olive oil and roast in the oven until golden crisp.

HANDS ON TIME
15 minutes

HANDS OFF TIME
15 minutes parboiling, plus
   1¼ hours roasting

SERVES 6–8
₰₰₰₰₰

1.4kg potatoes, preferably
   Maris Piper, scrubbed
   but unpeeled
3–4 tablespoons plain flour,
   or gluten-free flour,
   if needed
120ml extra virgin olive oil,
   plus more if needed
Sea salt flakes and freshly
   ground black pepper

Roughly cut each potato into 3 pieces (roughly 5cm each), cutting off each end at a slant so you're left with a triangle-shaped wedge in the middle. Try to cut the pieces as evenly sized as you can, so that they cook at the same rate.

Toss the chunks of potato into a large saucepan and cover with water, add a generous pinch of salt and set over a high heat to bring to the boil. Once the water begins to gallop, reduce the heat a little and let simmer for 10–15 minutes, until the potatoes are cooked and tender.

Drain the potatoes in a colander and shake them about a bit to roughen up the edges, then turn out into a roasting dish (or better still, distribute across a couple of dishes so they're not overcrowded).

₰₰₰₰₰

Heat the oven to 190°C / 170°C fan / Gas 5.

Sprinkle the flour over the potatoes, then shake the dish(es) so the potatoes are well coated. Drizzle over the olive oil and season generously with both salt and pepper. Set in the oven and roast for 60–75 minutes, turning halfway through, until golden and crisp.

Cheesy Fondue Roast Potato Bake

A magnificent way to repurpose leftover roast potatoes. I especially like this when made with 'Hedgehog' Potatoes (see overleaf), but we don't often seem to have many of those left over. Regular roast potatoes, or even cold baked potatoes, chopped into chunks, will all do nicely. I've also been known to roast potatoes solely for the purpose of making this dish.

The principle here is simple: potato, laced with sweet-sour pickled red onion and baked in a creamy, cheesy sauce until golden and melted on top. You can play around with the recipe as you please, and might want to toss in a few chunks of more strongly flavoured cheese, such as blue cheese or goat's cheese, as well. You could crumble in some chestnuts or walnuts; you could add cornichons directly to the bake, instead of serving them on the side; and equally you could add some fried pancetta, leftover shredded roast ham (such as the ham at page 124) or slices of speck or prosciutto, for something with more of a cheesy bubble-and-squeak quality about it.

HANDS ON TIME

10 minutes

HANDS OFF TIME

20 minutes for pickling the onion, 35 minutes baking

SERVES 6–8

❦❦❦❧

½ red onion, sliced

1 tablespoon red wine vinegar

1 teaspoon caster sugar

500g leftover roast potatoes

150g mild Cheddar, grated

60ml single cream

60ml white wine

Sea salt flakes

Cornichons or gherkins, to serve (optional)

Set the sliced onion in a small bowl together with the vinegar, sugar and a generous pinch of salt and leave to quick-pickle for at least 20 minutes.

Arrange the potatoes in an oven dish. Scatter over half the grated cheese, drizzle over half each of the cream and wine, then top with half the drained and pickled red onion. Now scatter over the remaining cheese, drizzle over the last of the cream and wine, then the last of the onion. Cover the tray with foil and set aside until you're ready to bake. Once assembled, the dish will happily keep, covered, for up to 4 hours somewhere cool.

❦❦❦❧

Heat the oven to 200°C / 180°C fan / Gas 6.

Set in the oven for 20 minutes until the cheese is melted, then remove the foil and set back in the oven for a further 10–15 minutes, until lightly golden on top and all the liquid has been absorbed. Serve the bake with a separate dish of cornichons or gherkins alongside, if you like.

'Hedgehog' Potatoes

It was our younger son, Achille, who christened these 'hedgehog' potatoes. Only in part because 'hasselback', the correct nomenclature, was too much of a mouthful for him, but also because – with their spiny, golden crisp backs – they do have a rather endearing and hedgehog-like quality about them. In our household, they've gone by 'hedgehog' ever since.

No matter how many you make, it's never enough: the potatoes, salty-crisp and golden, are so absurdly moreish that everyone requests seconds and then thirds. All of which makes the task of slicing each tiny little potato repeatedly across its back, then rubbing it in oil, well worth the modicum of effort required. If you use the wooden spoon trick I've outlined below (picked up from Nigella's version of this dish in *Nigella Summer*), it is far less of a faff than it sounds and so takes significantly less time than you think it will.

My other insistence is that you roast these on a baking tray rather than a roasting dish: the low sides allow hot air to circulate and crisp up the edges very nicely, rather than steaming them as you might in a deeper dish. Lastly, the sage is by no means a necessity, but it infuses the potatoes with a subtle, musky flavour I associate strongly with Christmas stuffing, and that is all-round very pleasing.

HANDS ON TIME
20 minutes
HANDS OFF TIME
45 minutes
SERVES 6

750g baby new potatoes
4 tablespoons olive oil
Small bunch of sage
Sea salt flakes

Sit the first potato inside the bowl of a wooden spoon, then use a sharp knife to slice into it repeatedly at roughly 3mm intervals, cutting right down almost to the bottom of the spud, but not quite all the way, so the whole thing holds nicely together. The wooden spoon stops you from cutting all the way down, and makes this a much quicker and easier process than it sounds. Repeat this process with all the potatoes, then arrange cut side up on a shallow baking tray.

Drizzle over the olive oil, then rub all the potatoes, gently prising the slices open and rubbing oil into the crevices as much as you can. Sprinkle generously with salt, then tear off the sage leaves and stuff a leaf in the sliced flesh of some of the potatoes. (You don't need to stuff a sage leaf into every single potato, though there is no harm in doing so.) You can prepare the potatoes up to 3 hours before roasting, then set aside until you're ready to put them in the oven.

Heat the oven to 200°C / 180°C fan / Gas 6.

Set the baking tray in the oven to roast for 45 minutes, until crisp and golden and the flesh of a potato feels tender when you poke at it with a knife or fork.

Panettone, Chestnut and Sage Stuffing

One of my favourite things about Christmas is stuffing. And while I know that the very name 'stuffing' implies that it should come stuffed inside something else, I can (and will happily) eat it all by itself, as is, and in extravagant quantities. Indeed, I prefer it baked in a roasting tray (or even in individual dollops in something like a muffin tray), because it creates extra surface for crispy bits. This particular recipe is a combination of some of my favourite flavours: sweet, raisin-studded panettone, buttery chestnuts and earthy, aromatic sage leaves. Together, it makes for the most exquisite combination.

To get ahead, you can make your stuffing up to two days before you plan on serving it, then just store in the fridge. Alternatively, it freezes very nicely and will keep for up to three months.

HANDS ON TIME

15 minutes

HANDS OFF TIME

45 minutes

SERVES 6–8

150g panettone, cut into
   1cm cubes

2 tablespoons extra virgin
   olive oil

1 onion, chopped

Small bunch of sage leaves,
   coarsely chopped

1 egg

300g unsweetened
   chestnut purée

130ml vegetable stock

Sea salt flakes

Heat the oven to 200°C / 180°C fan / Gas 6.

Spread out the cubes of panettone on a baking tray and toast in the oven for 5 minutes, until crisp and lightly golden. Set aside to cool a little.

Heat the olive oil in a medium frying pan, then add the onion, chopped sage and a generous pinch of salt. Fry gently for 3–5 minutes, until the onion is soft and translucent, then take off the heat.

In a large bowl, lightly beat the egg, then add the chestnut purée and the stock and mix together to combine. Now add the toasted panettone, cooked onion and sage and bring the mixture together with a wooden spoon. Spoon the stuffing into an ovenproof dish (I used a 15cm square dish). The stuffing will keep like this, covered and in the fridge, for up to 2 days. When ready to bake the stuffing, bring the dish to room temperature and uncover.

Heat the oven to 200°C / 180°C fan / Gas 6.

Set the dish in the oven to bake for 45 minutes, until golden and crisp on top and warm in the middle.

Nonna's Stuffing

I have some vague recollection of my mother tearing a Jamie Oliver recipe out of a magazine once upon a time, which I think was the starting point at least for this rustic, rich stuffing laced with fresh herbs, buttery chestnuts and salty cured bacon. But by virtue of the fact that she makes this without fail every year for Christmas lunch, the recipe has, to my mind at least, long since become hers. So I give it to you here exactly as my mother has it, neatly written out, in the folder where she keeps all her Christmas recipes, untouched and unchanged except for writing out in full those bits which she has scribbled down in shorthand. For me, it wouldn't be Christmas Day without it.

HANDS ON TIME

30 minutes

HANDS OFF TIME

70 minutes

SERVES 8–10

ᕬᕬᕬᕬ

1 loaf of ciabatta
   (about 250g)

3 red onions, peeled
   and quartered

4 garlic cloves, peeled
   but left whole

8 pancetta slices, plus
   more to top the stuffing

200g cooked chestnuts

Leaves from a small bunch
   of sage

Leaves from a small bunch
   of thyme

3–4 tablespoons extra virgin
   olive oil

500g sausagemeat, or
   chipolata sausages

Tear up the ciabatta into golf ball-sized pieces and scatter over a roasting tray. Arrange the onions, garlic, pancetta, chestnuts and herbs on top of the bread and drizzle over the olive oil. Roast in the oven for 30 minutes, until the pancetta is crisp and the onion is lightly roasted, then set aside and let cool completely.

Now, pulse the cooled, roasted ingredients for a few minutes in a food processor (or chop finely by hand). Combine all the ingredients with the sausagemeat in a large mixing bowl, or, if you are using sausages, then squeeze the meat out of the skins and bring everything together with your hands. Pack the stuffing into a roasting tray and drape the extra slices of pancetta over. Once assembled, you can store the tray of stuffing, covered and in the fridge, for up to 36 hours.

ᕬᕬᕬᕬ

When you're ready to cook it, heat the oven to 200°C / 180°C fan / Gas 6.

Set the roasting tray in the oven, uncovered, and roast for 35–40 minutes, until the pancetta slices on top have turned crisp and a knife comes out hot when inserted into the middle of the tray.

Sticky Roast Sprouts with Dates and Pistachios

I cannot overemphasise how utterly sublime sprouts cooked this way taste: the leaves charred and crisp, then tumbled in a sticky sweet-and-sour sauce of mashed dates and balsamic vinegar... almost irresistibly moreish. The addition of a handful of coarsely chopped pistachios is by no means essential, although I do have a soft spot for the many muted shades of green that the nuts and leaves create together, and I find the buttery crunch of the nuts adds another layer of texture to the dish.

This is one of those recipes where everything really comes together at the last minute. While you could, in theory, roast the sprouts in advance and simply reheat them in their sauce as needed, I find that in doing so you lose some of the charred crispness of the leaves, which is what makes this dish so utterly delectable.

HANDS ON TIME
10 minutes

HANDS OFF TIME
20 minutes

SERVES 8

800g Brussels sprouts, trimmed

40g salted butter

2–3 tablespoons balsamic vinegar

100g dates, pitted and chopped

4 tablespoons extra virgin olive oil

90g pistachios, coarsely chopped (optional)

Sea salt flakes and freshly ground black pepper

Cut the sprouts in half and toss on to a baking tray, spreading them out in a single layer.

In a large pan, melt the butter over a medium heat. Once melted, increase the heat and add the balsamic vinegar and chopped dates, along with a generous pinch of salt and a very generous grinding of black pepper. Let bubble away for 2–3 minutes, until the sauce is thickened into something that looks like bubbling molasses. Remove from the heat.

Heat the oven to 220°C / 200°C fan / Gas 7. Line a large baking tray with foil.

Drizzle the oil over the sprouts, season very generously with salt and roast for 15–20 minutes, until crisp and tender. Meanwhile, reheat the date sauce.

Add the roasted Brussels sprouts to the pan of date sauce and stir to coat, then sprinkle with pistachios, if you like, before serving.

Martin's Ruby Red Cabbage

It was over dinner that I discovered my friend Martin (who loves Christmas almost as much as I do) cooks his red cabbage in lashings of Ribena. Intrigued, I instantly went home to try his method out and now I won't cook red cabbage in any other which way. You can't taste the blackcurrant from the cordial, instead what it gives you is a sticky, buttery spaghetti-mess of sweetness with an intensely deep red colour. I serve this piping hot on Christmas Day; but an alternative way of doing things, if you like, is to serve it at room temperature, almost more of a salad, with a smattering of shimmering pomegranate seeds scattered over the purple-hued tangle of shredded cabbage. I find this smattering of pomegranate seeds is a great way of zhuzh-ing up any red cabbage leftovers, too.

HANDS ON TIME
10 minutes, then stirring
    from time to time for an
    hour or so
HANDS OFF TIME
An hour or so, but while
    stirring a bit too
SERVES 8
᥄᥄᥄ᠺᡉ
30g salted butter
1 red cabbage (1–1.1kg),
    thinly sliced
500ml undiluted Ribena
Sea salt flakes

Melt the butter in a large pan over a medium heat, then add the sliced cabbage, give everything a good stir, cover and let sweat for 25–30 minutes, until the cabbage is cooked right down. Every now and then, lift the lid up and give everything a good stir, to check that it isn't sticking to the pan.

Now, add the Ribena, bring to a gentle boil, then let simmer away, uncovered, for a further 30–40 minutes until all the dark red liquid has evaporated and the cabbage is tender and sticky. Season to taste with salt.

᥄᥄᥄ᠺᡉ

You can prepare the cabbage 4–5 days ahead of time, then just reheat gently on the hob when ready to serve, with a splash of water to loosen, if needed.

See previous page for a photograph.

Especially Good Maple-Roast Parsnips

You can bung parsnips in the oven as is, with a generous dash of olive oil and even a little maple syrup, and they will of course come out tasting good: that combination of floury parsnip with sweet syrup and a generous snowing of salt flakes is an excellent one. But – and I insist upon this 'but' – I firmly believe that it's well worth the extra faff of parboiling your parsnips, because that will give them that wonderfully fluffy centre and ensure a golden, devilishly moreish crunch on the exterior. You could omit the step of dusting with flour (if cooking for someone with a gluten sensitivity you should do so, or replace the plain flour with a gluten-free alternative), but I find it creates sticky, crisp caramelised 'bits' at the edges of the parsnips which are – to my mind – the very best bits of all. If you don't have a bottle of maple syrup to hand, you can just as well use honey in its place and indeed some might even prefer it, but I personally love the smokiness of maple syrup here.

HANDS ON TIME

15 minutes

HANDS OFF TIME

30 minutes

SERVES 4–6

❧❧❧

500g parsnips

1 heaped tablespoon
   plain flour (or see recipe
   introduction)

3 tablespoons olive oil

2 tablespoons maple syrup

Sea salt flakes

Heat the oven to 200°C / 180°C fan / Gas 6.

Trim and cut the parsnips into sticks, as evenly sized as you can (though don't worry too much about this), then toss into a saucepan, cover with cold water and season generously with salt. Set the pan over a high heat and bring to the boil. When the water begins to gallop, reduce the heat and let simmer for 6–8 minutes, until the parsnips feel tender when you insert a knife or fork into them.

Drain the parsnips in a colander and toss them around a little to rough up their edges, then turn out into a roasting dish and spread them into a single layer. Sprinkle over the flour and, using your hands, toss the parsnips about so they're all lightly coated. At this point, you can set the parsnips aside for 3–4 hours.

❧❧❧

Drizzle over the olive oil, salt generously and set in the oven to roast for 20 minutes. Take out of the oven, drizzle over the maple syrup and set back in for a further 10 minutes, until lightly golden all over and caramelised in parts.

See overleaf for a photograph.

Wilted Kale with Marmite Butter

You can't taste the Marmite in this, so for anyone who might find themselves on the cusp of overlooking this recipe because they're not Marmite people, I urge you to reconsider and to approach this dish with an open mind. What the dollop of Marmite gives is just the perfect amount of rich, umami-filled saltiness to coat the dark, glossy, frilly green leaves, that are cooked to just-tender with an al dente crunch when you bite into a stalk.

I buy those bags of pre-sliced kale for this, both for speed and for ease. If you like (and are feeling super-organised), you can pre-make the Marmite-flavoured butter, then chill, in pre-portioned little pats wrapped in baking paper, in the fridge, ready to add to a pan of lightly sautéed greens, or indeed to smear on toast. Lastly, it's worth emphasising that this recipe works just as well with cavolo nero, or cabbage, or even sprouts.

HANDS ON TIME

15 minutes

HANDS OFF TIME

None

SERVES 6

≈≈≈≈

120g salted butter, at room
    temperature

1 tablespoon Marmite,
    or Vegemite

4 tablespoons olive oil

360g kale, sliced, coarse
    stalks removed

180ml cold water

Combine the butter and Marmite together in a small bowl and mix with a fork or spoon until well combined.

Heat the oil in a large pan over a medium heat. Toss the kale into the pan and fry gently for 3 minutes or so, until the leaves have cooked down a little. Now add the measured water, increase the heat and let cook for another 3 minutes or so, until the water has completely evaporated and the leaves are cooked. Taste them to test if they're ready; I like mine with a little crunch.

Now add the Marmite butter and give everything a good stir so the butter melts completely and all the leaves are coated in its gloss. Take off the heat and serve.

≈≈≈≈

If you like, you can prepare the kale 1–2 days in advance, then just reheat in a pan over a medium-high heat to serve.

Roast Savoy Cabbage with Pancetta, Chestnuts and Gorgonzola

For years, pretty much the only way I cooked cabbage was coarsely shredded then wilted in a pan with heaps of butter, salty, fatty lardons (or pancetta) and a crumbling of sweet, creamy chestnuts. And I still love cabbage cooked that way. But then I discovered this method of roasting it in a delicate, pancetta-laced sauce with melted Gorgonzola and chestnuts, so the green leaves crisp and char moreishly at their edges. And now, all I want to do is eat cabbage cooked like this.

Additionally, and on an entirely practical level, this recipe works nicely for big meals, because you do everything in the one pan (thankfully minimising washing up) and you can in large part prepare everything for it in advance, then just pop it in the oven when you're ready.

HANDS ON TIME
20 minutes
HANDS OFF TIME
1 hour
SERVES 6–8

᧞᧞᧞᧞᧞

30g salted butter
300g pancetta, chopped
1 leek, finely sliced
200ml single cream
Leaves from a small bunch
   of thyme
1 Savoy cabbage
3 tablespoons olive oil
100g chestnuts
100g Gorgonzola
Sea salt flakes

In a large, ovenproof pan, melt the butter over a medium heat, add the pancetta and fry for 2–3 minutes until lightly coloured, then add the finely sliced leek and fry gently for a further 5–6 minutes until translucent. Remove from the heat, add the cream and thyme leaves and give everything a good stir.

Quarter the cabbage, then drop each of the 4 wedges into the creamy sauce. Roll them around so they are lightly coated in cream all over, then arrange snugly together in the pan, rounded-side down.

Drizzle the olive oil over the cabbage wedges and sprinkle over 1 teaspoon of salt flakes. Crumble the chestnuts and Gorgonzola over, then spoon some of the pancetta-leek-cream sauce over everything. Cover with foil and set aside somewhere cool for up to 12 hours until you're ready to roast the cabbage.

᧞᧞᧞᧞᧞

Heat the oven to 200°C / 180°C fan / Gas 6.

Set the cabbage, still covered in foil, in the oven to bake for 30 minutes, then remove the foil and roast for a further 20–30 minutes, until the cheese is completely melted and the cabbage leaves are crisp and have become deliciously charred at their edges.

Wild Rice, Lentil, Chestnut and Pomegranate Salad

I make this dish, a simplified and festive twist on my favourite wild rice and lentil salad from *A Table for Friends,* often in the winter. Something about the tumble of Christmassy green spinach and sparkling red pomegranate feels wonderfully appropriate for the holiday season. It's one of those pleasingly versatile recipes that you can easily scale up or down, and which doubles as a side or a light main course alongside anything from poultry to pork to pretty much whatever. Play around with the flavours as you like: add crumbled Stilton or Gorgonzola or feta; toss in some shredded red cabbage, radicchio or red chicory to play Santa-red to the festive green of the spinach; even toss through some shredded leftover roast turkey (or butter beans for a vegan alternative) to make more of a meal of it.

I use bags of pre-cooked Puy lentils, but if you would like to cook them from dried, simply follow the method given for Good Luck Salad (see page 192). Once assembled, this will sit somewhere cool (or in the fridge) for half a day; after that the spinach wilts a little. To make it up to two days ahead, just leave the spinach out and toss in at the last minute.

HANDS ON TIME

10 minutes

HANDS OFF TIME

30 minutes

SERVES 6

⤴⤴⤴⤴⤴

200g extra long grain
   black wild rice, rinsed
   and drained

1 litre water

4–6 tablespoons extra virgin
   olive oil

250g cooked Puy lentils (or
   see recipe introduction)

180g cooked chestnuts

150g pomegranate seeds,
   plus more (optional)
   to serve

3 handfuls of baby spinach
   leaves

Sea salt flakes and freshly
   ground black pepper

Toss the wild rice in a saucepan. Cover with the measured water and add ½ teaspoon of salt. Bring to the boil over a high heat. When the water begins to gallop, reduce the heat to a gentle simmer, cover and cook for 25–30 minutes. The rice should be chewy and some of the grains may burst open. Drain off any liquid, then tip into a large bowl and season generously with some of the oil and salt while the rice is still warm, so it absorbs all their flavours.

Add the cooked lentils to the bowl with the cooked rice, then crumble in the chestnuts and toss together. Drizzle over the remaining olive oil and toss together again so all the ingredients are coated and glossy. Season to taste with salt. At this point, the salad will keep, covered, for up to 2 days in the fridge.

⤴⤴⤴⤴⤴

To serve, bring the salad to room temperature and toss in the pomegranate seeds and baby spinach leaves. Dress with a few more pomegranate seeds on top, if you like, before bringing to the table.

Red Chicory and Candied Pecan Salad

Pure indulgence: creamy dressing, crisp, crimson-hued leaves and salty-sweet pecans. It might seem like an extravagance to have candied pecans – coated, as they are, in spices and brown sugar – in a salad, but it is Christmas after all. There is, of course, no real need to candy your pecans: for a lower effort and, no doubt, much healthier version, you could just as well toss in a couple of handfuls of the nuts, waxy and naked, just as they are. You could even, were you wanting to gild the lily, add a crumbling of blue cheese, Stilton or Gorgonzola, and/or a handful of dried cranberries to your crisp chicory leaves.

Equally, if you do choose to go down the candied nut route – and I strongly urge you to do so – then consider tripling or even quadrupling the quantities when you make them. You can use some for the salad and save the rest to serve with drinks (they'll keep happily in a jar or airtight container for a few weeks).

HANDS ON TIME

15 minutes

HANDS OFF TIME

20 minutes cooling

SERVES 6

⤳⤳⤳

FOR THE CANDIED PECANS

20g soft brown sugar

½ teaspoon ground cinnamon

⅓ teaspoon sea salt flakes

⅓ teaspoon vanilla extract

½ tablespoon cold water

60g pecans

FOR THE SALAD

2 tablespoons mayonnaise

2 tablespoons red wine vinegar

4 tablespoons olive oil

4–5 heads of red chicory

Sea salt flakes

To make the candied pecans, line a baking sheet with baking paper. Combine the sugar, cinnamon, salt, vanilla and measured water in a pan and set over a medium heat. Stir for roughly 1 minute, until the brown sugar melts into a bubbling sauce.

Now, add the pecans, stirring constantly until all the nuts are coated in the sauce. As the nuts heat up in the pan, the sauce will slowly coat them and turn shiny. Keep a careful eye on the nuts so they cook, but don't burn. This shouldn't take more than 2–3 minutes.

Carefully transfer the nuts to the prepared baking sheet, spreading them out in a single layer. Leave them to cool completely before serving. (The nuts will keep happily, stored in a sealed container, for up to 3 weeks.)

⤳⤳⤳

When ready to serve, make the salad dressing by whisking the mayonnaise, vinegar and olive oil together in a small bowl with a fork. Season to taste with salt and whisk again to break up any lumps.

Tear the leaves off the heads of chicory and toss them in a generous salad dish. Drizzle with the creamy dressing, add the candied pecans and serve immediately.

Christmas Salad

This salad just *looks* like Christmas, with its many hues of glossy red, topped with a crumbling of snowy white, salty feta cheese. And hence the name. You can prepare the beetroot well in advance and, in fact, the longer it sits in its syrupy juices, the more flavoursome it becomes. Most often, I'll serve this alongside a main course, but like many of the salads in this chapter, it also works well as a starter, either plated up individually or as a big dish in the middle of the table for everyone to help themselves.

HANDS ON TIME

10 minutes

HANDS OFF TIME

30 minutes to 3 days
   marinating

SERVES 6–8

130ml olive oil

3 tablespoons maple syrup

3 tablespoons balsamic
   vinegar

Juice of 1½ lemons

16 cooked beetroot, thinly
   sliced into rounds

350g feta cheese

3–4 heaped tablespoons
   pomegranate seeds

Handful of walnuts,
   coarsely chopped

Sea salt flakes

In a bowl, combine the olive oil, maple syrup, balsamic vinegar and lemon juice with a generous pinch of salt, then whisk lightly with a fork.

Add the beetroot slices to the bowl with the dressing, then toss together so everything is well coated in glossy juices. Cover and set to one side to macerate for at least 30 minutes. (You can leave the beetroot to rest in the fridge for up to 3 days.)

When ready to serve, arrange the slices of beetroot, overlapping, on a serving dish. Crumble over the feta, then scatter with pomegranate seeds and walnuts.

Orange, Carrot and Pistachio Salad

This salad comes as a welcome, vibrant pop of fierce colour on the plate, at a time of year when everything can feel quite dark and drab. Better still if you can find blood oranges; the deep red of their flesh and juice adds an even more festive hue to the salad. This is a dish you can prepare in advance, then keep, dressed and covered, in the fridge (or somewhere cool) for up to three days, if needed. Then just scatter the green nuts over the carrots and citrus before serving. If you wanted to add even more colour and a hint of sharpness to the plate, then you could scatter over a few shimmering pomegranate seeds (never amiss at Christmastime) too.

HANDS ON TIME
10 minutes

HANDS OFF TIME
None

SERVES 6

1 teaspoon cumin seeds

4–5 carrots

4 small oranges

3–4 tablespoons extra virgin olive oil

60g pistachios, coarsely chopped

Sea salt flakes

Heat a nonstick pan over a medium heat and add the cumin seeds. Toast for 1–2 minutes, until the seeds begin to darken and give off a strong, earthy aroma, then take the pan off the heat.

Using a mandolin or a sharp knife, slice the carrots into rounds, 1–2mm thick, and set in a salad dish. Peel the oranges, remove any white pith and slice into rounds, as thinly as you can. Add the orange slices to the carrot.

Drizzle over the olive oil, add the toasted cumin seeds, season generously with salt and toss together so everything is lightly coated in dressing.

Sprinkle over the pistachios and serve immediately.

Red Cabbage Panzanella

I wouldn't go quite so far as to suggest that this panzanella might be taken as a substitute for traditional stuffing, but it does undoubtedly sit in that same family. The crisp chunks of toasted bread, steeped in flavoursome olive oil, the buttery chestnuts and the slivers of almost sweet red cabbage, when mixed together, make for what you might describe as an Italianate cousin to the British Christmas classic. And it's more of a throw-together kind of recipe than either the Panettone, Chestnut and Sage Stuffing or Nonna's Stuffing (see pages 166–167).

You can make this up to two days ahead of time, then just store, covered and set somewhere cool, until you're ready to serve. If you're in a hurry and tossing it together last minute, you can skip the toasting of the bread in the oven, especially if the sourdough is on the slightly stale side; just make sure to serve and eat within a few hours, otherwise the bread turns too soggy if it hasn't been toasted.

HANDS ON TIME

10–15 minutes

HANDS OFF TIME

None

SERVES 6

⤐⤐⤐

300g sourdough, weighed
   without crusts
60ml olive oil, plus
   2 tablespoons, plus
   more to season
30ml balsamic vinegar
1 red cabbage, finely sliced
180g cooked chestnuts
70g pomegranate seeds
Sea salt flakes and freshly
   ground black pepper

Heat the oven to 200°C / 180°C fan / Gas 6.

Tear the bread into small chunks and arrange on a baking tray, then toast in the oven for 10 minutes or so, until crisp. Toss the toasted bread into a large salad bowl, then drizzle the 60ml olive oil and the balsamic vinegar over it. Cover and set aside to rest.

Meanwhile, heat the 2 tablespoons of olive oil in a pan, add the cabbage and fry gently for 5 minutes, until the cabbage has softened a little but the strips are still holding their vibrant colour, texture and crunch. Take off the heat and allow to cool a little, before tossing together with the seasoned bread.

Crumble in the chestnuts, scatter over the pomegranate seeds and season the salad with a little more oil, salt and pepper to taste.

⤐⤐⤐

The panzanella will happily keep in the fridge for up to 48 hours (leave out the pomegranate seeds until just before serving).

Red Cabbage, Feta, Hazelnut and Mint Salad

This is a different and rather good way of incorporating red cabbage, that traditional British staple, into Christmas lunch, especially helpful when you're short on time or stovetop space, or would like to minimise on washing up. Instead of simmering the cabbage until buttery-soft (as at page 170), you just toss the crisp, shredded pieces with a little olive oil, mellow vinegar and a handful of nuts. It makes for a delightfully light, fresh and zingy salad that can feel like a blessed relief alongside all the other, richer components of the meal.

HANDS ON TIME
10–15 minutes, depending
   on knife skills
HANDS OFF TIME
None
SERVES 6

᙭᙭᙭᙭

½ red cabbage
Leaves from a small bunch
   of mint, coarsely chopped
2 tablespoons olive oil
2 tablespoons apple
   cider vinegar
150g feta
40g toasted hazelnuts,
   coarsely chopped
Sea salt flakes

Use a mandolin or a very sharp knife to slice the cabbage into fine strips and toss into a large salad dish. Add most of the chopped mint (saving a little to dress the salad at the end), then drizzle over the olive oil and vinegar.

Toss again and season to taste with salt flakes. The cabbage will happily sit like this for up to 24 hours.

᙭᙭᙭᙭

Lastly, crumble over the feta cheese, hazelnuts and the last of the mint before serving.

See previous page for a photograph.

Shaved Fennel, Grapefruit and Pomegranate Salad

A gloriously fresh combination of ingredients: crisp aniseedy fennel; bitter, almost marmalade sweet grapefruit; pops of sharp pomegranate seeds. Tumbled together, it makes for a delectable, delicate shade of Christmassy red. If you wanted, you might consider tossing in a few fresh baby spinach leaves or a handful of coarsely chopped nuts (toasted flaked almonds or crumbled pistachios) to mix things up.

HANDS ON TIME
10–15 minutes

HANDS OFF TIME
None

SERVES 6

2 fennel bulbs

1 small red grapefruit

3 tablespoons extra virgin olive oil

2 tablespoons maple syrup

100g pomegranate seeds

Sea salt flakes and freshly ground black pepper

Thinly slice the fennel, either using a mandolin, if you have one, or a sharp knife. Peel the grapefruit and chop the segments into small pieces, collecting and saving any juices. Toss the fennel and grapefruit together in a salad bowl or serving dish.

In a small bowl, lightly whisk the oil, maple syrup and reserved grapefruit juice together, then season to taste with salt and a good grinding of black pepper. Sprinkle over the shimmering pomegranate seeds and toss everything together one last time.

Once assembled, the salad will keep nicely in the fridge for up to 12 hours, or 24 hours without the pomegranate seeds (which you can sprinkle in at the last minute).

See overleaf for a photograph.

Shaved Brussels Sprouts with Pecorino, Cranberries and Pecans

The flavour and texture of Brussels sprouts change completely when you eat them raw and, as here, thinly shaved. Rather than 'sprouty', they taste light, lacey and minerally. This way of doing sprouts is a refreshing antidote to the glorious indulgence and stodge of a traditional Christmas meal. I love the addition of cranberries here, shimmering dark gems amid the tangle of light green, bringing a much-needed hit of sharp flavour, just as the pecans add their essential nutty, almost-sweet crunch. You can toss the shaved, frothy sprouts with any combination of dried fruit and/or nut you like: finely chopped dates, or raisins, in place of cranberries; or toasted hazelnuts and slivers of crisp apple. I eat a quieter version of this (without the dried fruit and with the addition of toasted flaked almonds in place of sweeter pecans) on repeat through the winter months and I love it.

My one insistence is that you grate your own cheese: as much as I love a ready-grated Parmesan or pecorino (and I do), here you really need the texture of the rougher, newly grated slivers of cheese rather than the almost powdered variety in pre-grated bags.

The only nuisance in making this salad is the shaving of the Brussels: I either do this by thinly slicing them with a knife, or you can use a mandolin. It was a game-changer for me when I discovered that you can use a setting on the food processor for blitzing these, which changed it from a recipe that I lazily (and greedily) used to only cook for myself to a favourite that I'll happily churn out for a crowd of many.

HANDS ON TIME
10–20 minutes
HANDS OFF TIME
None
SERVES 8–10

600g Brussels sprouts
Small bunch of parsley,
    leaves coarsely chopped
40g pecorino
5 tablespoons extra virgin
    olive oil
Juice of 2 lemons
90g dried cranberries
60g pecans, coarsely
    chopped
Sea salt flakes

Slice the sprouts as finely as you can, using a mandolin or a sharp knife. In a salad bowl, toss the shaved sprouts together with the parsley and grate in the pecorino.

Drizzle over the olive oil and squeeze in the lemon juice, then toss together well so all the greens are coated in dressing. Taste and season with a little salt, if needed (the cheese is quite salty, so it might not be). Toss in the cranberries. At this point, the salad will keep in the fridge for up to 24 hours.

Crumble in the pecans and toss, one last time, to serve. I eat any leftovers of this the next day because I love it, but it will be a little wilted...

Good Luck Salad

I call this 'good luck' salad because it's filled with ingredients that double as culinary talismans. There are the lentils, which Italians swear by for good luck: one mouthful as the clock strikes midnight on New Year's Eve will bring wealth and prosperity in the coming year. And then there's pomegranate, also a symbol of prosperity. In Greece, you smash a pomegranate on the doorstep on New Year's Eve for good luck: the further the seeds scatter and the brighter they shine, the more blessed the year will be. You could call this superstition, but I almost always make this at some point over our New Year, usually to serve with cotechino, either served as is or baked into a pastry roll (see page 132).

I've split this recipe into two parts: the cooking of the lentils and the assembling of the salad. Once assembled, this salad will happily sit somewhere cool (or in the fridge) for half a day; after that the radicchio will begin to soften a little and lose its delectable crispness. If you would like to make it further ahead (which you can do up to two days before you plan on serving), then just leave the fresh leaves and pomegranate seeds out and toss them in at the last minute.

HANDS ON TIME

15–20 minutes

HANDS OFF TIME

1 hour

SERVES 4

❦

200g dried Puy lentils (or 500g cooked weight)

5 tablespoons olive oil

¼ red onion

3 tablespoons red wine vinegar

Generous pinch of caster sugar

3 cooked beetroot, chopped into 1cm pieces

Handful of hazelnuts, coarsely chopped

100g pomegranate seeds

½ head of radicchio di Chioggia or Verona, torn

Sea salt flakes and freshly ground black pepper

Put the lentils in a sieve, rinse them, then transfer to a large saucepan with 1.5 litres of cold water and a generous pinch of salt. Bring to the boil for 30 seconds, then reduce the heat to low and cover the pan. Simmer gently over the lowest heat for 18–20 minutes, until cooked but still firm in the centre. For this salad, you want them very much al dente. Drizzle 2–3 tablespoons of the olive oil over the lentils and season generously, then put the lid back on and let sit for a further 5 minutes. Drain and let cool to room temperature.

Finely slice the onion and set in a small bowl. Pour over 1 tablespoon of the red wine vinegar, add the generous pinch of sugar, mix well with your fingertips and leave to marinate for 15–20 minutes, or longer, if you like.

Combine the beetroot, nuts and lentils in a salad bowl. In a smaller bowl, whisk the remaining oil (or all 5 tablespoons olive oil, if using pre-cooked lentils) with the remaining 2 tablespoons vinegar and a very generous pinch of salt. Drizzle over the lentils and toss. Lastly, add the drained red onion. At this point, it will keep, covered, in the fridge for up to 2 days.

❦

Add the pomegranate seeds and radicchio, toss everything together, then season to taste with more salt and give everything a last toss before serving.

Cinnamon and Cranberry Bundt

This is a Good Cake: the sponge is soft, heady with spice and a warming hint of orange, with pockets of jelly-like, sherbet-y sweetness from the cranberries that pepper it throughout, shining like rubies suspended in cake. It's not overly sweet, which makes it a good breakfast choice, especially if you're the kind of person who is partial to cake for breakfast (which I am). Equally, once dressed up and coated in a thin layer of sugary, orange-scented icing and topped with shimmering cranberries, this cake takes on a character that is fancy enough for afternoon tea, or even to serve as pudding to follow on from a festive meal. I also quite often make it for bake sales and sell it by the slice: it slices nicely. Like I said: it's a good cake.

Much as I love the extravagant-looking confections which they turn out, I often find bundt tins a little problematic to work with, as I'm rather too haphazard in the way I cook to properly grease and dust all the nooks and crannies. The best way round this that I've found is to use a silicone bundt mould and grease it very lightly with butter or oil (a haphazard job is just fine here) before pouring in the cake batter: this makes it easier to turn the cake out than from a regular tin. Two caveats: always wait a good twenty minutes before turning out the cake, as if it's too warm it can be prone to collapsing; and set the mould on a baking tray before you add the batter, so it's easier to move in and out of the oven without spilling or upsetting the batter in the jiggly-wiggly silicone.

Lastly, a note on decoration: I like a mix of frosted and glazed cranberries here, just scattered over the crest of the iced cake, which gives a lovely contrast of textures and shades of festive red. If you're in a hurry, just dip the berries in the sugar syrup to give them a nice, sweet gloss, then scatter over the cake.

HANDS ON TIME
20–25 minutes
HANDS OFF TIME
1 hour 10 minutes baking,
   plus 2 hours cooling
SERVES 8–10

Heat the oven to 180°C / 160°C fan / Gas 4. Lightly butter or oil a 1.2-litre nonstick bundt tin. Gently melt the 110g butter in a small saucepan over a medium heat: once liquid, take off the heat and set aside to cool.

In a large mixing bowl, beat the eggs and the sugar together until they become fluffy and pale in colour. Add the 50ml oil in a steady trickle, beating constantly, until well combined. Now gradually beat in the cooled melted butter, then, lastly, beat in the yogurt and orange zest.

In a separate bowl, sift the 240g flour, the cinnamon and salt and stir to combine evenly, then fold into the cake mixture. Lastly, dust the cranberries with the ½ tablespoon flour, then gently fold them through the cake batter.

Pour the batter into the prepared bundt tin and bake in the middle of the oven for 60–70 minutes. After 30 minutes, cover the tin with foil, to stop the cake from browning too

FOR THE CAKE

110g salted butter, plus more
    (optional) for the tin
50ml sunflower oil, plus
    more (optional) for the tin
2 eggs
270g caster sugar
150g plain yogurt
Finely grated zest of 1 orange
240g self-raising flour,
    plus ½ tablespoon
2 heaped teaspoons ground
    cinnamon
Generous pinch of fine
    sea salt
130g frozen cranberries

FOR THE GLAZE

40ml water
30g caster sugar, plus more
    (optional) to dust
70g frozen cranberries
260g icing sugar, plus more
    if needed
Juice of 1 orange, plus more
    if needed

much. To test if the cake is ready, insert a knife into the middle and see if it comes out clean. Let cool for 15 minutes in the tin (if you turn it out too soon it risks collapsing), then turn out on to a wire rack and let cool completely.

Meanwhile, prepare the glazed cranberries. In a medium saucepan, combine the measured water with the 30g caster sugar. Set over a medium heat, bring to the boil, then let simmer for 2–3 minutes until you have a clear, syrupy liquid. Stir in the cranberries to fully coat in the syrup, then remove from the heat. Gently lift the red berries out of the syrup, using a slotted spoon (or very gently lifting them up using a fork) and transfer to a wire rack to dry out (roughly 1 hour). This gives the berries a lovely gloss and also helps sweeten their sharp taste. At this point, if you like, you can roll some of the cranberries in a little caster sugar on a small plate to get a frosted effect.

Once the cake is completely cooled, you can make the icing: sift the icing sugar into a mixing bowl, then add the orange juice, a little at a time, stirring until smooth each time and checking the consistency as you go: you want a thick, pourable icing. You can add more juice to thin it out, or more icing sugar to thicken it up, as needed. Drizzle the icing over the cooled bundt and top with the glazed and/or frosted cranberries.

Panettone Woodland Cake

A way to dress up a panettone to look like a scene from Narnia. Play around with it as you like: add figurines, rosemary sprig 'Christmas trees', fresh and frosted cranberries, meringue mushrooms or Crispie Christmas Trees (see pages 197, 215 and 276)...

I use gelatine to stabilise the cream and give structural integrity, for a towering cake with deep, thick layers of cream. If you skip the gelatine, you'll get a more haphazard structure with cream spilling out extravagantly between the tiers, which is not without a certain charm. You can also fold crumbled *marrons glacés* into the cream (in the bottom two tiers only, to leave the top snowy white), chocolate shards, or toasted flaked almonds.

HANDS ON TIME

20 minutes

HANDS OFF TIME

1 hour to set

SERVES 8–10

⋘⋙

1 × 750g panettone

4 gelatine leaves

90ml milk

100ml honey

600ml double cream

20g desiccated coconut

Discard the paper wrapping from the panettone, then use a bread knife to slice off and discard the 'muffin top' (to make good use of leftover panettone, see pages 79, 80, 92 and 154). You're aiming to make a flat surface on top. Now, cut the panettone horizontally into 3 layers. Set aside.

Put the sheets of gelatine in a small bowl and cover with cold water. Set aside to soften for 5 minutes. Meanwhile, warm the milk in a small saucepan over a medium-low heat. When it is just at the point of boiling (you should see the tiniest bubbles gathering at the surface around the edge of the pan), take it off the heat. Drain the gelatine and wring out any excess liquid, then stir into the warm milk and add the honey. Stir until you have a sweet milky syrup with no clumps of gelatine, then set aside to cool a little.

Now, in a large bowl, whip the cream until soft peaks form, then whisk in the honeyed milk, in a steady trickle.

Set the base layer of the panettone on a cake stand or serving dish. Spread roughly one-third (or just over) of the cream on in a thick, even layer, leaving a 1cm border around the edge to allow for the next layers squidging it slightly. Carefully add the second layer and repeat, then top with the last panettone tier. Spread on the last of the cream, using the back of a spoon or a knife to create gentle peaks. Sprinkle the coconut (like snow) over the top. Decorate with woodland elements (see recipe introduction), if you like. Set in the fridge for at least 1 hour before serving.

⋘⋙

The cake can be made up to 48 hours in advance and will keep happily in the fridge until you are ready to serve it.

Gingery Christmas Cake

I've been baking my own Christmas cakes every year to give as gifts to friends and loved ones for pretty much as long as I can remember. The recipe I rely on most often is my mother's and you can find a much-loved and much-used version of it in *A Table for Friends*. I've loosely adapted it here to incorporate a pop of pepperiness, by soaking the dried fruits in ginger wine instead of brandy, and adding chunks of sweet stem ginger layered throughout the cake. While ginger is perhaps not canonical in fruit cake, it does unequivocally taste like Christmas and I, for one, love this warming, lightly spiced twist on the well-worn classic as much as, if not more than, the original recipe. Nonetheless, if you prefer something more traditional, swap out the ginger wine for brandy and the stem ginger for 100g glacé cherries and, if you like, toss in 100g or so of coarsely chopped blanched almonds too, then bake following the method below.

When it comes to decoration, there are many variations upon a theme to work with. A traditional British Christmas cake, for example, comes enrobed in a thick layer of marzipan and then a second layer of snowy white, glossy royal icing (for a version of this classic method, see the Black and Gold Cake on page 206, or page 223). My go-to, on the other hand, is to top each cake with a 1–2cm-thick round of marzipan, then adorn it with whole glacé fruits, which I stick on with a little apricot jam (gently warmed to make a sticky syrup). But not everyone loves marzipan: I have a friend who religiously picks the layer of marzipan off his cake each year. And with that in mind, you'll see that the method here, where you bake a sticky mess of glacé cherries, syrupy ginger and mixed nuts into the top of the cake and it comes out in a decorative layer not unlike a Florentine biscuit, offers a light, yet still appropriately luxurious, alternative. Not only does it look effective, but there is the added time-saving bonus that you don't need to decorate it once it comes out of the oven.

HANDS ON TIME
5 minutes preparing the
    fruit, 20 minutes making
    the cake
HANDS OFF TIME
1–2 days soaking the fruit,
    2 hours baking
SERVES 8–10

For the cake, put the chunks of ginger, peel, currants, raisins and sultanas into a large bowl, pour over the ginger wine, cover and let steep for 24–48 hours. The longer you are able to leave the fruit, the more flavour and moisture it will give the cake.

When you're ready to make your cake, heat the oven to 180°C / 160°C fan / Gas 4. Butter a 23cm round cake tin, line it with baking paper, then cut a second circle of baking paper the same diameter as the base of the tin (set this aside to cover the cake while it bakes).

Beat together the butter and sugar until they become paler and fluffy, then add the treacle and beat until smooth. Add the eggs, one at a time, whisking them lightly with a fork before you add them to the cake batter, then beat until

FOR THE CAKE

170g stem ginger in syrup,
   drained and chopped

80g mixed peel

190g currants

190g raisins

190g sultanas

220ml ginger wine

200g salted butter, softened,
   plus more for the tin

200g dark muscovado sugar

1½ tablespoons black treacle

4 eggs

1 teaspoon mixed spice

2 teaspoons ground ginger

200g self-raising flour

Large pinch of fine sea salt

FOR THE TOPPING

130g stem ginger in syrup,
   drained and halved

50g blanched hazelnuts

50g blanched almonds

90g Brazil nuts

90g flaked almonds

170g glacé cherries

110g golden syrup

well combined. Sift in the spices, flour and salt and mix with a wooden spoon. Lastly, add the ginger wine-soaked fruit, along with any remaining liquid in the bowl.

Scoop up 100g of the cake batter and set to one side. (If you don't want to follow my Florentine-like topping suggestion, see recipe introduction, then omit this step.) Spoon the remaining batter into the prepared tin and gently even out the top with the back of the spoon, to make a flat surface. Now, make a slight dip in the centre of the cake – you want as flat a surface as possible and this counters the oven spring of the cake – and cover with the reserved baking paper circle. Bake the cake in the oven for 1¼ hours.

If you are going to ice and decorate the cake in the traditional way (be it with marzipan and glacé fruits, or marzipan and royal icing), then leave it in the oven for a further 15–20 minutes, until it feels dry on top and a knife comes out clean when inserted in the middle.

If you are going to top the cake with fruit and nuts, then make the topping while it bakes in the oven: combine the ginger, nuts, cherries, golden syrup and reserved cake batter together in a mixing bowl, mixing it into a sticky mess of fruit and nuts. Remove the top layer of baking paper from the part-cooked cake (once it has had its 1¼ hours in the oven) and spoon the fruit and nut mixture over the top of it, distributing it evenly over the surface.

Loosely cover the top of the tin with foil and set back in the oven for 40 minutes more. Then remove and discard the foil and bake for a further 10–15 minutes, until the nuts are lightly golden and a knife comes out clean when inserted in the middle of the cake. Let cool completely in its tin, then turn out and wrap with foil: the cake will keep for up to 2 weeks, or can be frozen for up to 2 months.

Black and Gold Cake

The first time I tasted Caribbean 'black' cake – so-called because it's rich and black with rum and dried fruits – was on holiday with my mother in Barbados. It was sublime and I was instantly overcome by the need to recreate something similar at home. I turned to Felicity Cloake's 'How to Make the Perfect...' column in *The Guardian,* as I so often do when I want to learn how to cook something new, and the recipe below is very loosely adapted from her own version of the rum-laced cake. To make it even more Christmassy, I've taken the liberty of adding a layer of snowy, crisp white royal icing. This is perhaps not canonical (nor indeed are the speckles of shimmering gold leaf which I couldn't resist using), but it does look pretty and festive, and the icing sugar-snap-crisp and stark white colour offer a delectable contrast to the heavy and pudding-like texture of the cake.

It's fair to say that to bake this cake is an exercise in patience and delayed gratification, as to make it properly takes days. By that I don't so much mean that it's especially labour-intensive, nor that the process requires any grand patisserie skills (quite the opposite), but it must be done in stages and each of these stages needs time to settle and develop. You need time for the fruit to soak in rum (this is what gives the cake its distinctively punchy, boozy flavour, so you skip this step at your peril); time for a slow, gentle bake to give it that pudding-like texture so different from the drier, crumblier British fruit cake; time for the cake to cool and soak up the extra rum you splash over its top once baked; time for the snowy white icing to harden completely before gilding with patches of extravagant gold leaf. So while I accept that this is perhaps not the recipe for those in a hurry, I must insist that you don't let the timings put you off. Not only is this a cake that is pure joy and deeply rewarding to bake – as the kitchen fills with its scent of sweet, heady alcohol, spices and citrus zest – but it's also well worth the effort, for something that both tastes and looks so utterly sublime.

HANDS ON TIME
20 minutes preparing the fruit, 25 minutes making the cake, 35 minutes decorating

HANDS OFF TIME
Overnight soaking fruit, 5 hours baking, 3–4 hours cooling, 24 hours for the icing to dry

SERVES 10–12

To make the cake, combine the dried fruit, cherries and peel in a large saucepan, cover with the Marsala and simmer gently over a medium-low heat until all the liquid has been absorbed. Take off the heat, pour over the 300ml rum, then cover and let soak overnight.

Heat the oven to 180°C / 160°C fan / Gas 4. Butter a 23cm cake tin and line with baking paper.

Tumble the dried fruit into a food processor, along with any boozy juices, and blitz to a paste.

In a large mixing bowl, cream the butter and sugar together until fluffy and paler. Add the treacle, zests and vanilla, then beat until combined. Now add the eggs, one at a time, beating until combined. In a second bowl, sift the flour, baking powder and spices, then fold this into the cake mix in

FOR THE CAKE

200g pitted prunes

230g currants

230g raisins

170g glacé cherries

70g mixed peel

450ml Marsala

300ml rum, plus 30ml to
   brush the cake

250g salted butter, plus more
   for the tin

250g dark muscovado sugar

3 tablespoons black treacle

Finely grated zest of 1 lemon

Finely grated zest of 1 orange

1 teaspoon vanilla extract

6 eggs

150g plain flour

1 teaspoon baking powder

1 teaspoon ground cinnamon

½ teaspoon mixed spice

FOR THE ICING

500g marzipan

70g apricot jam

1 tablespoon water

3 egg whites

600g icing sugar, sifted

1 teaspoon liquid glucose

1 teaspoon lemon juice

Edible glue

15–20 sheets of edible
   gold leaf

4 parts, trying to keep as much air as possible in the batter. Lastly, fold in the macerated fruit paste, adding it in 3 parts.

Pour the cake batter into the prepared tin and smooth the top. Bake for 60 minutes, then reduce the oven temperature to 160°C / 140°C fan / Gas 3 and bake for a further 4 hours, until a knife comes out clean when inserted into the middle of the cake.

Once cooked, use a toothpick to make holes all over the top of the cake and use a pastry brush to brush over the 30ml rum. Let cool completely in its tin.

To ice the cake, roll the marzipan out between 2 sheets of baking paper into a 2.5mm-thick disc large enough to cover the top and sides of the cake. Warm the jam together with the measured water in a small saucepan over a gentle heat, until it turns liquid and hot, then use a pastry brush to glaze all over the sides and top of the cake to create a tacky surface. Drape the marzipan disc over the cake and gently press it down to snugly cover the sides, trimming away any excess and patching up gaps as needed (don't worry, you won't see this layer, so it doesn't need to be perfect).

Now make the royal icing: in a spotlessly clean mixing bowl, whisk the egg whites until frothy, then add the icing sugar, a spoonful at a time, whisking all the while. Lastly, whisk in the liquid glucose and lemon juice and whisk until you have a thick, glossy white icing that holds stiff peaks.

Spoon the frosty white icing over the top and sides of the cake, then spread it out evenly all over, making sure every last little corner and crevice is covered. Now use a fork to create a snowy texture in the thick, glossy layer of icing. Let the icing firm up somewhere cool and dry (not the fridge) for 24 hours. Lastly, use a paint brush to dab a small amount of edible glue on to a small patch of the white icing and gently stick a sheet of edible gold leaf on to it; then press down and even out with the brush. Repeat this process in a haphazard pattern all over the pristine white cake with the remaining sheets of gold.

Pandoro Tower

....

Pandoro is the distant cousin of panettone: it too is a bready, pillowy sweet cake, enjoyed at Christmas; but whereas panettone is typically studded with candied peel and raisins, pandoro is plain, scented just with a little vanilla, then doused in an extravagant cloud of powdered sugar. Pandoro also has an unusual shape: a star-shaped pyramid, which when you cut it crossways, as here, then twist the pieces round clockwise at different angles, looks both rather effective and bears a distinct resemblance to a Christmas tree.

This is wonderfully simple to make: you just layer the slices of cake with an airy mascarpone cream, which I've allowed for here in very generous proportions because everyone always wants more! My only caveat is that, once assembled, it doesn't hold its shape forever and quite quickly begins to look like the leaning tower of Pisa. I wouldn't assemble it more than a couple of hours before you plan to serve. If you make the cream in advance (even up to a couple of days beforehand), then store in the fridge in an airtight container, it takes just moments to assemble the cake before dinner. If you're anxious about its structural integrity, insert a couple of wooden skewers down the middle of the cake to hold the tiers together, then trim the ends to the height of the penultimate tier and hide them under the top tier. Or simply slice the pandoro as per the method here, then reassemble into a snowy tower, but omit the cream which you can instead serve in a big bowl on the side: this still looks wonderfully effective but the cake won't risk going soggy while it sits out and will comfortably hold its shape, even without dowels.

HANDS ON TIME
25 minutes
HANDS OFF TIME
None
SERVES 8–10

~~~~~

3 eggs, separated
80g caster sugar
380g mascarpone
1 × 750g pandoro
Icing sugar, to dust

In a spotlessly clean bowl, whisk the egg whites until they begin to turn fluffy, then slowly add half the sugar, a spoon at a time, whisking all the while, until stiff peaks form.

Combine the yolks and remaining sugar together in a separate bowl and beat until light, pale and fluffy. Now beat in the mascarpone until smooth. Lastly, fold in the stiff egg whites. Chill in an airtight container in the fridge for up to 3 days.

~~~~~

Cut the pandoro crossways into 4-5 slices and set the base piece on a cake stand or serving dish. Spoon one-quarter of the mascarpone cream over, then add the second slice of pandoro, rotating slightly, so the points don't match up. Repeat until you have rebuilt the pandoro tower. Dust generously with icing sugar before serving.

Flourless Chocolate Orange Cake

The world's ugliest cake. I say this with love, as it is also one of the world's most glorious-tasting cakes, which is why, in spite of its appearance, I come back to it time and again. I feel I must insist on its ugly duckling-ness, lest you be disappointed when it comes out of the oven all higgledy-piggledy and with a crisp, crackled top. That's exactly how it should look. Just let it cool completely in its tin, then chill it for a while before attempting to extricate it (or it might crumble). If it does, just patch it together and drench in icing sugar before serving. I promise you, looks aside, everyone will demand seconds, then thirds.

I make this using Lindt orange-scented dark chocolate, peppered with tiny speckles of candied orange. But you could use any orange chocolate, or plain dark chocolate and use more orange extract. Chocolate and orange taste like Christmas to me, but if it's not your thing, just omit the orange extract to make a devilishly rich, bitter dark chocolate cake.

This improves with age and peaks around the three-day mark, so you can – and indeed should – make it in advance. You can then store it in the fridge for up to five days, total.

HANDS ON TIME

25 minutes

HANDS OFF TIME

1 hour 20 minutes baking,
    plus 3 hours cooling

SERVES 8–10

~~~~~

250g salted butter, plus more
    for the tin

250g orange-scented
    chocolate (see recipe
    introduction), broken
    into pieces

5 eggs

250g caster sugar

½ teaspoon orange extract

Icing sugar, to dust

Heat the oven to 140°C / 120°C fan / Gas 1. Remove any oven racks above the shelf where you will put the tin, as the cake rises a lot as it bakes. Grease and line a 23cm springform tin.

Gently melt the butter and chocolate in a pan over a very low heat, stirring constantly so it doesn't burn. As soon as it's melted, take the pan off the heat and set aside to cool.

Separate the eggs and whisk the yolks together with half the sugar, using electric beaters, for at least 5 minutes until pale and creamy in colour and trebled in volume. Now whisk in the orange extract.

In a second, spotlessly clean bowl, whisk the whites until they become frothy, then add the last half of the sugar, spoonful by spoonful, whisking all the while.

Gently fold the egg whites into the creamy yolks, then fold in the cooled melted chocolate. Pour the batter into the prepared tin and set in the oven for 1 hour 20 minutes, until the top feels firm to the touch. The cake should not wobble when you gently jiggle the tin. Switch the oven off, close the door and let the cake cool in there for at least 1 hour.

Leave to cool completely in its tin and store in the fridge, ideally overnight, or for at least 2 hours, before trying to turn it out. It will keep happily in the fridge for up to 5 days.

~~~~~

Dust with icing sugar before serving.

Chocolate and Chestnut Yule Log

I'm not going to lie: a yule log, whichever which way you look at it, takes time and a little patience to make. But to its credit it can (and indeed must) be made in stages, which eases things; moreover, no single one of those stages is especially tricky nor lengthy to execute, just a matter of taking things step by step. And there are shortcuts you can take: you don't need, for example, to make your own little meringue mushrooms to decorate the cake. A light dusting of icing sugar over the chocolatey log, and perhaps a few redcurrants dotted here and there, looks plenty effective, and will significantly speed up the process. Or you can have fun sourcing ready-made sugar paste decorations for your cake online (Etsy, I find, is a wonderfully fruitful resource in these instances). Or fashion the mushrooms out of marzipan (shop-bought for ease, or homemade if you prefer, see page 272), which offers a more instant-gratification base material to work with than the meringue.

And while I wholeheartedly accept that this recipe might read a little on the laborious side, I can promise you a cake that is pillowy-light, chocolatey but not overly sweet, laced with whipped cream and sugared chestnut and glossed in a fudgy, dark chocolate ganache. And should these delectable components not feel like quite enough to tempt you, there is a special intangible magic that comes with a cake that looks like an enchanted woodland log where Christmas fairies might live. It never fails to capture the imagination of children and grown-ups alike.

HANDS ON TIME
20 minutes for the
   mushrooms, 25 minutes
   for the sponge, 30 minutes
   to fill, 40 minutes to
   assemble

HANDS OFF TIME
3 hours for the mushrooms,
   15 minutes baking, 3 hours
   cooling, plus about 2 hours
   setting and resting time

SERVES 10–12

Start by making the cake: heat the oven to 180°C / 160°C fan / Gas 4. Grease and line a 42 × 30cm Swiss roll tray. Sift the flour, cocoa, baking powder and salt together into a mixing bowl. In a second, large mixing bowl, whisk the egg whites until they become frothy, then add 100g of the sugar, a spoonful at a time, until stiff, glossy peaks form. In a third mixing bowl, whisk the egg yolks, remaining 100g sugar, oil and vanilla together until they become a pale, fluffy and voluminous mass.

Fold the egg whites into the fluffy yolks, then fold in the sifted dry ingredients one-third at a time. Spread the batter evenly into the prepared tray and gently bang it on the kitchen counter a couple of times to pop any air bubbles and level it out. Bake for 15 minutes, until the sponge springs back lightly when you press on it with your finger. While the sponge is still warm, lift it out of its tin and, starting with a shorter side, gently and slowly roll the cake up, using the baking paper to help you. Let the cake cool completely, still rolled up and sitting on the baking paper.

FOR THE CAKE

2 tablespoons sunflower oil,
    plus more for the tray
160g plain flour
2 heaped tablespoons
    cocoa powder
1 teaspoon baking powder
½ teaspoon fine sea salt
6 eggs, separated
200g caster sugar
1 teaspoon vanilla extract

FOR THE FILLING

290ml double cream
130g icing sugar
200g unsweetened
    chestnut purée

Now make the filling: whip the cream and the icing sugar in a large mixing bowl until soft peaks form, taking care not to overwhisk, then fold in the chestnut purée. Gently and slowly unroll the sponge cake and spread the chestnut cream over it, leaving a 1–2cm border around the edge. Gently roll the sponge back up (this time without the baking paper). If the sponge splits a little as you roll it, don't worry too much: you won't notice once the cake is iced. Carefully lift the cake up and place it on a chopping board or serving dish (once the cake is iced it will be much harder to move). Cover with clingfilm and set in the fridge to chill for at least 30 minutes, or up to 2 days.

Make the topping by gently warming the cream in a small saucepan over a medium heat: bring it to just before the boil (you should see the tiniest bubbles begin to form at the edge of the pan), then take the pan off the heat, add the chocolate and stir until completely melted. Set the chocolate ganache in the fridge for 30–60 minutes to thicken, until you have something that is the consistency of thick honey.

While the cake is chilling, you can get on with making the mushrooms for decoration. Heat the oven to 140°C / 120°C fan / Gas 1. Line a baking sheet with baking paper.

In a spotlessly clean bowl, whisk the egg white and cream of tartar until frothy, then add the sugar half a spoonful at a time, whisking all the while, until it forms stiff and glossy peaks. Spoon into a piping bag with a round tip (roughly 5mm in diameter). Pipe blobs of various sizes (ranging from a 5p coin to 20p coin), with the piping bag held directly above the area you're piping and pulling up on the bag quickly to make little pointed shapes that will be the mushroom tops. Lightly dust with cocoa powder. Next, pipe the stems by pulling up gently on the piping bag as you apply even pressure: you're trying to create little towers on which you can balance the mushroom tops. Pipe the stems to different heights so you can create variation in the scene. Bake for 1 hour, then turn the oven off and leave in there to cool for a second hour. You can make these up to 2 weeks in advance and then store in an airtight container.

FOR THE TOPPING

220ml double cream
220g dark chocolate,
    finely chopped
A few sprigs of redcurrants
A few sprigs of rosemary
Icing sugar, to dust

FOR THE MERINGUE
MUSHROOMS (optional,
see recipe introduction)

1 egg white
Small pinch of cream
    of tartar
50g caster sugar
½ teaspoon cocoa powder
30g dark chocolate,
    broken into pieces

To assemble the mushrooms, bring a pan of water to the boil, melt the chocolate in a heatproof bowl over the simmering water, being sure the bowl does not touch the water (or melt it in the microwave). Dab a little melted chocolate on the centre-base of each mushroom top and carefully stick a stem to it. Then set each mushroom standing upright while the chocolate hardens and sets (this should take no more than 30–60 minutes and you can pop them in the fridge to speed up this step, if you like).

Take the cake from the fridge. Diagonally slice a 8–10cm section from one end and place the angled piece against the side of the roll, to make a little branch. Slowly spoon the ganache over the cake, spreading it out evenly and covering the whole area, including the ends. Use kitchen paper to clean away any messy chocolate from the board or serving dish, then set back in the fridge for 30 minutes or so for the icing to harden a little. The cake will keep like this for up to 3 days.

To decorate the cake, use a toothpick to create textured lines, like tree bark, all over the cake. Gently prop the meringue mushrooms against the cake and add a few sprigs of redcurrant and rosemary here and there. Lastly, before serving, dust with a little icing sugar, like snow.

Black Cherry and Ricotta Cheesecake

You can, somewhat conveniently, now buy jars of amarena cherries from many online retailers and I generally like to keep a couple of jars (at least) on hand, to add to this and that, when needed. I find them especially useful around Christmastime, to spoon over and zhuzh up anything from a scoop of vanilla ice cream, to trifle, to a plain pannacotta, to pavlova (see page 262). They add an instant touch of holiday mood with their glossy, deep red juices that look every bit as festive as the cherries taste sherbet-y sweet.

And while there is nothing strictly 'Christmas' about this cheesecake – with its light, airily fluffy ricotta filling set against a dark, devilishly chocolatey biscuit base – I do still find myself making the recipe often at this time of year, for the very reasons listed above: once you've piled syrupy cherries, gleaming and ruby-like, over the top of the thick layer of baked ricotta, the whole thing somehow looks and feels just the right amount of merry.

HANDS ON TIME

30 minutes

HANDS OFF TIME

55 minutes baking, plus
    2 hours cooling

SERVES 10–12

100g salted butter, plus more
    for the tin

300g chocolate bourbon
    biscuits

50g caster sugar, plus
    2 tablespoons

160g dark chocolate,
    finely chopped

2 eggs

600g ricotta

2 tablespoons cornflour

260g amarena cherries, plus
    120g to top the cake

100ml double cream

50g condensed milk

Grease and line a 23cm springform cake tin.

Combine the biscuits and the 2 tablespoons of sugar in a food processor and blitz to a chocolatey crumble. In a small pan, gently melt the butter and chocolate together, then stir the melted chocolate into the powdered biscuits. Tip the mixture out into the prepared tin and press it down firmly over the bottom and sides, taking it halfway up. Set in the freezer to harden for 30 minutes.

Heat the oven to 180°C / 160°C fan / Gas 4.

In a mixing bowl, whisk the eggs and the 50g sugar with electric beaters until light, fluffy and voluminous, then whisk in the ricotta. Sift over and stir in the cornflour. Drain the 260g cherries and reserve 50ml of their syrup. Add the reserved syrup to the mixture, along with the cream and the condensed milk, then stir to combine. Arrange the cherries over the biscuit base, then spoon over the ricotta filling.

Set in the oven (sitting it on a baking tray to catch any melted butter that might ooze out of the tin) and bake for 30 minutes, then reduce the oven temperature to 160°C / 140°C fan / Gas 3 and bake for a further 20–25 minutes until lightly golden on top and firm to touch in the middle. Let the cheesecake cool completely.

To serve, carefully remove the cake from its tin and spoon the last 120g of the amarena cherries over its golden baked top.

Christmas Cupcakes
with Brandy Buttercream

These taste inimitably like Christmas: headily spiced sponge, fiery from ginger and sticky with molasses, smothered in airy, ambrosially sweet, brandy-laden buttercream. (Though leave out the brandy if you are making these for small children.) I like to sprinkle sugary silver balls – so reminiscent of my childhood and the 1980s – over these, as that is how my mother decorates baked goods at Christmas. But you can try a sprig of redcurrants, pieces of crystallised ginger shimmering in their sugar coating, or just leave them snowy white.

The buttercream is a version of my mother's brandy butter and, in larger quantities, can be served with Christmas pudding or mince pies, or smeared on a slice of panettone.

HANDS ON TIME

20 minutes

HANDS OFF TIME

20 minutes, plus cooling

MAKES 12

~~~~~~

FOR THE CUPCAKES

180g self-raising flour

2 teaspoons ground ginger

2 teaspoons ground
   cinnamon

½ teaspoon ground nutmeg

½ teaspoon mixed spice

½ teaspoon fine sea salt

120g salted butter, softened

90g muscovado sugar

160g molasses

2 eggs

120ml whole milk

FOR THE ICING

150g salted butter, softened

150g icing sugar, sifted

35ml brandy

Silver sugar balls (or see
   recipe introduction),
   to decorate

Heat the oven to 180°C / 160°C fan / Gas 4. Line a cupcake tray with paper liners.

Sift the dry ingredients into a large bowl and stir to combine. In a second large bowl, cream together the butter and sugar until light, fluffy and smooth. Now, beat in the molasses, then the eggs, one by one, and lastly the milk.

Adding a little at a time, stir in the flour mixture, until just combined, taking care not to over-mix.

Divide the batter equally between the prepared liners, filling each up to three-quarters full (the cakes will rise in the oven). Bake in the middle of the oven for 18–20 minutes until a knife inserted in the middle comes out clean and, if you press down gently on the top, it springs back. Allow to cool in the tins for 5 minutes, then transfer to a wire rack until completely cold. They will keep happily, un-iced, in an airtight container for 1 week, or frozen for up to 3 months.

To make the icing, combine the butter and sifted icing sugar in a large bowl and beat until smooth. Pour in the brandy and beat again until combined and creamy-smooth. The brandy-laced icing will keep in a sealed container for 2–3 weeks, or, if you prefer, it will freeze well.

~~~~~~

Dollop or pipe the buttercream on to the cooled cupcakes and decorate with silver balls. Once assembled, the cakes will keep for 5–6 days.

Easy Cake Decorating Ideas

Beyond aesthetics, how you decorate your cake boils down to a matter of taste: if you love fruits and buttery nuts, a Florentine-style decoration (see page 202) or the Jewel Box method here is just the ticket. For those who enjoy a layer of golden marzipan as well, the finish of the Black and Gold Cake (see page 206) is best. I love something halfway between: a layer of thick marzipan topped with glacé fruits (see below), which looks effortlessly celebratory.

The methods here are just a starting point for you to play around with and take in your own creative direction. Quantities are based on a 23cm diameter cake, or can easily enough be adapted to go bigger or smaller, as needed.

GLACÉ FRUITS AND GOLDEN MARZIPAN

There are myriad variations you could create using the same basic principle as this. Use any fruits you like, or swap glacé fruits for dried fruits (apricots and figs are good). Once decorated, the cake keeps for weeks. If it starts to look a bit tired, brush it with apricot glaze to bring it back to life.

200g marzipan
100g apricot jam
70g pecans
170g glacé cherries, 3 small glacé pears, ½ glacé peach, 1 glacé fig, 1 glacé apricot, 1 slice glacé pineapple

Set the marzipan between 2 sheets of baking paper, then roll it out into a sheet as thick as a £1 coin. Cut out a circle very slightly wider than the diameter of the cake. Spoon the jam into a small pan, add 1–2 tablespoons water and set over a medium heat until it bubbles lightly. Brush it on the top of the cake, then gently lay on the marzipan. Brush the glaze over the marzipan, and stick on the nuts and fruits. Start with a circle of pecans round the edge, then a circle of cherries. Stick 2 pears in the centre, then cut the rest of the fruit into chunks to fill the gaps. Use the jam to give it all a lovely gloss (reheat gently with a splash of water if it has set).

JEWEL BOX

Taking inspiration from the Italian Christmas cake (of sorts), the *certosino*, but also reminiscent of British Dundee cake. Use any mix of glacé fruits you like, chopped into chunks, intermingled with cherries and waxy blanched almonds. Or a mix of glacé cherries (red and green) and nuts will give the same, ornate jewel box effect.

140g mixed glacé fruits (pear, peach, apricot or pineapple)
2 tablespoons runny honey
80g glacé cherries
30g blanched almonds

Chop the glacé fruits into chunks. Warm the honey in a small saucepan until liquid. Brush the glue-like liquid all over the top of the cake and decorate with chunks of glacé fruits, cherries and almonds, so the entire cake is covered, like a jewel box.

SNOWY WHITE FONDANT

This is how my mother used to decorate her Christmas cakes when I was growing up and it will forever hold a nostalgic quality for me. Once you've draped your cake in a blanket of smooth sugar fondant, you can leave it as is, pure and minimalist, or spray with edible gold dust, or gild with gold leaf. I love the opulent simplicity of shimmering gold and silver sugared almonds, stuck on with edible glue.

One caveat on timing: if you're making the cake in advance, allow a week for the marzipan to dry before adding icing. Otherwise, the oils of the marzipan will seep into the fondant after a week, so you will need to eat it relatively quickly.

500g marzipan
200g apricot jam
1kg white ready-to-roll icing
Icing sugar, to dust
Edible glue
Silver and gold sugared almonds

Roll the marzipan out between 2 sheets of baking paper into a 2.5mm thick disc large enough to cover the top and sides of the cake. Warm the jam (see opposite), then brush the cake, top and sides. Drape the marzipan over and gently press it down to cover the sides, trimming away excess and patching up any gaps. You can (indeed, should) do this in advance. Let it sit for a few days (ideally, 1 week) to dry.

Lightly knead the icing, then roll out between 2 sheets of baking paper into a 36cm-wide round. Dust your hands in icing sugar, then drape the icing over the cake, centring it neatly, and easing to fit around the sides. Use a sharp knife to trim away excess. Dust your hands again, then use a circular action to 'polish' the top and sides of the cake, smoothing out any bubbles, creases or bumps.

Use a small paintbrush to dab edible glue here and there on to the surface of the cake, then stick on the sugared almonds, to decorate.

Maxim's Mince Pies

So-called not because this is my friend Maxim's recipe, but because he relishes a mince pie with such joyful enthusiasm, and was so very delighted by these specifically, they shall forever, in our home, be known affectionately as his. As to the nuts and bolts of the recipe, I owe an eternal debt to Orlando Murrin (whose recipe in *Good Food: Christmas Made Easy*, edited by Mary Cadogan, I rely upon) for this foolproof method. It's a pastry recipe for people who don't like making pastry: quite literally, as easy as pie. Rather than rolling it out and cutting it into rounds (which is where things tend to go wrong for me, as bits of pastry inevitably stick to places they're not meant to), simply use your fingers to press chunks of dough into the tin, to make a shell. And while, by rights, this seemingly crude method should give chewy, tough and inferior pastry, by some Christmas miracle it absolutely doesn't. You get a golden, buttery, exquisitely crisp sugar-dipped crust.

HANDS ON TIME
30 minutes
HANDS OFF TIME
20 minutes, plus cooling
MAKES 12
꧁꧂
350g plain flour
100g caster sugar, plus
   1 tablespoon
225g cold salted butter,
   chopped
480g mincemeat (see page
   286 for homemade), or
   shop-bought
1 egg, lightly beaten

Heat the oven to 200°C / 180°C fan / Gas 6.

To make the pastry, combine the flour and 100g caster sugar together in a mixing bowl, then rub in the cold butter until the mixture resembles crumbs. Combine the pastry into a ball: you don't need to add any liquid for this, just keep rubbing it with your hands to bring it together and you will end up with a firm, shortbread-like dough. Use the dough immediately or chill it for later, if you prefer.

Divide the pastry into 24 pieces: 12 roughly the size of a walnut, 12 slightly smaller. Roll the pieces into small balls, then press a walnut-sized ball of pastry into a nonstick muffin tin, lining the bottom and the sides of the hole. Spoon in a dollop of mincemeat, to fill it, then take a slightly smaller pastry ball and form it into a lid. Drape it over a pie and seal base and top together. Repeat to make 12 pies. Of course, if you prefer, you could roll out the pastry in the conventional way. At this point, the pies can be frozen for up to 1 month.

Use a pastry brush to lightly glaze each of the pies with egg, then sprinkle over the 1 tablespoon of sugar.

Bake for 20 minutes, until lightly golden. Leave to cool in the tin for 5 minutes, then carefully lift the pies out of the tin and set on a wire rack to cool completely. The mince pies will keep in an airtight container for 3–4 days.
꧁꧂
To serve warm, reheat in a medium oven for 5 minutes, then serve with a dollop of Boozy Amaretto Butter or drizzle of Easy Peasy Hot Brandy Custard (see page 293).

Puff Pastry Mince Pies

Some people prefer their mince pies made with puff pastry, and on some days, I'm inclined to agree. The puff pastry, flaky and buttery as it is, somehow gives you an airier, fluffier pie than its more widely celebrated shortcrust counterpart. My mother, for example, likes there to be both shortcrust and puff pastry mince pies on the table at Christmas, which is why I've included recipes for both in this book. Though you'll notice that this method, much like the one opposite, is for a good 'cheat's' mince pie which is simpler and less labour-intensive to make, yet every bit as gratifying to eat, as any version which involves making puff pastry from scratch. My only insistence is that you buy all-butter puff pastry, which really does taste better.

Unlike a classic, shortcrust mince pie – which is a hardy beast and will happily keep for a few days with little, if any, impact on its taste – puff pastry really should be eaten within twenty-four hours of baking, or it tends to turn a little soggy. By the same principle, these mince pies really are best enjoyed still warm from the oven. You can assemble the pies ahead of time and store them, ready-to-bake, for up to twenty-four hours in the fridge, or bake them off and gently reheat before serving: both methods work well.

HANDS ON TIME
15 minutes
HANDS OFF TIME
25 minutes, plus cooling
MAKES 12

⟶⟶⟶

3 × 320g sheets of
   ready-rolled all-butter
   puff pastry
480g mincemeat (see page
   286 for homemade), or
   shop-bought
1 egg, lightly beaten
1 tablespoon caster sugar

Heat the oven to 200°C / 180°C fan / Gas 6.

So as to avoid the pastry melting or becoming sticky as you work, you might want to work with a sheet at a time and keep the others in the fridge. Unroll a sheet of pastry, then cut a round that is a little larger than a nonstick muffin tin hole. Drape the pastry round over the muffin tin hole and gently press it down, so the base and sides are covered.

Spoon a dollop of mincemeat into the pastry case, so that it's filled, then cut a second pastry round, this time smaller, and drape over the top of the pie. Use your fingers to gently seal the top to the base. Repeat this process with the remaining pastry and mincemeat, to make 12 mince pies.

Once the pies are assembled, you can keep them, in their tin and ready to go, in the fridge for up to 24 hours.

⟶⟶⟶

Use a pastry brush to lightly glaze each pie with egg, then sprinkle over the caster sugar. Bake in the oven for 20 minutes (25 minutes if straight from the fridge), until puffed up and lightly golden on top.

Let cool in the tin for 5–10 minutes, then carefully lift out and serve warm. Alternatively, you can bake the pies in advance, then gently reheat and serve (see opposite).

Salted Caramel Pecan Pie

I conceived this recipe as a no-bake pie in large part to avoid dealing with temperamental pastry, as well as to save oven space at a time of year when it comes at such a premium. However, I've since decided I'm very partial to the biscuit base and wouldn't have this any other way. You can make it with pretty much whatever biscuits you like: Oreos for full Thanksgiving Americana; chocolate bourbons for a deeper, chocolatier taste; even shortbread for something richer and somewhat reminiscent of a millionaire's shortbread. But my favourite is the humble digestive, not overly sweet, so it balances the fudgy intense salted caramel and the glossy layer of chocolate. A bit like eating a Snickers bar.

You can make this well in advance and it will keep, chilled, for days. I serve it straight from the fridge so the case holds its shape well when sliced, but also because, chilled, the caramel takes on a seductive soft-chewy texture which I'm especially partial to.

HANDS ON TIME

25 minutes

HANDS OFF TIME

2 hours chilling

SERVES 8–10

FOR THE BASE

450g digestive biscuits (or
    see recipe introduction)
160g salted butter, softened

FOR THE FILLING

100g salted butter
140g soft brown sugar
90g golden syrup
270g condensed milk
140g pecans, coarsely
    chopped
120ml double cream
170g dark chocolate,
    finely chopped
Sea salt flakes

First make the base: combine the biscuits and the butter in a food processor and blitz until you have something of the consistency of wet sand. Press the biscuity rubble evenly into a deep 28cm fluted pie dish with a removable base, taking care to press it evenly over the bottom of the tin and into all the nooks and crannies on the sides, then set in the freezer for 10–15 minutes to harden.

Meanwhile, make the caramel: gently melt the butter in a heavy-based saucepan over a medium heat, then stir in the sugar, syrup and condensed milk. Increase the heat and bring to a bubble, then stir constantly with a wooden spoon for 5 minutes or so, until the sauce is thick and smooth and a rich caramel colour. Take off the heat, add a generous pinch of salt and stir well. Add the pecans and give everything a good stir to combine so all the nuts are well coated.

In a second pan, heat the cream just to the point before the boil (you should see the tiniest bubbles come to the surface round the edge of the pan), then take off the heat, tip in the chocolate and stir constantly until melted. Spoon the caramel-coated nuts into the tart base, spreading them out evenly with the back of the spoon, then pour the chocolate over. Set the pie back in the fridge, still in its tin, to chill for 2 hours, or up to 4–5 days.

Gently remove the pie from its tin and set on a serving dish.

Pistachio Cream and Ginger Pie

I love the warming peppery gingernut base here against the mellow creaminess of the filling. But above all, I love how effective the two look together: soft green and milky tones twirled in a feathered pattern that almost – and I emphasise 'almost' – looks too pretty to eat. Like the other sweet pies in the book (see pages 232 and 236), this too is a no-bake recipe, sparing precious oven real-estate when there is often so much to bake, roast and reheat. You can make this in advance, if you like, then either freeze it or store in the fridge.

And while I love the delicate, sweet pistachio cream, you could swap it out for a dollop of chocolate-hazelnut spread such as Nutella, then top the pie with shards of chopped dark chocolate and/or toasted hazelnuts alongside the sugar-dipped chunks of ginger.

HANDS ON TIME

25 minutes

HANDS OFF TIME

2 hours chilling

SERVES 8–10

⋘⋘

FOR THE BASE

500g gingernut biscuits

120g salted butter, softened

FOR THE FILLING

2 gelatine leaves

500g mascarpone

2 eggs

50g caster sugar

110g pistachio cream

50g crystallised ginger, coarsely chopped

30g pistachios, coarsely chopped

Toss the biscuits into a food processor and blitz to crumbs, then add the butter and blitz again. Tip the biscuity rubble into a 25cm pie dish with a removable base, then press it into the nooks and crannies to cover the bottom and sides. Set in the freezer to harden for 10–15 minutes.

In a small bowl, soak the gelatine for 5 minutes in cold water. Meanwhile, heat 3 tablespoons of the mascarpone in a small saucepan until steaming, but don't let it boil.

In a large bowl, whisk the eggs and sugar with electric beaters for 4–5 minutes until you have a voluminous lemony mass, then whisk in the remaining mascarpone. Squeeze the water out of the gelatine and stir it through the warmed mascarpone until smooth, then whisk this into the rest of the mascarpone. Spoon into the pie case and spread it out.

Spoon the pistachio cream into a small, heatproof bowl and set in the microwave for 10–20 seconds: just long enough to loosen the cream to a soft consistency that is easy to drizzle. If you don't have a microwave, you can also do this in a small saucepan over a very gentle heat.

Drizzle the softened pistachio cream over the filling in vertical stripes, then drag a toothpick across the stripes to create a marbled effect. Set in the fridge for 2–3 hours until set, then carefully lift the pie out of its tin and set on its serving dish. At this point, it will keep happily in the fridge for 1–2 days, or freeze it (well wrapped) for up to 3 months.

⋘⋘

Before serving, scatter chunks of crystallised ginger and chopped pistachios over the pie. Serve chilled.

Egg Nog Cream Pie

Not for the faint of heart, but certainly for the merry of spirit. This is gloriously boozy, but also so light and fluffy that you can practically taste bubbles with each bite. I came upon the inspired idea while leafing through my much-loved copy of Claire Macdonald's *Seasonal Cooking*. Claire makes it with a pastry crust, which I've swapped out here for a chocolate biscuit base. I've also increased the alcohol to make the wibbly-wobbly custard filling more noggy. If you don't have bottles of whisky, brandy and rum to hand, don't go out and buy more, just increase any one single kind of alcohol to make up the difference. Or, to make a version suitable for children, leave out the booze and you will be left with a nutmeg-scented cream and chocolate concoction that will undoubtedly please everyone.

HANDS ON TIME

40 minutes

HANDS OFF TIME

2½ hours cooling
   and chilling

SERVES 8–10

FOR THE CRUST

450g chocolate bourbon
   biscuits

80g dark chocolate, chopped

100g salted butter, softened

FOR THE FILLING

8g gelatine leaves (5 leaves)

200ml whole milk

2 eggs, separated

80g caster sugar

1 teaspoon cornflour

⅔ teaspoon freshly ground
   nutmeg, plus more
   to serve

2 tablespoons rum

2 tablespoons whisky

2 tablespoons brandy

200ml double cream

Put the biscuits and chocolate in a food processor and blitz to form a crumb, then add the butter and blitz until the mixture starts to clump together and resembles wet sand. Press into a 25cm tart tin with a removable base and set in the fridge to harden and chill, while you make the filling.

Soak the gelatine in a small bowl filled with cold water.

In a small saucepan, gently warm the milk over a medium heat for 2–3 minutes, until tiny bubbles appear at the edge of the pan. In a large bowl, beat together the egg yolks with half the sugar, the cornflour and nutmeg. Pour a little hot milk in with the eggs and whisk until you have something that resembles a milkshake, then pour this back into the pan with the remaining milk. Heat gently for 4–5 minutes, stirring constantly, until thick enough to coat the back of a spoon, then remove from the heat and stir in the squeezed-out gelatine. Stir in the rum, whisky and brandy, then let cool completely.

In a second mixing bowl, whip the cream until soft peaks form, then gently fold into the custard. In a third, spotlessly clean bowl, whisk the egg whites until frothy, then add the last of the sugar, a spoonful at a time, whisking all the while. Whisk one-third of the glossy whites into the creamy, boozy custard, then gently fold in the rest. Pour into the chilled tart case and set in the fridge for 1–2 hours, until firm to touch.

Carefully release from the tin and chill until ready to serve. It will keep in the fridge for 3–4 days, or cover then freeze for up to 3 weeks (it takes 5–6 hours to defrost).

Dust with grated nutmeg before serving chilled.

Nutty Chocolate Torrone

At Christmastime, you'll see the sweet shop windows in Italy filled with different kinds of torrone: nougat-based, chocolate-based, peppered with nuts and glacé fruits and all good things. The recipe opposite is for a chocolate-based torrone, with three different kinds of nuts, so when you slice through the log you can see their different shades and forms, like mosaic pieces set into clay. You can build the torrone with whatever you fancy, or even make it completely nut-free: toss in some glacé cherries, crystallised ginger or candied peel; try it with other dried fruits such as figs, dried apricots or dried cranberries; you could even try crumbling in chunks of sweet biscuit or shards of chocolate-dipped honeycomb. Alternatively, you could try making the filling with pistachio cream in place of the chocolate-hazelnut spread (omit the milk chocolate for this version and double the quantities of white chocolate to 400g), for a pistachio-flavoured and -hued cream to fill the log's hardened dark chocolate shell.

Either which way you make this, it's a lovely recipe to serve by the slice, after dinner in place of (or in addition to) dessert, or to give as a gift. (This works with either the whole log wrapped in baking paper or cellophane, or simply a few slices bundled up in a paper or cellophane bag and adorned with a ribbon.) If you have a silicone loaf tin, then you could use that to mould the melted chocolate in; but I like to buy disposable foil loaf tins (roughly 1.2 litres in volume for the quantities here), which I can then easily cut away once the chocolate has set.

HANDS ON TIME

30 minutes

HANDS OFF TIME

1¼ hours chilling

MAKES 8–10 generous
   slices

300g dark chocolate,
   coarsely chopped

200g milk chocolate,
   coarsely chopped

200g white chocolate,
   coarsely chopped

200g chocolate-hazelnut
   spread, such as Nutella

70g pistachios, coarsely
   chopped

70g blanched hazelnuts,
   coarsely chopped

70g blanched almonds,
   coarsely chopped

Edible gold dust, to decorate
   (optional)

Heat a saucepan of water over a medium heat. Put the dark chocolate in a heatproof bowl and set over the pan of bubbling hot water, taking care not to let the water touch the bowl. Stir the chocolate from time to time, until melted and smooth, then remove the bowl and reduce the heat under the saucepan to a very gentle simmer.

Use a pastry brush to paint two-thirds of the melted dark chocolate, in a thick, generous layer, on to the sides and bottom of a 1.2-litre (or 2 × 600ml) disposable foil loaf tin(s), saving roughly one-third for later. Set in the fridge to chill for roughly 15 minutes, until it has hardened.

In a second, larger heatproof bowl, combine the milk chocolate and the white chocolate together, set over the pan of steaming water and, once melted into a sweet, creamy pool, take off the heat. Now, stir in the chocolate-hazelnut spread to make a thick, chocolatey cream. Lastly, stir in the chopped nuts.

Spoon the filling into the chocolate shell and set back in the fridge again to chill for a further 15 minutes. Then take the tin out of the fridge and brush the last of the melted dark chocolate over the chocolate cream filling, going well over the edges so the log is sealed. (If the dark chocolate has solidified in this time, just melt it again by setting the bowl back over the boiling water.)

Once assembled, set the torrone back in the fridge for at least 1 hour. Once the torrone has hardened, gently turn it out of its tin, spritz with a little edible gold dust, if you like, and slice to serve. The torrone will keep in the fridge for up to 2 weeks.

Hidden Orange Christmas Pudding

The real magic of this pudding lies on the inside: the whole orange which sits at its centre, a secret treasure, glistening, golden and incandescent, that makes a ceremony of cutting into the pudding, just as setting it on fire makes a ceremony of bringing it to the table. The pudding itself is unexpectedly light and fluffy for something that looks so dense and dark. It's not overly sweet, but wonderfully, comfortingly rich and intensely orangey (almost as if the pudding is laced with marmalade) from the Cointreau and the sweet juices of the whole orange cooking in its centre. The orange itself is sweet and tender to eat, the bitterness of its candied, tenderised citrus peel a sharp contrast to the dense richness of the pudding. If you would prefer a more mellow flavour, then you can swap the citrus-scented Cointreau out for stout.

The method you find below is the way my mother cooks her Christmas pudding, in a heatproof ceramic bowl and sealed with baking paper and a length of muslin cloth tied with string. This looks nice and, if you're giving the pudding to someone, is a lovely way to present it, though it can be a little fiddly to swap the paper and tie the string for the first and then second steamings of the pudding. I've since discovered plastic pudding bowls, which you can buy easily online and which come with little plastic lids, that are rather more user-friendly if somewhat less aesthetically pleasing. If I'm making the pudding to serve for dinner rather than give away, then I must admit that is what I use.

HANDS ON TIME

1 hour on the first day,
    20 minutes each on days
    2 and 3, 5 minutes on
    Christmas Day

HANDS OFF TIME

3 days, plus 12 hours
    steaming

SERVES 10–12

DAY 1

Put all the mixed fruit, dates and apricots, along with the muscovado sugar, in a large mixing bowl. Pour over the Cointreau, cover with a clean tea towel and leave to steep overnight (or longer, if you can). Put the butter in the freezer at the same time and leave there to freeze also.

Now make the candied orange: pierce the orange several times with a cocktail stick or skewer. Put it in a small saucepan and cover with cold water, then bring to the boil and simmer gently for 2 hours, topping up the water as needed, to keep the fruit covered. Drain and discard the cooking water from the pan; then pour the measured cold water into the pan. Add the caster sugar and star anise and heat gently, stirring constantly, until the sugar has dissolved. Bring to the boil. Now add the orange, cover with a lid and simmer for 1 hour. Remove the lid and simmer gently, uncovered, for a further 30 minutes. Remove from the heat, cover the pan and let cool overnight.

500g mixed dried fruit

100g dates, pitted and chopped

90g dried apricots, chopped

110g muscovado sugar

290ml Cointreau, plus 2 tablespoons, plus more if needed and to serve

110g salted butter, plus more for the bowl

1 orange

800ml water

800g caster sugar

3–4 star anise

50g plain flour

110g brown breadcrumbs

50g ground almonds

2 teaspoons mixed spice

1 teaspoon ground cinnamon

2 eggs

DAY 2

The next day, place the flour and breadcrumbs in a large mixing bowl and coarsely grate in the frozen butter. Toss the butter flakes and flour together. Add the ground almonds and spices, then add the soaked fruit, along with any juices.

In a small bowl, lightly beat the eggs with a fork, then add to the mixture, together with the 2 tablespoons of Cointreau. Stir to mix all together thoroughly. If the mixture is a little stiff, then just add a splash more Cointreau. Stir the pudding for luck (get the rest of the family to do this, too), then cover the bowl and leave the mixture to rest overnight.

DAY 3

The next day, spoon roughly one-third of the pudding mixture into a buttered 1.8-litre heatproof pudding bowl, pushing down to pack the mixture. Sit the orange in the centre of the pudding, then pack the rest of the mixture around and on top of the orange to make sure it's well covered. Cover with a double layer of baking paper and a double layer of foil, tied tightly with a string. I don't pleat the baking paper, I just cut it to size and then rather roughly tie it on.

Steam the pudding, in a deep pan half-filled with water and with the lid on, for 8–9 hours. Regularly check the water level and top up when needed. If you're nervous, you could sit it on a trivet – and I should recommend you do, to be on the safe side – but I've never used a trivet; I just put the bowl straight into the pan and it has always been fine. Lift it out of the pan and allow to cool, then remove and discard the baking paper and foil. Cover again in the same fashion: your pudding will now keep for up to a year.

On Christmas Day, steam the pudding for a further 3 hours, then lift out of the pan, remove the baking paper and foil and gently turn out, upside down, on to a heatproof serving dish with a lip. Warm a metal ladle of Cointreau over a candle on the table, set it alight – being very careful and using a long match – then pour over the pudding to serve.

Salted Caramel Zuccotto

While strictly speaking this is a zuccotto – a dome-shaped cake, filled with ice cream and enrobed in chocolate – I take disproportionate pleasure in the fact that it looks very much like a Christmas pudding. Even more delightful is the knowledge that this is a recipe which can be made weeks, if not months, ahead of time (without its redcurrant decoration) and then whisked out of the freezer and brought to the table as needed.

I have a soft spot for salted caramel ice cream, which is what I have used here, but obviously you can fill the Marsala-drenched panettone shell with whatever flavour ice cream you like. If you wanted to be extra fancy, you could even layer different flavours on top of each other, so that, when you slice into the zuccotto, you see stripes of colour down the middle.

HANDS ON TIME

40 minutes

HANDS OFF TIME

1¾ hours freezing

SERVES 12–14

⤞⤞⤞⤞

2 litres salted caramel
   ice cream

500g panettone

120ml Marsala

260g dark chocolate,
   finely chopped

150g salted butter

150g white chocolate,
   finely chopped

80ml double cream

Redcurrants, for decoration

Remove the ice cream from the freezer, open the lid and set aside to soften slightly. Line a 3-litre bowl with clingfilm.

Slice the panettone into roughly 2cm-thick pieces and press them into the bowl, so the entire surface is lined with cake, saving some for the top. Drizzle most of the Marsala over the panettone, again saving a small amount for the top. Spoon the softened ice cream into the panettone-lined bowl, then cover the top with the last few slices of panettone, so that the ice cream is sealed in. Drizzle over the last of the Marsala. Cover with clingfilm and set in the freezer for 1 hour, or longer, if you like.

Melt the dark chocolate and the butter together in a saucepan over a very low heat, stirring all the while to make sure the chocolate doesn't burn or catch. Once melted, take off the heat and set aside.

Turn the frozen panettone and ice cream cake out of its bowl and on to a serving dish, ideally with a little lip. Discard the clingfilm and pour over the hot buttery chocolate so the entire surface of the cake is covered. Set the pudding back in the freezer for 30–45 minutes, or longer, so that the chocolate can harden.

Lastly, warm the white chocolate and cream together in a small saucepan and over a low heat, until the chocolate is completely melted, then pour over the chocolate-covered panettone. Decorate with a few redcurrants and set back in the freezer until you're ready to serve.

Pomegranate Campari Jelly

This is a wibbly-wobbly jelly with a soft melt-in-your-mouth set rather than the more solid, gelatinous variety I so strongly associate with childhood tea parties. Plus it has sparkling booze in it, which of course makes the whole thing feel very grown-up. The joy of jelly is that you can (indeed, you must) make it in advance, which in part at least is what makes it such an ideal dinner party dessert. It's also low-effort, easy to make and both gluten- and dairy-free, so it's a good option when navigating dietary restrictions.

HANDS ON TIME
15 minutes
HANDS OFF TIME
Overnight setting
SERVES 8–10

16g gelatine leaves
    (10 leaves)
175ml Campari
175ml pomegranate juice
400ml prosecco
250ml water
300g caster sugar
Handful of pomegranate
    seeds, to serve

Set a 1.5-litre jelly mould on a small tray so it's easy to carry to the fridge once filled. I often use bits of scrunched-up foil to stabilise it on the tray, if the mould feels a little wobbly when set upside down on a flat surface.

Now, set the gelatine in a small dish, cover with cold water and leave to soak for 5 minutes. Pour the Campari, pomegranate juice and prosecco into a saucepan. Add the measured water and sugar and give it a good stir to help dissolve, then set over a medium heat. Do not stir once the pan is on the heat, as this will kill off the bubbles in the prosecco (you want as many of those in the jelly as you can get). Bring to the boil for about a minute or just under, until the sugar is completely dissolved, then take off the heat.

Carefully ladle roughly 250ml of the ruby-red liquid into a measuring jug and add the softened gelatine leaves, giving them a good squeeze in your hands to remove excess water beforehand. Whisk everything together until the gelatine has completely dissolved. Pour the rest of the liquid from the saucepan into your measuring jug before carefully pouring into the jelly mould. Carry to the fridge and leave to set overnight for a gentle, wibbly-wobbly texture. At this point, it will keep happily in the fridge for 2–3 days.

When ready to serve, carefully plunge the jelly mould into a dish of hot (not boiling) water, making sure it doesn't splash into the jelly. Hold it there for 3–5 seconds until you can see the edges begin to separate from the mould. Lift it out of the hot water immediately. Now set a serving dish on top, taking care to centre the mould on the dish, and, using both hands to hold the two together, flip it over. The jelly should slip out easily. Sprinkle over the pomegranate seeds to serve.

Gingerbread, Cranberry and Zabaione Trifle

If you are able to serve this in a glass dish then all the better, because part of the magic of a trifle, I can't help but feel, is to see and enjoy all the different layers. This Anglo-Italian variation on the theme of trifle, with its layer of dark, sticky gingerbread, ruby-red cranberry sauce, custard yellow, frothy zabaione and final stratum of soft, snowy whipped cream, is certainly no exception. Equally – and obviously – it will taste just as good however you serve it, so if all you have is a salad bowl, that will do well too. Don't let the absence of the right bowl put you off: this particular combination of cloud-like zabaione with dense, peppery gingerbread is enough to make even those who think they don't really like trifle (of which I count myself a member) change their minds.

A traditional trifle calls for a layer of custard, which I've replaced here with airy zabaione, infused with Amaretto liquor, instead of the more conventional prosecco or Marsala. The hint of sweet almond is a subtle and pleasing complement to the layer of sticky, spiced ginger cake. All together the cake, cream and zabaione are quite sweet, which is why I like the sharpness of cranberry sauce (be it from a jar or homemade, see page 291) here rather than a more canonical sweet jam, such as raspberry or apricot, but you could also use fresh fruit instead. A layer of frozen jammy raspberries would work well, as would blackberries or redcurrants. And if you crave the jellied sweetness of jam, far be it from me to stand in your way. As an added bonus, the trifle freezes very nicely; so you can, if you like, make it well in advance, then defrost in the fridge overnight and top with the last layer of whipped cream, to serve.

HANDS ON TIME
35 minutes
HANDS OFF TIME
1 hour (minimum) standing
   before serving
SERVES 8–10

Slice the ginger cake into 2–3cm-thick pieces and arrange in a trifle dish in a single layer, squishing the pieces of sticky cake together with your fingers so the entire area is covered. Now spoon the cranberry sauce over the cake, spreading it out evenly.

Fill a pan up to one-third full of water, set it over a medium heat and bring to the boil. Put the egg yolks and sugar into a heatproof bowl and whisk with electric beaters – plugged in (if they need to be) close to the stove – for 2–3 minutes, or until you have a light, fluffy and voluminous mass. As the mixture begins to froth up, set the bowl over the pan of gently simmering water, taking care that the hot water doesn't touch the bowl. Keep whisking until the mixture is thick enough for a trail of it to remain on the surface when drizzled over from the whisk. Slowly pour in the Amaretto, whisking all the while. This should take

580g ginger cake (I use
    Jamaica Ginger Cake)
300g cranberry sauce
12 egg yolks
200g caster sugar
140ml Amaretto
30g flaked almonds
900ml double cream

3–5 minutes, and as you add the liquid, the zabaione will double in size and thicken. Remove the bowl from the heat and let the zabaione cool to room temperature, whisking occasionally to prevent a skin from forming.

Toss the flaked almonds into a nonstick frying pan and set over a medium heat. Toast for 2–3 minutes, shaking the pan from time to time to move the shards of nuts about, until they are lightly golden. Take off the heat and set aside.

In a second bowl, whip 400ml of the double cream until soft peaks form, taking care not to over-whip. Gently fold the whipped cream into the cooled zabaione and spoon the yellow, Amaretto-scented custard into the trifle dish, over the cranberry sauce, spreading it out evenly. Store in the fridge, covered, for up to 36 hours. Alternatively, freeze for up to 3 months, then defrost overnight in the fridge before adding the whipped cream and nuts.

When ready to serve, whip the remaining cream to soft peaks, spoon it over the layer of zabaione and sprinkle over the toasted flaked almonds. You can prepare this up to 24 hours before serving and keep it in the fridge until you're ready for pudding.

Gorgonzola, Fig and Hazelnut Terrine

This is a delectable and savoury alternative to a sweet dessert: a cheese course of sorts that looks a little fancier and more striking than your standard Cheddar-and-Stilton-on-a-board-with-crackers (though there's nothing wrong with that). It's one of those dishes that looks impressive but where no actual cooking – in any strong sense of the word – is involved, just a matter of assembling a handful of ingredients together. And while it does require some forethought, as the terrine needs a good few hours in the fridge to set, it's a recipe that takes mere moments to throw together. I usually serve this in place of or in addition to dessert, but there is nothing stopping you from offering it with drinks before dinner, with a pile of crackers, so everyone can dig in and help themselves, or equally as a starter before Christmas lunch.

HANDS ON TIME
30 minutes
HANDS OFF TIME
6 hours (minimum)
SERVES 8–10

~~~~~

250g dried figs
20ml brandy
700g Gorgonzola dolce
60g toasted hazelnuts,
    coarsely chopped
350g ricotta
A few thyme sprigs
    (optional)

The night before, put the dried figs in a small bowl, add the brandy and top up with boiling water so the fruit is completely covered.

Line a 25 × 11cm loaf tin with baking paper.

Slice the Gorgonzola into pieces roughly 5mm thick and arrange them over the bottom and sides of the tin so it is completely covered (save a few slices for the top of the terrine). Use your fingers to gently press the cheese slices together, if necessary.

Cut a little less than two-thirds of the drained figs into thin strips and arrange over the layer of Gorgonzola, again covering both the base and sides. Combine the chopped hazelnuts with the ricotta in a small mixing bowl (saving a few of the nuts for decoration). Spoon the ricotta mixture over the Gorgonzola and figs, then even out with the back of a spoon.

Slice most the remaining figs into thin strips and arrange over the ricotta (save some for serving), then cover with a last layer of Gorgonzola. Set in the fridge to chill for at least 6 hours.

~~~~~

When you're ready to serve (or a few hours beforehand), turn the terrine out on to a serving dish or board and gently peel away the paper. Cut the remaining figs into chunks and scatter these with the remaining chopped hazelnuts over the terrine. Garnish with a few thyme sprigs, if you like, and serve with bread and crackers for spreading.

Saffron Poached Pears with Chocolate Caramel Sauce

I'm a big fan of poached pears and I usually prefer them served chilled, in their sugary infused juices, but in this particular instance I want the fruit hot and soupy and swimming in rich chocolate sauce. There is a warmth to the flavours here – from the tender, saffron-infused, golden fruit and the velvety, caramel-laced chocolate sauce – that is utterly irresistible. It tastes like pure comfort, during winter when we so crave comfort.

You can make as much or as little of the sauce as you like: certainly in our household it will always find a good use, splashed over a dollop of ice cream or simply devoured by the spoonful, as is. Typically, I calculate quantities based on 1 Mars bar and roughly 50ml of cream for each pear (and each person). While that is probably slightly more than you need, it's one of those instances where you really don't want to reach for seconds and find you've run out of sauce. You can make it in advance and have it sitting on the hob, then reheat it whenever needed so you can serve it piping hot (but not bubbling).

HANDS ON TIME

15 minutes

HANDS OFF TIME

15 minutes

SERVES 6

❤❤❤❤❤

FOR THE PEARS

50g caster sugar

1 teaspoon saffron strands

1 litre water

6 pears

FOR THE SAUCE

6 standard-sized (51g)
   Mars bars, chopped into
   small pieces

300ml double cream

Sea salt flakes

In a pan in which all 6 of the pears can fit snugly, combine the sugar and the saffron strands. Pour in the measured water, then set over a medium-high heat and bring to a gentle boil.

Peel the pears and cut a slice off each base so they can stand up like little soldiers, then gently lower them into the boiling golden water. Reduce the heat to low, cover the pan and leave to simmer for 20 minutes, turning the fruit every now and then so each side is imbued with saffron. Insert a butter knife into the bottom of a pear to see if the fruit is cooked: the knife should slide in with no resistance. Turn off the heat and let the pears cool. Once cooled, store the fruit, swimming in its bright yellow cooking syrup, for up to 1 week in the fridge and reheat before serving.

To make the chocolate sauce, combine the chopped Mars bars and cream in a small saucepan and set over a low heat, stirring constantly for 3-4 minutes with a small whisk until the chocolate bar has completely melted. Add a generous pinch of salt flakes. Reheat as required.

❤❤❤❤❤

When ready to serve, gently warm the pears and the sauce separately on the hob and serve piping hot.

Sugar Plum Sorbet

This is light and airy and sumptuously sugar-sweet to eat: a delicate palate cleanser, like rose-tinted glass. Unlike the recipe for Christmas Cake Ice Cream opposite, which is a no-churn recipe, to make this sorbet and to get it to the just-right consistency, it helps to use an ice cream maker. Though you will find that, with the machine, this is a recipe of such low effort that it takes mere moments to make. If you don't have an ice cream maker, you can churn the sorbet manually by checking on it and giving it a good stir every thirty minutes or so as it freezes. This will give you something of the consistency of crushed ice or a granita rather more than a creamy sorbet, but I still feel that it works well, perhaps even better. The shards of reddish-peach pink ice have a sparkling quality about them that, appropriately somehow, evokes pink tutus and sugar plum fairies.

HANDS ON TIME

15 minutes

HANDS OFF TIME

1 hour chilling, plus

    30 minutes churning,

    plus 30 minutes freezing

MAKES about 1 litre

⤳⸙⸙⸙⤸

190g caster sugar

750ml water

230g plums, halved

    and pitted

Heat the sugar and measured water together in a small saucepan over a gentle heat, until the sugar has dissolved and you have a clear syrup. Toss the plums into a food processor and blitz until you have a smooth purée, then add the syrup and blitz again to combine. Leave to cool, then pop into the fridge for about 1 hour, until chilled.

Pour the cold, sweet mixture into an ice cream maker and churn on the sorbet setting according to the manufacturer's instructions (usually 30–40 minutes), then freeze until ready to serve. Alternatively, pour straight into an ice cream container and freeze for 5–6 hours, opening it up and giving the mixture a good mix every 30 minutes or so as it freezes.

Christmas Cake Ice Cream

I believe I'm right in thinking that I first tore this recipe out of a magazine many years ago, though I can't now – to my shame – remember from which publication, and over time it has come to be a firm and much-loved part of my repertoire. From memory, the original recipe called for mincemeat, spooned straight into the custard ice cream base, but I like to make it with leftover fruit cake and/or pudding, though you could just as well crumble in chunks of fudgy brownies (see page 283) or even sticky, shop-bought ginger cake. This is a no-churn ice cream, so no fancy equipment is called for and very little by way of effort, but it creates an exquisitely fudgy texture with a hint of melted marzipan to offset the mellow vanilla of the thick double cream.

HANDS ON TIME

10 minutes

HANDS OFF TIME

6 hours, or overnight, freezing

MAKES about 900ml

600ml double cream

130g marzipan, cut into small pieces

320g leftover Christmas cake

Combine the cream and marzipan together in a saucepan and set over a medium-low heat. Heat until the marzipan has dissolved, stirring all the while to help crush and break down any lumps, but take care not to let the cream come to the boil.

Take off the heat and pour the velvety, marzipan-scented custard into a freezerproof container. Cover and let rest until cooled.

Once cooled, crumble in the Christmas cake and give the mixture a good stir. Seal and set in the freezer for 5–6 hours (or overnight) to freeze.

Christmas Pavlova

My friend David, who is both Australian and something of a culinary authority, insists
that it's not a Christmas pavlova without a generous drizzle of fresh, searingly sharp
passion fruit flesh, drizzled over the cream to cut through the richness and the sweetness
of it all. Good passion fruit, sadly, is hard to come by in the northern hemisphere, most
especially in the depths of winter, so I hope David will forgive me for suggesting
redcurrants – also juicy and sherbet-y tart – instead. The happy muddle of shades of
festive red, from the cheery Santa-bright of the berries to the rich, deep scarlet of the
sour cherries in syrup, as well as the pleasing resemblance of this dish to a holiday
wreath, add a good dash of 'Christmas', in my book, to the whole affair.

HANDS ON TIME

20 minutes

HANDS OFF TIME

2 hours baking and cooling

SERVES 6–8

⤷⤷⤷⤷⤶

3 egg whites

⅓ teaspoon cream of tartar

150g caster sugar

450ml double cream

250g amarena cherries

100g fresh redcurrants

40g pomegranate seeds

Heat the oven to 140°C / 120°C fan / Gas 1. Line a baking
tray with baking paper. Draw a wreath shape in pencil on
the baking paper (I use a plate and a mug to create the outer
and inner outline for this, respectively, but you can also do it
by eye).

In a spotlessly clean bowl, whisk the egg whites and
cream of tartar until frothy, then add the sugar, 1 spoonful at
a time, whisking all the while, until stiff, glossy peaks form.

Spoon the soft meringue on to the template to create a
wreath shape, then use the back of your spoon to create a
gentle hollow channel within the walls of the meringue,
where the cream and fruit will sit later. Bake in the oven for
1 hour, then switch the oven off without opening its door
and leave the meringue in there to cool completely for a
further hour. You can bake the meringue up to 4 days ahead
of when you plan to serve it and keep it in an airtight
container at room temperature.

⤷⤷⤷⤷⤶

To serve, gently lift the meringue ring off the baking tray,
peeling away the baking paper, and place on a serving dish.

Whip the cream in a mixing bowl until soft peaks form,
taking care not to over-whip it. Spoon the cream into the
channel you created over the meringue wreath and top with
the fruit. Store in the fridge for up to 8 hours before serving.

Gilded Gingerbread Tree Ornaments

It's become something of a family tradition to make biscuits to decorate our Christmas tree every year: it's an activity we started during that first lockdown Christmas and has now become a moment in the festive calendar that I look forward to hugely. I make a jug of (non-alcoholic) egg nog, we put on a Christmas playlist and the boys and I busy ourselves cutting gingerbread shapes – stars, snowflakes, angels, gingerbread men and so forth – for our tree. As to how to decorate the ornaments, each year takes us in a slightly different direction. You could top each biscuit with snowy white royal icing (see page 270), but my personal preference is to leave the richly spiced, nutty gingerbread naked, with only flashes of gold leaf here and there, so the biscuits twinkle as they hang from the tree.

If you're feeling super-organised, you might want to consider making the gingerbread dough in advance and freezing it (up to three months beforehand): then, when you're ready to make the ornaments, all you need do is defrost the dough, roll it out and cut the biscuits. Once baked, these will keep in a tin or airtight container for up to two weeks; once hanging on the tree, however, they do tend to become a little stale, though I happily (and greedily) help myself to biscuits from the tree well into the holidays.

HANDS ON TIME
25 minutes
HANDS OFF TIME
20 minutes, plus at least
    1 hour chilling
MAKES about 24

Combine the golden syrup, ginger preserve, sugar and butter together in a saucepan. Set over a medium-low heat and melt gently, stirring constantly. Once you have a liquid syrup, stop stirring and bring the syrup to boiling point. When the mixture starts to bubble away, take the saucepan off the heat and add the bicarbonate of soda. Stir to dissolve the bicarb and very quickly you'll see the mixture transform from a syrup into a smooth, frothy mass, taking on the colour of toffee or café au lait. Set aside and let cool for 10 minutes or so.

Meanwhile, sift the flour, spices and the fine sea salt into a large mixing bowl, stir to combine, then crack in the egg and stir again until just combined. Lastly, pour the cooled spiced sugar mixture into the dough and stir just to combine. You don't want to over-mix the batter now, or the biscuits will both spread out too much while in the oven and become too tough.

Now, bring the dough together with your hands and wrap in clingfilm, then set in the fridge to chill for at least 1 hour (or overnight if you prefer). I split the dough into smaller chunks before chilling, to make it easier when it comes to rolling it out.

120g golden syrup

40g ginger preserve

200g soft light brown sugar

200g salted butter

1 teaspoon bicarbonate
of soda

500g plain flour

4 teaspoons ground ginger

2 teaspoons ground
cinnamon

Generous pinch of fine
sea salt

1 egg

36–40 sheets of edible
gold leaf, to decorate (or
see recipe introduction)

When you're ready to bake the biscuits, heat the oven to 180°C / 160°C fan / Gas 4 with an oven rack in the centre, then line 2 baking trays with baking paper.

Set the dough between 2 sheets of baking paper and use a rolling pin to roll it out to 0.5–1cm thick. Use cookie cutters to cut it into shapes and gently lay each piece on a prepared baking tray, allowing at least 2cm between each biscuit. Scoop up any scraps of dough, then roll them back out and cut them, too, into shapes. Keep going in this way until you've used up all the dough.

Bake in the centre of the oven for 12–14 minutes, until lightly golden. It's hard to tell if they're done by their colour, as the dough is a light brown already, but the biscuits should feel dry to the touch and look lightly crisped at the edges. Don't worry if they still feel a little soft, as they will dry out and crisp up as they cool. Moving quickly, while the biscuits are still warm and pliable, use a chopstick (or skewer) to pierce a ribbon hole at the top of each, 0.5–1cm away from the top edge. (If you go too close to the edge, you risk the hole breaking open when you try and thread it with ribbon.)

Stick 1–2 sheets of edible gold leaf on each biscuit to decorate. To do this, gently peel away the top protective sheet of paper from the gold leaf, then press it, gold leaf side down, on to a biscuit. Gently lift away the sheet of backing paper from the leaf and, if you like, use a paint brush (or a soft-bristle pastry brush) to very gently soften the edges of the gold square.

Once the biscuits have cooled, tie a length of ribbon through each of the biscuit holes and tie it in a double knot at the top, to create a loop to hang from the tree.

Christmas Wreath Biscuits

Embellished with reddish-pink dried rose petals and sparkling silver balls, then tied with a colourful silk or velvet ribbon, these look glorious hanging from the tree. They're also good to eat: a thick, buttery biscuit, coated in icing with a hint of delicate rose flavour.

I use dried rose petals, or hibiscus, the kind you use to make tea, to decorate these, as I like the crimson offset against the dark, forest-green tree. But you could use any dried petals, in any colour you like, and it's worth doing a little online research for the plethora of options available. Equally, you could decorate these with silver balls, glittery sprinkles, rosemary sprigs, or leave them simply iced, covered in a blanket of what looks like snow.

If you want these to be a hit with children, try using rainbow-hued sprinkles in place of the (somewhat more subtle) dried rose petals.

HANDS ON TIME

45 minutes

HANDS OFF TIME

2 hours cooling, plus
   3 hours setting

MAKES 18–20

FOR THE BISCUITS

300g plain flour

120g icing sugar

1 teaspoon baking powder

120g cold salted butter, chopped

1 egg, lightly beaten

FOR THE DECORATION

1 egg white

200g icing sugar

⅓ teaspoon liquid glucose

⅓ teaspoon lemon juice

Dried rose petals, or hibiscus petals

Silver sugar balls

To make the biscuits, sift the flour, icing sugar and baking powder into a large bowl. Rub in the butter until the mixture resembles sand. Add the egg and use your hands to bring it together into a smooth dough. If it feels crumbly, work in a small amount of water. Shape into a ball, wrap in clingfilm and set to rest in the fridge for 30 minutes (or overnight).

Heat the oven to 200°C / 180°C fan / Gas 6 and line a baking tray with baking paper. Set the dough between 2 sheets of baking paper, then roll out to 3–5mm thick. Use a cookie cutter about 8cm in diameter to cut biscuits out, then use a second cutter about 4cm in diameter to cut a hole in the middle of each. Arrange on the tray, allowing at least 2cm between each, then gather together the scraps, roll them out and cut more biscuits until you have used it all.

Set in the middle of the oven to bake for 8–10 minutes, until lightly golden, then transfer to a wire rack to cool.

To make the royal icing, whisk the egg white in a spotlessly clean mixing bowl until frothy, then add the icing sugar, a spoonful at a time, whisking all the while, then whisk in the liquid glucose and the lemon juice.

Spread the icing evenly over each biscuit, as you would spread cream cheese on a bagel, then press ⅓ teaspoon of dried rose petals all over. Lastly, dot about ¼ teaspoon of silver balls, here and there, nestled among the petals. Set aside for a couple of hours so the icing hardens.

Tie ribbon through each wreath and hang from the tree. Once baked and iced, the biscuits will keep for a few weeks.

Candy Cane Hearts

This is an idea I stumbled upon in a very old issue of the Australian magazine *Taste*, and I cannot tell you how much joy it brings me. It's the simplest of tricks, but so effective and fabulously festive. I make these in quite large batches to decorate our Christmas tree, but you could also pack sets of four or six hearts, boxed in a tin or wrapped in cellophane, to give as a gift, or tie a tag with a name written on each and use them as place markers at your Christmas table.

HANDS ON TIME
20–30 minutes

HANDS OFF TIME
None

MAKES 6

12 large candy canes

Heat the oven to 190°C / 170°C fan / Gas 5. Line a baking tray with baking paper.

Place 2 candy canes on the prepared tray, facing each other and with the ends overlapping, so they make the shape of a heart. Depending on the size of the cane you're using, you can trim the ends to make the hearts smaller and chubbier, if you prefer. Arrange all 6 pairs of candy canes this way, allowing plenty of space between each heart.

Set the tray in the oven to bake for 1 minute, or until the ends start to melt. Take the tray out of the oven and gently press the ends together to seal the shapes. While the candy canes are still hot and pliable, use a very sharp knife to trim away any excess and to make the heart shape that you like, then let cool completely on the tray.

Loop a length of ribbon through the heart shape and tie it firmly at the top, so you can hang the hearts from the Christmas tree.

Miniature Marzipan Pears

A wonderful treat to give, boxed up in a tin or box, neatly packed in with tissue paper or straw, or even as a single pear in a cellophane bag, tied with a ribbon. Strictly speaking, perhaps this falls more into the realm of crafting than cooking, but it's the kind of simple crafting that even I (the least crafty of people) can enjoy playing around with to the most pleasing of results. It's also the kind of activity that you can involve the whole family (across all ages) in. You can of course make anything, but I find pears to be rewardingly easy to shape and they feel appropriately festive for this time of year.

It's unexpectedly simple to make marzipan and, once you've given it a try, there is no turning back. But you can just as well use shop-bought and no one would be the wiser.

HANDS ON TIME
20–30 minutes
HANDS OFF TIME
Overnight for marzipan
    drying, plus 2–3 days
    paint drying
MAKES 6–8 small pears

300g icing sugar
150g ground almonds
2–3 tablespoons cold water
6–8 cloves
Red, green and yellow
    food dye

Combine the icing sugar and ground almonds in a bowl, then add the water (start with 2 tablespoons, then add more if needed) and stir with a wooden spoon. Once you have a clumpy mass, turn it out to on to a work surface and massage it to a smooth texture, similar to modelling clay.

Divide into 6 or 8 roughly equal parts, then shape each into a pear by rolling between your palms. Flatten the base of each miniature pear a little, so they can sit nicely on a dish or in a box once finished (it also makes painting them easier if they can stand up). Now tease the top part of the ball upwards to shape the head of the pear, pinching it with your fingers to get the shape that you want (remember that no 2 fruits are the same, so higgledy piggledy here is good). Take care to smooth out any creases in the marzipan: you want as smooth and even a surface as possible.

Set the pears on a plate and gently press a clove, upside down, into the heads of the pear shapes to create stalks. If possible, allow the pears to dry out overnight, as that will make it easier to apply colour to their surfaces.

Now, using a dry paint brush, mix your colours: I start with a mix of yellow with a small amount of red in it and paint all over the pear, trying to create patches and texture by painting a little thicker in some spots than others. Then add a little of the yellow base colour to a small amount of green to create a pale brownish green and paint this on in patches. Now add a little of the brown/green to red and paint on patches; lastly finish with a little red if you like. Let dry for 2–3 days before storing in a tin or airtight container.

Chocolate Salami

The taste of this is somewhat reminiscent of rocky road, though the addition of a generous splash of rum gives it a slightly more grown-up edge. You can make a chocolate salami following the method below and throwing in pretty much whatever takes your fancy. I find that the combination of chocolate bourbon biscuits with lashings of melted dark chocolate makes for an intensity of chocolatey flavour, which the bluntness of the crumbled walnuts helps balance. You can make this using any kind of biscuit: shortbread, Oreos, digestives, chocolate digestives, even gingernut biscuits for a more richly spiced, almost peppery flavour. Then you might like to add in dried cranberries or cherries in place of the sweeter glacé variety, coarsely chopped dried figs, candied peel, raisins, almonds, pistachios... you name it. All of it gets tumbled together into a sticky mass that you roll into something that loosely resembles a salami. Don't panic if, when you're shaping your sticky mess of chocolate, it doesn't look anything like a salami; just trust me that by the time you've dusted everything down in white icing sugar and strung it up with string, it absolutely will. The good news is that meat salamis, just like the chocolate variety, come in all shapes and sizes.

Come Christmastime in Italy, you'll see chocolate salamis for sale in the shops: what the connection is with the holidays exactly, I've never really known, but undoubtedly it makes for a fun gift and an excellent stocking filler. It's also a nice treat to enjoy, sliced at the table, with a glass of sweet wine, for dessert. You might want to make a few smaller salamis too, for gifts, or to sell individually at a bake sale.

HANDS ON TIME

15 minutes

HANDS OFF TIME

2 hours chilling

MAKES 1 medium salami

150g chocolate bourbon
  biscuits, coarsely chopped

30g walnuts, coarsely
  chopped

30g glacé cherries,
  coarsely chopped

40g caster sugar

200g dark chocolate

100g salted butter

30ml rum

20g icing sugar, to dust

Combine the biscuits, nuts and cherries together in a mixing bowl with the sugar. Break the chocolate into pieces and gently melt it in a medium saucepan together with the butter. Pour the melted chocolate mixture over the biscuit rubble, add the rum and bring everything together with a wooden spoon (or your hands).

Spoon the chocolate mixture on to a sheet of baking paper and form it into something that resembles the shape of a salami. Roll it up tightly in the paper and set in the freezer for 2 hours, until solid.

Unwrap, then roll the salami in icing sugar and tie with kitchen string, as a salami would be tied. This will keep chilled for 7–10 days.

Crispie Christmas Trees

These are nothing more than chocolate rice pop treats, fashioned into something that looks, rather magically, like a Christmas tree. To make them, you can create moulds by making paper cones out sheets of baking paper, then stapling (or sticky taping) the ends together to hold everything in place. I lack the patience for this, so instead, for both ease and simplicity, I use large disposable piping bags: spoon the chocolate-laced cereal right down into the bottom of the cone, let it set and then cut away the plastic.

Like little trees, you can decorate these with ornaments: shards of candy cane, dried rose petals or silver sugar balls glued on to their surface with a dot of edible glue; but they look equally magical with just a dusting of edible glitter and a shower of icing sugar snow. Once assembled, these will keep happily for one or two weeks.

HANDS ON TIME

15 minutes

HANDS OFF TIME

1 hour chilling

MAKES 6 small trees

⤜⤜⤜⤜⤛

100g white chocolate, broken into pieces

100g rice pop cereal

100g dark or milk chocolate, broken into pieces

TO DECORATE (OPTIONAL)

Edible glue

Candy cane, coarsely chopped

Dried rose petals

Silver sugar balls

Icing sugar

Edible glitter dust

Edible gold dust

Bring a saucepan of water to the boil over a medium-high heat. Set the white chocolate in a heatproof bowl and set over the water (taking care the water doesn't touch the bowl). Stir until melted and smooth, then take off the heat.

Stir half the rice cereal into the white chocolate. Use your hands to open up a piping bag, inserting your fingers right into the tip to stretch it open, then spoon a small amount (half a spoonful or so) of the chocolatey crispies into the bag and gently massage them right down into the tip: take your time with this, you want to make sure that the 'tree' comes out with a pointy tip. Then add a couple more spoonfuls of the chocolatey mixture and massage it down. Use the palm of your hand to flatten the bottom of the tree (so it will stand up straight), then twist the piping bag to seal. Repeat to make 3 white chocolate trees. They don't need to be equally sized; if anything it looks nicer to have different heights. Set in the fridge for 30–60 minutes to chill and harden.

Now, repeat the process with the dark or milk chocolate and the remaining cereal, to make 3 more little trees.

Once the crispy trees have set, cut away the piping bags. Set the trees standing upright.

If you would like to decorate them, use a paint brush to dab on a small amount of edible glue and carefully stick on a shard of candy cane, dried rose petals or silver sugar balls: this can be fiddly, but work patiently and hold each piece to the tree for a moment to help the glue set. Dust with icing sugar and edible glitter and/or gold dust, if you like.

Peppermint Meringues

These are intensely minty, with a chewy middle that is somehow also reminiscent of the nostalgic sticky sweetness of a candy cane. The merry and kitsch swirls of bright red through the snowy white peaks are of course entirely optional, but I just can't resist how festive they look. If, however, you would prefer something a little more subtle (or would rather not use food colouring), then bake the meringues as is, pristine, virginal white, then finely chop a couple of candy canes and sprinkle the shards, like shimmering gems, over them before serving, for a more elegant take on a childhood holiday favourite. If you really wanted to gild the lily, you might also want to consider brushing each meringue with a little gold leaf, by dabbing on a small amount of edible glue and then gently sticking a sheet of gold leaf to it (see photo at page 213). Just one or two patches of gold on each is more than enough to add a little extravagant shimmer.

This is an especially good recipe for bake sales, because though they take a while in the oven, they're quick and simple to make, with only one mixing bowl to wash up, and come innately individually portioned. You can also make them to whatever size you prefer: from tiny, bite-sized meringues to the extravagantly blowsy ones that you see here and which I love most. Equally, don't feel that you need a bake sale as an excuse to make these: a tin of striped pepperminty meringues is a lovely gift (and indeed they will keep for a couple of weeks in a sealed tin). Or I will pile them high on a cake stand and serve as is for pudding after dinner, perhaps with a bowl of whipped cream or crème fraîche on the side.

HANDS ON TIME
20 minutes

HANDS OFF TIME
2 hours baking and cooling

MAKES 10–12 large
meringues

Oil or butter, for the trays
6 egg whites
⅓ teaspoon cream of tartar
300g caster sugar
¾ teaspoon peppermint
extract
3–4 drops of red food
colouring gel

Heat the oven to 140°C / 120°C fan / Gas 1. Grease and line 2 baking trays.

Pour the egg whites and cream of tartar into a large, clean mixing bowl. The bowl must be immaculate, as even a spot of grease will stop the whites from peaking. Using electric beaters, beat on a medium-low speed until the whites begin to froth, then add the sugar, a spoonful at a time, whisking all the while, until the mix becomes stiff and glossy. Now, add the peppermint extract and whisk it in.

Gently fold in the red food colouring, creating swirls. Use 2 spoons to dollop the mixture on to the prepared trays, leaving a few centimetres between each and twirling the spoon round with each dollop to finish the meringue off with a spiky peak.

Set in the middle of the oven and bake for 1 hour. Switch the oven off and leave the meringues in there (without opening the door) for a further hour, to cool completely. Once baked, the meringues will keep happily for 2–3 weeks.

Cocoa and Panettone Truffles

Spiced, sweet (albeit not overly so) and deliciously fudgy. I love the rich bitterness that rolling these in cocoa powder gives, but you could also try desiccated coconut if you wanted something lighter and with a bit of a crunch, or multi-coloured sprinkles if you're making the truffles with younger children in mind. These are quick to throw together and an ingenious way of making good use of leftover panettone: a sweet treat to serve with coffee after dinner. Also a small box (or cellophane bag) of these will make for a lovely gift to give to pretty much anyone, and one which you can throw together easily at the last minute. Once rolled and dipped in their coating, the truffles will keep happily in the fridge for up to one week.

HANDS ON TIME

15 minutes

HANDS OFF TIME

30 minutes chilling

MAKES 20

200g panettone

60ml double cream

160g dark chocolate, finely chopped

4 tablespoons cocoa powder, to dust (or see recipe introduction)

Blitz the panettone in a food processor to make crumbs.

In a small saucepan, gently warm the cream until just before the boil (you should see the tiniest bubbles forming at the edge of the pan), then take the pan off the heat and stir in the chocolate until melted. Add the panettone crumbs to the thick chocolate sauce and stir to combine, then use the palms of your hands to roll the sticky chocolate mixture into 20 small walnut-sized balls.

Chill the truffle balls in the fridge for 30 minutes or so, until solid, then roll each in cocoa powder to coat all over.

Once assembled, the truffles will keep in the fridge for up to 1 week.

Christmas Brownies

This is a version of my favourite chocolate brownies from *A Table Full of Love*, here laced with candied peel, peppery ginger and fudgy marzipan, then topped with brushstrokes of shimmering gold leaf. They are extravagant in every sense of the word. It's a good recipe for bake sales and for gifting, as it's easy to scale up and make en masse. It's also a hardy, foolproof recipe that is nigh-on impossible to go wrong with and so can be delegated to any willing helpers (even, and especially, small ones). They keep nicely for at least a week, if not two, making timings infinitely less sensitive than with other baked goods.

The gold leaf may feel like a little too much and is by no means necessary... but if not at Christmas, then when? I buy sheets of edible gold leaf online: while it's not, as you might expect, what I would describe as cheap, it's also not nearly as pricey as one might suppose... and it's worth noting that a very little of it goes a long way.

Children and grown-ups alike will go wild for these.

HANDS ON TIME
20 minutes

HANDS OFF TIME
35 minutes baking, plus a few
   hours chilling

MAKES 36 small or
   24 larger brownies

150g dark chocolate,
   finely chopped

300g salted butter

90g cocoa powder

6 eggs

600g caster sugar

90g strong white bread flour

¾ teaspoon baking powder

150g crystallised ginger,
   coarsely chopped

150g candied orange peel,
   coarsely chopped

120g marzipan, coarsely
   chopped

10–12 sheets of edible
   gold leaf

Edible glue, if needed

Heat the oven to 180°C / 160°C fan / Gas 4. Line two 25 × 18cm brownie tins with baking paper.

In a small saucepan, gently melt the chocolate and the butter together over a very low heat, stirring all the while to make sure the chocolate doesn't catch. Add the cocoa and stir to combine, then set aside to cool.

In a large mixing bowl, whisk the eggs and sugar with electric beaters until light and creamy in colour. Now, gently whisk the cooled melted chocolate into the eggs. Fold in the flour and the baking powder. Lastly, fold in the ginger, orange peel and marzipan.

Divide the batter between the 2 prepared tins. Bake for 30–35 minutes until the tops feel firm to the touch and a light chocolate crust has formed.

Let cool completely in the tins before turning out. Even better, if you can, let them chill in their tins in the fridge for a few hours or overnight.

Carefully apply the sheets of gold leaf, by lifting each sheet from the paper and draping it over the area you want to apply it (I do this in a random pattern on the block of brownies). It should stick immediately, but you can help press it down with the back of a knife, or use a dab of edible glue, if needed. Cut into small squares before serving.

The brownies will happily keep in an airtight container for up to 2 weeks.

SAUCES

Homemade Mincemeat
(and Why it's Worth it)

I remain an evangelical convert to the many virtues of homemade, as opposed to shop-bought, mincemeat: it's improbably simple to make, but also tastes so very much better than anything you can buy, something to do (I think) with the chunkier texture. So I do urge you to give this recipe a try, especially if you've not made mincemeat before. All that said, if push comes to shove and you can't face making your own, adding a generous splash of brandy or rum to a jar of shop-bought will go a long way towards livening it up.

There are so many things you can do with mincemeat beyond, of course, making mince pies (see pages 228–229). See right for lots more ideas.

HANDS ON TIME
30 minutes
HANDS OFF TIME
None
MAKES about 2.2kg

300g raisins
300g currants
180g mixed peel
240g glacé cherries
300g dried figs, coarsely
   chopped
180g blanched almonds,
   very coarsely chopped
80g walnuts, very coarsely
   chopped
6 Pink Lady apples,
   coarsely grated
450g muscovado sugar
1 teaspoon ground ginger
1½ teaspoons ground
   cinnamon
1 teaspoon freshly ground
   nutmeg
230g salted butter
300ml brandy

Sterilise 8–9 × 240g jars, by heating the oven to 160°C / 140°C fan / Gas 3. Wash the jars in hot, soapy water, rinse, then set to dry in the oven for 10–15 minutes.

Stir all the ingredients except the brandy together in a large pan and set over a low heat, until the butter is melted. Cook gently, stirring frequently, for 10 minutes or so, until you have a dark, sticky mass of fruit and the nuts look almost caramelised in the syrupy juices.

Take the pan off the heat, pour in the brandy and give everything a good stir so the flavours can intermingle. Carefully spoon the mincemeat into the prepared jars and seal. You can eat the mincemeat immediately, or store in the sealed jars for up to 6 months.

Sticky Christmas buns Swap out the filling on page 72 for 80–100g mincemeat.

Ice cream sundae Spoon mincemeat, with its syrupy juices, over vanilla ice cream, then top, if you like, with toasted nuts or candied pecans (see page 181).

Homemade mincemeat and marzipan ice cream Swap out the Christmas cake in the recipe at page 259 for mincemeat to swirl through the marzipan-laced cream.

Festive pain au raisin (of sorts) Heat the oven to 200°C / 180°C fan / Gas 6. Spread the mincemeat (roughly 400g) over a 320g sheet of ready-rolled, all-butter puff pastry, leaving a small (1–2cm) margin at the edges. Roll into a thick sausage, as snugly as you can, slice into 2–3cm rounds, then arrange on a baking tray. Brush the tops of the swirls with lightly beaten egg, sprinkle over a little sugar if you like and bake for 20–30 minutes, until lightly golden.

Mincemeat galette Heat the oven to 200°C / 180°C fan / Gas 6. Unfurl a 320g sheet of ready-rolled, all-butter puff pastry on to a baking sheet, then spoon over mincemeat and spread out evenly, leaving a 2-3cm border. Turn the edges of the pastry over the edges of the filling, brush the pastry with lightly beaten egg, sprinkle with sugar, if you like; then bake for 20-30 minutes, until the pastry is golden and the edges puff up.

Baked apples Heat the oven to 220°C / 200°C fan / Gas 7. Core apples, stuff the holes with mincemeat, dot with a little butter and sprinkle with sugar, then bake in the hot oven for 35–40 minutes.

Bread, butter and mincemeat pudding Heat the oven to 160°C / 140°C fan / Gas 3. Slice about 500g bread, butter the slices generously, then use them to make sandwiches filled with mincemeat. Cut into chunks and arrange snugly in an ovenproof dish. Warm 120ml milk and 120ml double cream together in a small saucepan and bring to just before boiling point. Whisk 4 egg yolks and 3 tablespoons of caster sugar together in a small bowl, then whisk into the warmed cream. Pour over the bread, let rest for 5-10 minutes so the flavours can settle in nicely, then bake in the oven for 25-30 minutes, until the custard is softly set.

Brioche Bread Sauce

Bread sauce is an idiosyncratically British phenomenon, but, for many of us, it wouldn't be a proper Christmas lunch without it. It's almost unbelievably rich and a suitably indulgent complement to all the festive trimmings that we so love on Christmas Day. Traditionally, you make it with leftover bread, ideally white for that creamy consistency and colour, but I love it with brioche, which gives an added layer of irresistible, mellow sweetness to the flavours.

HANDS ON TIME

15 minutes

HANDS OFF TIME

None

SERVES 6–8

150g brioche, weighed
    without crusts

460ml whole milk, plus
    more (optional) to reheat

20g salted butter

150ml double cream, plus
    more (optional) to reheat

1 small red onion, peeled

8–10 cloves

½ teaspoon freshly
    ground nutmeg

2 bay leaves

Sea salt flakes and freshly
    ground black pepper

Cut the bread into small (3–5cm) pieces. Combine the milk, butter and 2 tablespoons of the cream together in a small saucepan. Stud the onion all over with the cloves, then add to the pan together with the ground nutmeg and bay leaves. Set over a medium heat and bring to the boil.

When the milk begins to bubble, add the brioche to the pan, reduce the heat to low and give everything a good stir. Let it simmer away over a gentle heat until the bread has completely disintegrated and you have something the consistency of creamy porridge.

Take off the heat, remove and discard the studded onion and bay leaves and stir in the remaining cream to thin out the sauce a little. Season to taste, then serve.

You can make the sauce in advance, then store in the fridge in an airtight container for up to 3 days, or freeze for up to 3 months. When you're ready to serve, spoon the sauce – which will have thickened considerably – into a saucepan, dilute with a generous splash of milk or cream and reheat gently. Serve warm.

Cranberry and Marsala Sauce

I like my cranberry sauce sharp, with just a hint of sugar to round off the tart edges, which is why I like to make my own rather than relying upon shop-bought, which I often find cloying. Feel free to add more sugar if you like your cranberry sauce on the sweeter side.

HANDS ON TIME
20–25 minutes
HANDS OFF TIME
None
SERVES 8–10

≈≈≈≈≈

340g fresh cranberries
120g caster sugar
100ml Marsala

Combine the berries, sugar and Marsala together in a small saucepan and set over a medium-low heat. Let everything simmer away gently for 15–20 minutes, until the cranberries have mostly popped and you're left with a jelly-like, ruby-red sticky mess.

≈≈≈≈≈

Serve warm or at room temperature.

Make-Ahead Gravy

Making gravy the 'proper' way is a step too far when trying to seamlessly bring together all the other elements of Christmas lunch at the same time. Therefore, I favour this make-ahead method. The gravy keeps for a few days in the fridge, ready to reheat gently on the hob and – if you would like and for an added flourish – whisk in some of the meaty cooking juices (with any excess fat removed) just before serving. Not that it's needed, as the Worcestershire sauce gives a moreish, burnt-bits, rich and salty quality.

HANDS ON TIME
10–15 minutes
HANDS OFF TIME
None
SERVES 6–8

≈≈≈≈≈

30g salted butter
2 tablespoons plain flour
60ml Marsala
600ml chicken stock
2 teaspoons Worcestershire sauce
Small bunch of sage leaves

Melt the butter over a low heat in a small saucepan, add the flour and whisk to combine. Whisk for 2–4 minutes until the mixture turns light brown, then add the Marsala and whisk, cooking until the sauce thickens a little.

Now add the stock, Worcestershire sauce and sage, bring to the boil, then simmer for 10–15 minutes until slightly thickened (you don't want it too thick now, as it thickens when reheated). Strain, discard the sage and store, covered, in a sealed container in the fridge for up to 3 days.

≈≈≈≈≈

When ready to serve, gently reheat the gravy in a saucepan until hot. Whisk in some of the cooking juices from the roast, if you like, then serve immediately.

Boozy Amaretto Butter

It wouldn't be Christmas for me without boozy butter, in extravagant quantities, to go with pudding, mince pies, Christmas cake, pandoro and panettone. Even with a slice of Flourless Chocolate Orange Cake (see page 212), this ambrosial butter doesn't go amiss.

You can, of course, make this with brandy as is the convention, or even whisky, rum or bourbon. All are equally good, but I have a soft spot for Amaretto, which is a little sweeter, and somehow perfectly Anglo-Italian in character. I like the addition of ground almonds, to round off the sweetness and give a slightly gritty texture which feels more robust than a straight whipped buttercream, but leave them out if you're looking for a lighter butter.

HANDS ON TIME
10 minutes
HANDS OFF TIME
None
MAKES about 600g

❧

220g icing sugar
60g ground almonds
250g salted butter, softened
120ml Amaretto

Combine the icing sugar, almonds and butter together in a large mixing bowl and beat until creamy and smooth. Slowly add the Amaretto in a steady trickle, beating all the while.

❧

The butter will keep, stored in a sealed jar, for up to 3 weeks, somewhere cool or in the fridge. Serve at room temperature.

Easy Peasy Hot Brandy Custard

I call this a custard, as it is thick, rich and velvety-smooth. But, whereas making custard involves whisking egg yolks to thicken the cream, then constant stirring in a delicate balancing act to ensure it thickens but doesn't curdle, this is just a matter of warming three ingredients over a gentle heat into a creamy, decadently boozy sauce. Easy peasy.

HANDS ON TIME
5 minutes
HANDS OFF TIME
None
SERVES 6–8

❧

300ml double cream
90g marzipan, chopped into
    small pieces
30ml brandy

Gently warm half the cream and the marzipan together in a small saucepan over a medium heat, stirring from time to time, until the marzipan is melted, then pour in the rest of the cream and heat until it is all warmed through. Stir in the brandy and serve.

❧

You can make the custard in advance, then keep for up to 3 days, in a sealed container, in the fridge. When ready to serve, just give it a good stir and warm gently over a medium-low heat.

Making Good Use of Leftovers

While the build-up to Christmas is, I know, manic – and it can feel challenging to look beyond Christmas Day – it's a worthwhile investment of time and energy to give a little thought to those days between Christmas and New Year well ahead of time. When you're making your big plan and compiling your shopping list(s), remember that having a well-stocked fridge and pantry means you can easily and happily improvise breakfast, lunch and supper at the last minute.

It's also worth thinking creatively about leftovers. Christmas is a time for excess, but that over-indulgence feels more comfortable and less excessive when it doesn't come with waste too. It's worth remembering that more things than you might imagine taste good either served at room temperature or reheated. So if you have leftover bits and bobs in the fridge, even if it's not quite enough to make a meal out of, it's worth adding them to your menu as an extra for sharing.

A number of recipes can also be made up out of leftovers. Here are a few ideas of what to do with ingredients that you might have going spare.

TURKEY

Bang bang turkey Whisk together 125g peanut butter with 1 tablespoon soy sauce, 1–2 tablespoons maple syrup and the juice of ½ lemon until smooth. Add a splash of cold water, if needed, for a more liquid sauce, then drizzle the sauce over shredded cold turkey and serve with crisp green salad leaves, coarsely chopped.

Turkey tonnato Put 250g drained canned tuna with 4 heaped tablespoons mayonnaise, 3 anchovy fillets, 4 gherkins, 1 tablespoon capers and 8–10 drops of Tabasco in a food processor and blitz until you have a smooth, creamy sauce. Drizzle over shredded cold turkey and top with a few more capers to serve.

Turkey, cranberry and kale salad Toss a few handfuls of kale leaves into a salad bowl, drizzle over a generous glug of olive oil, a squeeze of lemon juice and a generous pinch of salt, then massage until the leaves wilt a little. Add a bag of cooked quinoa (or grain of your choosing), a handful of dried cranberries and some shredded cold turkey; you might want to toss in a few crumbled walnuts or pecans, if you have them to hand, too.

A Christmas sandwich Good bread with leftover stuffing, cold turkey, a couple of crisp salad leaves and a generous dollop of cranberry sauce. If you're able to fry a rasher or two of bacon and add it, still hot and dripping from the pan, too, it really lifts the whole thing to another level.

Wild rice, lentil and turkey salad Make the Wild Rice, Lentil, Chestnut and Pomegranate Salad at page 178, then toss in shredded cold turkey.

STALE BREAD

Red Cabbage Panzanella (see page 186)

Red Berry Breakfast Panzanella (see page 76, using regular bread)

Brioche Bread Sauce (see page 290, using regular bread)

Nonna's Stuffing (see page 167)

French toast Follow the method for Panettone Perduto (see page 79), replacing panettone with stale bread.

Spaghetti with breadcrumbs Blitz stale bread to make breadcrumbs. Toast in a pan with a splash of hot oil and a garlic clove. Cook spaghetti al dente, then drain, drizzle with olive oil and top with breadcrumbs.

POTATOES

Cheesy Fondue Roast Potato Bake (see page 163)

Potato and saffron salad Coarsely chop leftover roast or baked potatoes and mix with a generous dollop of saffron mayonnaise (see page 109).

PANETTONE

Panettone Perduto (see page 79)

Panettone Grilled Cheese Sandwich (see page 80)

Gorgonzola-Walnut Panettone Crostini (see page 92)

Panettone, Chestnut and Sage Stuffing (see page 166)

Cocoa and Panettone Truffles (see page 280)

Panettone croutons To add to a good shop-bought soup.

Toasted panettone Toast panettone and serve with butter, jam or **Boozy Amaretto Butter** (see page 293).

Panettone bread and butter pudding Heat the oven to 160°C / 140°C fan / Gas 3. Cut 500g panettone into pieces and arrange snugly in an ovenproof dish. Warm 120ml milk and 120ml double cream in a small pan and bring to just before boiling. Whisk 4 egg yolks and 3 tbsp caster sugar in a small bowl, then whisk into the warmed cream. Pour over the panettone, let rest for 5-10 minutes so the flavours can settle, then bake for 25-30 minutes, until softly set.

EGG WHITES

Peppermint Meringues and **Christmas Pavlova** (see pages 279 and 262)

EGG YOLKS

Holiday Mood Egg Nog, Mayonnaise, Bread Butter and Mincemeat Pudding, Panettone Bread and Butter Pudding (see pages 86, 109, 287 and above).

Making
Merry

There are many ways of celebrating the holidays with the people you care about, beyond Christmas Day itself. In fact, the excuse to gather friends and family is one of the things I love most about 'Christmas', intended in the wider sense as a mood, rather than as a single day in the calendar year.

Different years call for different occasions: festive lunches, kitchen suppers, more formal dinners, holiday parties, or quick exchanges of gifts over tea and cake. Even within the arc of a single holiday season, it is nice to celebrate in different ways with all the groups of people in your life who mean something to you. In this section, you'll find menu suggestions for all such occasions and tips on how to put everything together: hosting, celebrating and making merry.

When it comes to planning a menu for a Christmas party, there is no reason why you couldn't cook a full festive roast; indeed, any of the menus (or recipes) proposed for Christmas Day would work just as well for a holiday party. But, as much as I enjoy turkey, there is only so much of it I can eat; moreover, I like to play around in the kitchen, flirting with new traditions and reworking classics. There are practical considerations to think about, too: we don't always have as much time to cook for friends on a weeknight, say, as we would for Christmas lunch, but that doesn't mean that it can't still be special, festive or memorable.

With that in mind, in these pages, you'll find menus not so much canonical as seasonal, with a bit of festive flair. A wibbly-wobbly, fire truck-red Campari and pomegranate jelly, or a ruby-red beetroot tart – both so Christmas-y in colour – or a flourless chocolate cake that tastes like the Terry's Chocolate Orange at the bottom of your stocking. You'll find menus designed to fit comfortably within the constraints of our busy, demanding lives. Above all, you'll find menus that abide by the underlying philosophy of the more, the very much merrier!

Excellent Edible Gifts

(and Other Ideas of What to Give the Person Who Has Everything)

There was never a moment when I stopped believing in Father Christmas. At some point in my teens, I think, the formality of Santa leaving a stocking just for me fell by the wayside, and, in its place, grew a new family tradition of swapping stockings with each other. As I drifted into adulthood, the notion of Father Christmas just came with me. This is perhaps a reflection of my innately gullible nature, but I also take it as evidence of the fact that if you want something to be true intensely enough, you can – to the most surprising extent – believe it into being.

One of the weightier criticisms levelled at the celebrations surrounding Christmas is the consumerism of it all. The excess of gifts especially – that frenzy of shopping, buying and packing just for the sake of having something to give – is something even I, a self-proclaimed Christmas fanatic, recognise as over the top. And yet, I love giving presents: a happy part of growing up is the discovery that to give a gift feels even better than to receive one (though, of course, it's always spoiling to receive a present). So one small thing I do to counterbalance the materialism of the season is to make gifts myself: almost always something edible. It's a simple way to show someone you love them, that you're thinking of them this Christmas, that you care. Better still, it's perfect for the person who already has everything: something delicious to eat will always be gratefully received, especially over the festive period when, with the hosting and celebrating, we all have extra hungry mouths that we need to think about. So edible gifts are as practical as they can be spoiling. A small step, perhaps, towards redeeming the honour (and joy) of holiday gift-giving.

In terms of what to make, I find that lots of a single item is far easier to manage than conjuring up something different for each person. Or, if the monotony of baking near-industrial quantities of a single recipe feels too much to bear, then choose two, even three different recipes, but no more or the whole business becomes a logistical nightmare. Trust me: I've been there. Then you can make each gift feel individual with a special card, note or label.

Every year, for example, I set a day or two aside to make twenty- or thirty-odd Christmas cakes: once baked and decorated, I keep one for Christmas Day to share with my family. I earmark a couple more as emergency supplies for when I am hosting over the holiday period and need to rustle something up at the last minute (one less dessert to think about). The rest, I box up and give to friends. That's pretty much all my 'Christmas shopping' done. Fruit cakes work especially well for mass baking, as they're hardy cakes which will keep happily for weeks at a time. By the same token, Christmas pudding – presented in a nice, heatproof bowl and wrapped in muslin – can be a useful, and therefore especially valuable, gift. And in the spirit of two birds with one stone, that's also dessert for Christmas lunch sorted. At the lower-effort end of the spectrum, jars of homemade mincemeat (perhaps with a simple recipe for mince pies attached) make good presents: you can jazz the jars up with an illustrated label, or a piece of festive fabric tied over the lid, if you like.

I've included here a list of recipes from the centre section of this book which work well as edible gifts. They keep well, at the very least for a few days, so you don't need to worry about too fast a turnaround between baking the gifts and passing them on, nor pressure the recipient to open and eat their present the moment you give it to them. By the same principle, the biscuit tree ornaments and Candy Cane Hearts (see pages 266, 270 and 271) make great presents, delicately wrapped in tissue paper or sealed in cellophane bags, boxed in small, disposable cake boxes (which you can buy easily online) or presented in tins, either new or – I especially like – vintage (Ebay is a great source for these).

A sachet of Candy Cane Hot Chocolate Sticks (see page 66)

A jar or box of Pistachio, Almond and Parmesan Cantucci (see page 91)

A Black and Gold Cake on a gold cake board and in a cake box tied with a festive ribbon (see page 206)

A tin or cake box of Christmas Brownies tied with a ribbon (see page 283)

A Hidden Orange Christmas Pudding wrapped in muslin with a note for cooking instructions (see page 242)

A sachet of Candy Cane Hearts (see page 271)

A small box or tin of Miniature Marzipan Pears (see page 272)

A Chocolate Salami wrapped in baking paper and tied with twine (see page 275)

A tin or box of Peppermint Meringues (see page 279)

A jar (or jars) of Homemade Mincemeat with a recipe for making your own mince pies (see page 286)

A jar of Cranberry and Marsala Sauce (see page 291)

A whole Nutty Chocolate Torrone wrapped in baking paper and then decorative wrapping paper, if you like, or a couple of slices in a cellophane bag tied with ribbon (see page 238)

A jar or sachet of Candied Pecans (see page 181)

A tin or box of Maxim's Mince Pies (see page 228)

A box or tin of Gilded Gingerbread Tree Ornaments, Christmas Wreath Biscuits, or just a few of the biscuits bundled in tissue paper and tied with a ribbon (see pages 266 and 270)

A jar of Boozy Amaretto Butter (see page 293)

A box or tin or sachet of Cocoa and Panettone Truffles (see page 280)

A Gingery Christmas Cake presented on a cake board and set in a sturdy cake box tied with a festive ribbon (see page 202)

PANETTONE CLASSIC

Lievitato naturalmente, con uvetta e scorze di arancia candita
Naturally leavened, with raisins and candied orange peels

CHIOSTRO
DI SARONNO • SPECIALITÀ

FAREISA FABBRI
FRUTTO E SCIROPPO

Useful Things to Have at Hand in the Kitchen

....

EDIBLE GOLD LEAF

You can buy this online and it gives an instant festive lift to all baked goods, however sad or unappetising they might start off looking. It's also a lovely touch to add as a decoration to fruit.

MEAT THERMOMETER

If you're cooking a roast, this is an essential piece of kit, as it lessens any anxiety over whether the meat is done or not. If you don't have one already, I can't recommend buying one strongly enough: it's small and won't take up much space in your kitchen, and you'll use it throughout the year.

SUGAR THERMOMETER

More niche than the meat thermometer, but very useful if you're making preserves or more elaborate bakes; also a very small piece of kit.

DISPOSABLE FOIL LOAF TINS

I buy these in bulk online. They're the sort of thing that, once you have them on hand, you find yourself using the whole time. Specifically I use these for making terrines (such as the Nutty Chocolate Torrone and the Nut and Cranberry Terrine, see pages 238 and 142). However, they're also great for storing leftovers (which you can reheat still in the tin to save on washing up) or for transporting dishes from one place to another (if you're going to a potluck meal, for instance).

BRANDY AND/OR RUM, BUT AT LEAST BRANDY

Everything at Christmas seems to have brandy in it, so it's well worth having a good stock at home before December kicks off.

POMEGRANATE SEEDS

The moment you scatter pomegranate seeds over a dish, it instantly looks festive. You'll find lots of recipes containing pomegranate in this book, but generally they're wonderful for scattering over salads, desserts and even roasts. You can of course scoop the seeds out of whole fruit, but the little packets of ready-prepared seeds are just so very convenient that I rarely do.

AMARENA CHERRIES

For the same reason as pomegranate seeds: deep red and delectably glossy, you can drizzle them over anything from yogurt to chocolate cakes to pavlovas or cheesecakes (see pages 262 and 218) for instant 'Christmas'.

PANETTONE

I love panettone and you'll see from the recipes in this book that I include it in both savoury and sweet dishes. But beyond that, having a panettone on hand (if properly wrapped and sealed, they keep for-seemingly-ever) offers an instant, low-effort and innately festive pudding. Bring it to the table whole, then slice and serve as is, or with a generous dollop of Boozy Amaretto Butter or drizzle of Easy Peasy Hot Brandy Custard (see page 293).

MOSTARDA DI CREMONA

A classic Italian preserve of whole glacé fruits – figs, peaches, cherries, mandarins and the like – in a mustard-scented sugary-syrup. It might sound eccentric, but trust me when I say that it is utterly delectable, most especially with roasts, leftover cold cuts, or with cheese. The fruits look beautiful, so the mostarda doubles as decoration as well as a fabulously festive condiment. You can buy it in jars at Italian delicatessens or online.

CANDY CANES

Another recipe for instant Christmas, whether you're using them to bake with, to ornament your Christmas tree, as table decorations, or to slip into presents. I buy mine in bulk from the pound shop, but you can also get them online or from most supermarkets once the festive season gets started.

CHOCOLATE GOLD COINS

Scatter these over the table and you've instantly got a wonderfully festive set-up. I like to keep a big jar in the kitchen and find them just generally useful for zhuzh-ing up the table, but also for slipping into gifts or adding to stockings.

DISPOSABLE CAKE BOXES

If you're doing lots of baking over the holiday season, you'll find these useful: for cakes of course, but also for gifting, as well as for transporting bits and bobs (brownies, biscuits and the like) to bake sales.

Decorating the Table

Everyone has a different idea of what a Christmas table should look like and we each have our own family traditions and sensibilities to abide by, too. So my thoughts here come with the strong caveat that there is no right or wrong way of doing things, and that any Christmas table – by virtue of the fact that it is Christmas and people we love are gathered round it – will look magnificent. But if you are in charge of laying and decorating the table and if you, like me, enjoy a more-is-more kind of affair, it is well worth thinking, roughly at least, about how you want to do things, then sourcing and planning as much as you can well in advance. This means that, when the day comes, the process of laying everything out is a simple and intuitive business.

As much as I love the holidays, I resist Christmas-themed crockery to wheel out once a year. I can't help but feel it is a waste, especially when there is so much you can do with bits you likely already have. Here are a few of my go-tos:

AN EXCESS OF SWEETS, PILED HIGH DOWN THE CENTRE
These look wonderful and set the tone for a holiday that is all about joyful extravagance, indulgent excess and treating yourself to that which you wouldn't dream of on any other day of the year. Favourite sweet treats of mine – that both taste good and look striking – include: **BOWLS OF SUGARED ALMONDS (IN GOLD AND SILVER); GOLD CHOCOLATE COINS**, spilling out of small bowls and dotted over the table; plenty of sweet **SUGAR MICE**; small plates piled high with **TURKISH DELIGHT**; glasses filled with **CANDY CANES**; little dishes of **MINIATURE MARZIPAN PEARS** (see page 272 for the recipe); small plates piled high with **CHOCOLATES**; small dishes of **QUALITY STREET** chocolates in their crinkly, rainbow-hued wrappers; **NUTTY CHOCOLATE TORRONE** (see page 238), sliced and piled up on a small plate; **AMARETTO BISCUITS** in their pretty paper wrappers, piled high into bowls and spilling out on to the table; small dishes of **DATES, CANDIED PEEL** by the slice, **DRIED FIGS** and other **DRIED FRUITS**; little dishes of sugar-dipped **CRYSTALLISED GINGER**; clusters of **CRISPIE CHRISTMAS TREES** (see page 276) arranged on small side plates and cake stands for height; a **CHRISTMAS CAKE** on a cake stand at the centre of the table; a dish of **BOOZY AMARETTO BUTTER** (see page 293), or other boozy butter of your choosing, piled high and scattered with silver sugar balls in abundance.

CANDLES
You want to create a mix of heights with your candles: tealights and tapers poised in candlesticks of varying heights. There is no need to go out and buy special candlesticks, though you may want to splash out on gold or red or green

candles for the occasion. I also have a soft spot for those spinning tealight holders which rotate when the flames are lit: dancing angel candles look particularly delightful down the middle of the table. They are also a nice touch around the house generally, so when they're not in use on the dining table, they can double up as festive decoration in another room.

TOWERING CENTREPIECES

These look truly magnificent, in a retro way gloriously reminiscent of the 1970s and 1980s. In fact, if you find yourself leafing through cookbooks from that era, you'll find the tables filled with this sort of over-the-top, quasi-Georgian decoration, together with the plates of jellied aspic and other such now-deeply unfashionable dishes. To build a towering centrepiece is simple enough: you can buy styrofoam cones easily online. Once you have your cone, cover it (I usually use either tissue paper or foil). This doesn't need to be an especially neat job, and strictly speaking you could skip the step, but the covering means that any little naked gaps peeking through the tower – as guests start to eat away at it – look a little more intentional, while also protecting the cone's surface from sticky food, so you can re-use it. Once your cone is ready, you can cover it with pretty much whatever you like. I've done towers of **TURKISH DELIGHT, MACAROONS, MARSHMALLOWS** or **GLACÉ CHERRIES** (especially effective in a mix of red and green in a candy-stripe pattern). Or make a centrepiece of **BABY TOMATOES AND MINIATURE MOZZARELLA BALLS,** or **STUFFED OLIVES AND CHUNKS OF CHEESE**, so everyone can help themselves. Or cover a small tower in **COCOA AND PANETTONE TRUFFLES** (see page 280) dusted in desiccated coconut or icing sugar. You can make a tower out of whatever you like to eat, though smaller items, which can be nestled closely together to cover the surface, are more pleasing to work with. To assemble the centrepiece, simply push toothpicks into whatever you're sticking on the tower, then press it firmly into the cone. Depending on what you're adding, sometimes the toothpicks might be too long and stick out the other end, so just snap them to the right length. You can also make towers using citrus fruit, such as **LEMONS** or **MANDARINS**. For these heavier, bigger decorations, you might find you need two or three toothpicks for each fruit, to support their weight. You can then use bits of greenery – bay leaves, eucalyptus or what have you – to fill any gaps; the easiest way to attach these is with U-shaped floral pins, from a florist or online, pressed firmly over the greenery and stuck into the cone, like a large staple.

POTS OF PAPERWHITES, OR AMARYLLIS, OR POINSETTIAS

December isn't a good time of year for flowers, which is why I rely more heavily on fruit, sweets and greenery for decoration. But you can find Paperwhite narcissus, as well as amaryllis, and while both have a painfully short life, they look magnificent for as long as they're in flower. I like them cut short in tumblers

or small vases and dotted in among the other table decorations, or potted in nice terracotta pots and placed on the table. Similarly, you can place small potted poinsettias here and there down the centre of the table for decoration too.

CRACKERS

I can't help but feel it's not really a Christmas table if it doesn't have Christmas crackers on it, and a few dotted down the middle of the table, perhaps amidst a smattering of chocolate gold coins, is often decoration enough (or certainly goes a long way towards setting a very festive tone). Or you can set a single cracker on each place setting, then, if you like, write a guest's name on it (in gold or acrylic marker) or tie a little decorative gift tag with their name to one of the bows. You can of course buy crackers from the shops but for tips on how to make your own (and/or make the shop-bought type look more bespoke and fancy) see page 50.

RIBBONS TO TIE YOUR NAPKINS

A lovely little touch that brings an instant sense of celebration to the table, but is very simple to execute. You could use up scraps of ribbon left over from gift-wrapping, or repurpose ribbons from last year's gifts, for a cheerful mix-and-match approach. Or if you have in mind a specific colour scheme, you might want to buy ribbon especially for the occasion. There are different ways you can tie the ribbon and fold the napkin, of course. Typically, I start with a napkin folded and ironed into a square shape and then fold the left and right corners behind, slightly at an angle, to make a diamond shape that is wider at the bottom than it is at the top. Finally, I loosely tie a bow round the middle of the napkin. More simply, you can roll your napkin up and tie a bow in the middle, much as you would add a napkin ring. Another attractive way is to fold your napkin into a rectangle with a longer side closest to your guests. Pinch the napkin together in the middle to make a bow-like shape, then tie the centre with ribbon, leaving the two ends flowing like tails of a bow. If you want to embellish things further, you could slip a candy cane, a long cinnamon stick or a sprig of festive greenery under the ribbon on top of each napkin.

A SMALL GIFT ON EACH PLACE SETTING

This doesn't need to be anything extravagant, and is by no means necessary, but can make a lovely touch. The gift could be anything from a favourite bar of chocolate prettily wrapped, to a snow globe, or edible tree ornament that you have made (see pages 304–305 for inspiration). You can then tie a tag with each guest's name on it to their gift, so it also doubles as a place marker.

A FESTIVE MENU

There is no need to write out menus on Christmas Day, but they can look pretty on the table and also make for a nice memento. I keep many of my menus from over the years and frame them. You can design a menu online, using one of the many platforms that offer this service, then have them printed; or you can write it out by hand and even decorate it, if you like. You could also write the menu inside a Christmas card, or on the back of a festive postcard, written for each of your guests.

GILDED FRUITS

I use fruit to decorate the table throughout the year. I take whatever is in season and pile it high on plates, cake stands and in small dishes and dot it down the table to very pleasing effect. This works especially well at Christmas, with a mix of pomegranates, grapes, pears, whole walnuts, mandarins and so forth. Over Thanksgiving, I like to add in apples and gourds, too. If you want to be a little extra, you can add a few touches of edible gold leaf to the fruits: just gently press the gold side of a sheet of gold leaf on a piece of fruit. This works well on apples, pears and pomegranates, but not so well with citrus, as their peel is oily and porous. Gently lift away the protective sheet of paper and use a paint brush to very gently soften the edges of the gold leaf and press it down on to the fruit, along with any scraps that might be lifting up. If the gold leaf won't stick (some kinds are more temperamental than others), you can fix it with a little dab of edible glue. There's no need to decorate each piece of fruit, but a few touches of gold here and there, strategically placed, add a very magical glimmer.

Thanksgiving

Something I envy of my American friends, a beautiful holiday centred around those things I treasure most in life: friendship, good food and an excuse to share the two. While I can't claim Thanksgiving as part of my own cultural heritage, I have, over the years, adopted it as a holiday. And as is often the case when you choose something for yourself rather than inheriting it, I'm evangelical about it.

Growing up in Venice, we often celebrated Thanksgiving with Italo-American friends. They cooked turkey, of course, but the rest of the meal was a hodge-podge of what is delicious and what loosely resonates with the Thanksgiving canon. We might have roast sweet potatoes one year, but roast persimmons (in peak season in Italy in November) the next. No two menus were the same and I enjoyed this laissez-faire approach, especially in contrast with the rigid (albeit comfortingly so) traditions of Christmas. The menus here are in keeping with that spirit: eclectic and celebratory. But most involve some kind of pie, because I'm not sure it's technically Thanksgiving – and my American friends, please do correct me if I'm wrong – if there isn't some kind (if not two kinds) of pie.

As to the table, I go all out: squashes and gourds, in gnarly, eccentric shapes and variegated colours. Among them, I might scatter apples and pears, perhaps the odd persimmon, keeping that autumnal colour palette, then add lots of candles. Dried flowers, with their faded rich tones, look beautiful, especially in a setting like this: dot a few sprigs here and there in small bud vases, or larger bunches in old jam jars down the table. You want a mix of colours, shapes and textures: yellow glixia, helichrysum, yellow achillea, ammobium and statice (in different colours), even dried wheat, all work beautifully. You can then keep them in vases to enjoy around the house for months. If you're doing a seating plan, consider marking each place setting with a postcard, on the back of which you've written something about the person that you're thankful for; or collect dried leaves and write each guest's name on a leaf in gold pen. And then, of course, there's the food. Thanksgiving is all about the food: plentiful, bountiful, glorious. If I can squeeze it all on the table, it almost acts as decoration in itself; if there is too much, I lay the table with the flowers and candles, then put all the food out on a separate table (in our case, that's our kitchen island, but you could use a sideboard or a small trestle table), so everyone can help themselves.

VEGETARIAN THANKSGIVING

Gnocchi and Pumpkin Gratin (see page 154),
    made with vegetarian cheeses, if needed
Shaved Brussels Sprouts with Pecorino,
    Cranberries and Pecans (see page 191),
    made with vegetarian pecorino, if needed
Wilted Kale with Marmite Butter
    (see page 173)

~~~~~

Saffron Poached Pears with Chocolate
    Caramel Sauce (see page 256)
Christmas Cake Ice Cream (see page 259),
    perhaps made with sticky gingerbread
    instead of Christmas cake

VEGAN THANKSGIVING FEAST

Creamy Chestnut Soup with Pomegranate,
    with no crème fraîche (see page 106)

~~~~~

Stuffed Pumpkin with Wild Rice, Cranberries
    and Chestnuts (see page 157)
Especially Good Maple-Roast Parsnips
    (see page 171)
Sticky Roast Sprouts with Dates and
    Pistachios (see page 169, use vegan butter)
Shaved Fennel, Grapefruit and
    Pomegranate Salad (see page 189)
Red Chicory and Candied Pecan Salad,
    swapping out the mayo in the dressing
    for vegan mayo (see page 181)

~~~~~

Saffron Poached Pears (see page 256, but
    swap the chocolate sauce for this version)
    Vegan chocolate sauce: combine 120ml
    water, 2 tablespoons maple syrup, 50g
    cocoa powder and 2 tablespoons chopped
    dark vegan chocolate in a pan over a
    medium heat and whisk. Let simmer for
    5 minutes until thickened, then add
    1 teaspoon vanilla extract and a generous
    pinch of sea salt flakes

THANKSGIVING DINNER FOR A FEW

Pomegranate-Glazed Turkey with Cranberry
    and Marsala Sauce (see pages 118 and 291)
A buttery mashed potato
Especially Good Maple-Roast Parsnips (see
    page 171)
Red Chicory and Candied Pecan Salad
    (see page 181)
Make-Ahead Gravy (see page 291)

~~~~~

Salted Caramel Pecan Pie (see page 232)
Christmas Cake Ice Cream, perhaps made
    with leftover Christmas Brownies
    or Flourless Chocolate Orange Cake
    (see pages 259 and 212) instead of
    Christmas cake

THANKSGIVING DINNER FOR A BIGGER CROWD

Rolled Turkey Breast with Chestnut
    and Sage Stuffing with
    Cranberry and Marsala Sauce
    (see pages 120 and 291)
Stuffed Pumpkin with Wild Rice,
    Cranberries and Chestnuts (see page 157)
Cheesy Fondue Roast Potato Bake
    (see page 163)
Orange, Carrot and Pistachio Salad
    (see page 185)
Wilted Kale with Marmite Butter
    (see page 173)
Make-Ahead Gravy (see page 291)

~~~~~

Pistachio Cream and Ginger Pie (see
    page 235)
Salted Caramel Pecan Pie (see page 232)

Weekend or Holiday Brunch

....

I don't often host brunch, but around the holiday season I do. Just as with holding a tea party (see page 322), it is a great way of gathering grown-ups and children together and it can be refreshing, too, to have the excuse to cook and eat something very different from the usual starter–main course–dessert menu. You'll find in the FEASTING section lots of ideas and recipes for festive breakfasts that you could take inspiration from at any point over the holiday season, be it in the build-up to Christmas, on the day itself, or in those gloriously languorous days between Christmas and New Year (see pages 66–83).

Equally, if you don't feel like cooking, brunch is an especially good hosting option to choose, because you can happily just assemble bits and bobs from the shops, put them out on plates and still have it feel welcoming, festive and special.

A few of my go-tos: **PASTRIES**, fresh from a bakery, or better still those you can buy frozen and just bung in the oven to bake. **BOWLS OF GRANOLA AND YOGURT** for everyone to help themselves. **A GOOD LOAF OF BREAD FOR TOASTING** (you could put out the bread with a knife and let everyone slice and toast away as they like) with a wide array of **GOOD SPREADS AND JAMS** (some could even be festive-themed, if you really wanted to get carried away). That's pretty much all you need, but you might consider adding: **FRESH FRUIT** (whatever you like) or **LEFTOVER POACHED FRUIT** (such as Saffron Poached Pears, see page 256) or a **COMPOTE**; a dish of **SMOKED SALMON**, maybe with **EGGS** of some kind and/or a dish of **CREAM CHEESE** and a small bowl of **CAPERS**. **PANETTONE OR PANDORO** as is, for everyone to slice into, possibly with a dish of **BOOZY AMARETTO BUTTER** or brandy butter, for an extra – and spoiling – festive touch. (If you can face making your own brandy or Amaretto butter, as per the simple instructions at page 293, I really – and greedily – feel that it's worth it, but if not shop-bought does fine.) As to decorating the table, you could place a cracker on each place setting; or a Candy Cane Hot Chocolate Stick (see page 66) in each guest's cup or mug (perhaps with a label with their name tied to it) makes a very special touch.

HOLIDAY BRUNCH
FOR A CROWD

Candy Cane Hot Chocolate Sticks, with mugs
of warm milk (see page 66)

Sticky Marzipan Breakfast Buns
(see page 72)

Cheesy Ham and Croissant Bake
(see page 83)

Sliced oranges topped with
pomegranate seeds

HOLIDAY BRUNCH FOR
A SMALLER GANG

Panettone Perduto (see page 79)

Saffron Poached Pears (see page 256), with or
without their Chocolate Caramel Sauce

Yogurt topped with granola or toasted nuts

Candy Cane Hot Chocolate Sticks, with mugs
of warm milk (see page 66)

A FESTIVE BREAKFAST
FOR TWO

Panettone Grilled Cheese Sandwich
(see page 80)

A plate of fresh fruit

A pot of hot coffee

BREAKFAST IN BED

A warm mince pie (see pages 228–229)

A mug of fresh ginger tea (3–4 slices of root
ginger in boiling water) with honey

Handful of chocolate gold coins

Hot, buttered crumpets with Marmite

(MOSTLY) MAKE-AHEAD
CHRISTMAS MORNING
BREAKFAST FOR A CROWD

Nutella Christmas Wreath (see page 69)

Red Berry Breakfast Panzanella
(see page 76)

Greek yogurt

Candy Cane Hot Chocolate Sticks,
with mugs of warm milk (see page 66)

A LOW-EFFORT CHRISTMAS
DAY BREAKFAST

Panettone

Pistachio Cream Croissants (see page 70)

Candy Cane Hot Chocolate Sticks, with mugs
of warm milk (see page 66)

A MORE ELABORATE
CHRISTMAS DAY BREAKFAST

Sticky Marzipan Breakfast Buns with
chocolate chips instead of marzipan
(see page 72)

Cheesy Ham and Croissant Bake
(see page 83)

Scrambled or soft boiled eggs

Fresh fruit and yogurt

Toast

Candy Cane Hot Chocolate Sticks, with mugs
of warm milk (see page 66)

Afternoon Tea

....

I love a good afternoon tea, and over the holiday period I find it's a format that works particularly well. Like any big holiday party, it allows you to gather lots of people together at the same time, but the timings – afternoon rather than evening – can be a nice way to include younger friends and family members too. On a personal note, I love baking (and eating) sweet things, so a menu of primarily cake and sandwiches is pretty much my dream, but you should of course weight the menu towards savoury, or more towards cake, as you like. Depending on numbers and how you like to do things, you can either hold a seated afternoon tea – much like a supper party but in the afternoon – or lay the dining table up with food and let everyone help themselves and mill around.

You by no means need to, but it might be nice to have a theme around which to centre your afternoon tea. Perhaps it could be a tree-decorating party, so you have your boxes of baubles and so on ready to go and bring everyone together to decorate the tree with you. By the same principle, you could also make it a paper chain-making tea party (see page 46 for instructions). Put rolls of paper down the middle of the table, then allow a pair of scissors for each place setting (tie some ribbon to the handles of these to make them look extra-pretty, and perhaps even a label with each guest's name) and a roll of sticky tape for every two or three places. Add cake and sandwiches down the middle of the table, a festive playlist in the background and you're ready to go. Following much the same template, you could host a cracker-making party (see page 50 for instructions), or Christmas ornament-making party (see pages 45–47 and 266–70 for instructions and inspiration), or a marzipan fruit-making party (see page 272). Alternatively, you could combine afternoon tea with the showing of a classic Christmas movie.

A GROWN-UP TEA PARTY
Gorgonzola-Walnut Panettone Crostini (see page 92)
Olga's Sticky Sausages (see page 88)
Gingery Christmas Cake (see page 202)
Pomegranate Campari Jelly (see page 248)
Peppermint Meringues (see page 279)

A CHILDREN'S CHRISTMAS TEA PARTY
Fairy bread, made with silver sugar balls
Roast ham and chutney sandwiches
Spiced Hot Apple Juice (see page 96)
Christmas Brownies (see page 283)
Christmas Cupcakes with Brandy Buttercream, replacing the
brandy with vanilla extract (see page 221)

PAPER CHAIN-MAKING PARTY
Pistachio, Almond and Parmesan Cantucci (see page 91)
Gorgonzola-Walnut Panettone Crostini (see page 92)
Mulled Wine and/or Spiced Hot Apple Juice (see pages 89 and 96)
Cinnamon and Cranberry Bundt (see page 196)

A LESS 'PARTY' MORE 'TEA' PARTY
Gingery Christmas Cake (see page 202)
Cheddar and cranberry sauce finger sandwiches
A pot of proper tea

AN EXTRA-FESTIVE TEA PARTY
Smoked salmon finger sandwiches
Maxim's Mince Pies (see page 228)
Boozy Amaretto Butter (see page 293)
Panettone
Gilded Gingerbread Tree Ornaments, made as cookies
rather than as ornaments (see page 266)

Festive Kitchen Suppers

My favourite way to celebrate is supper round the kitchen table with a handful of people I love. Not so showy as a big party perhaps, but a more intimate setting that allows us proper and precious time together. Spending time with the people I love – family, of course, but importantly also those friends who feel like family – is ultimately what makes the holidays happy for me, and so I have learned to prioritise it. I might not get round to sending out Christmas cards (in fact, I rarely do), but I do try to make time to celebrate in a meaningful way with friends. Most often, this means over a nice meal.

On a practical level, I've figured out a way of doing this that both works well for me and that fits comfortably into the busy-ness of the month of December, and that feels, all things considered, both pretty effortless and pretty special, with minimum time spent in the kitchen and maximum time eating, chatting and generally feeling festive. These are the menus that you'll find in the next couple of pages.

While the spirit of these suppers is cosy and while I prioritise actually doing them over making them so much work that I can't find time for them, it can be nice to add a few special festive touches (see pages 312–316 for some more ideas for table decoration). While I might not go all out and fully decorate the table, I might tie the napkins with red velvet ribbons (you can re-use these on multiple occasions) and add a sprig of holly or a candy cane to each. I might go so far as to make everyone something small (a bundle of Christmas Brownies packed in a clear cellophane bag and dressed with festive ribbon, for example, or a jar of Cranberry and Marsala Sauce, see pages 283 and 291) and label it with their name, then present it prettily on their place setting. If I don't have time to bake, even a little bundle of candy canes, tied with ribbon or twine and labelled with each guest's name, can be a really lovely touch.

MAKE-AHEAD VEGETARIAN FESTIVE DINNER FOR 6—8

Beetroot and Horseradish Galette
   (see page 149)

Wild Rice, Lentil, Chestnut and Pomegranate
   Salad (see page 178)

Red Chicory and Candied Pecan Salad
   (see page 181)

Flourless Chocolate Orange Cake
   (see page 212)

FESTIVE DINNER FOR 6—8

Roast Poussins with Crisp Prosciutto and Sage
   (see page 127)

'Hedgehog' Potatoes (see page 164)

Christmas Salad (see page 182)

Panettone, Chestnut and Sage Stuffing
   (see page 166)

Egg Nog Cream Pie (see page 236)

VEGETARIAN FESTIVE DINNER FOR 4

Camembert and Cranberry Pithivier
   (see page 146), made with vegetarian
   Camembert, if needed

Sticky Roast Sprouts with Dates and
   Pistachios (see page 169)

Wilted Kale with Marmite Butter (see
   page 173)

Red Cabbage, Feta, Hazelnut and Mint Salad
   (see page 188), made with vegetarian feta,
   if needed

Maxim's Mince Pies with Boozy Amaretto
   Butter (see pages 228 and 293)

FESTIVE DINNER FOR 4

Pork Tenderloin with Persimmons and
   Pomegranate (see page 131)

'Hedgehog' Potatoes (see page 164)

Martin's Ruby Red Cabbage (see page 170)

Shaved Brussels Sprouts with Pecorino,
   Cranberries and Pecans (see page 191)

Sugar Plum Sorbet (see page 258)

FOOLPROOF AFTER-WORK FESTIVE DINNER FOR AS MANY AS YOU LIKE

Roast Poussins with Crisp Prosciutto
   and Sage (see page 127)

Cheesy Fondue Roast Potato Bake
   (see page 163)

Wilted Kale with Marmite Butter
   (see page 173)

Red Cabbage Panzanella (see page 186)

Salted Caramel Zuccotto (see page 247)

A COSY, COMFORTING VEGETARIAN SUPPER

Camembert and Cranberry Pithivier
   (see page 146), made with vegetarian
   Camembert, if needed

Martin's Ruby Red Cabbage (see page 170)

Good Luck Salad (see page 192)

Panettone, Chestnut and Sage Stuffing
   (see page 168)

Peppermint Meringues (see page 279)

Continued overleaf

A SIMPLE MAKE-AHEAD SUPPER (IDEAL FOR WEEKNIGHTS)

Creamy Chestnut Soup with Pomegranate (see page 106), with a nice loaf of brioche

Red Chicory and Candied Pecan Salad (see page 181)

Gorgonzola, Fig and Hazelnut Terrine, if you like, but you don't need it (see page 255)

Flourless Chocolate Orange Cake (see page 212)

A FANCIER MAKE-AHEAD SUPPER (ALSO IDEAL FOR WEEKNIGHTS)

Beetroot and Horseradish Galette (see page 149)

Red Cabbage Panzanella (see page 186)

Shaved Brussels Sprouts with Pecorino, Cranberries and Pecans (see page 191)

Wilted Kale with Marmite Butter (see page 173)

Sugar Plum Sorbet (see page 258)

Christmas Brownies (see page 283) piled high

COSIEST SPOILING SUPPER

Gilded Miniature Baked Potatoes with Crème Fraîche and Caviar (see page 110), using big potatoes for baking

A side of smoked salmon

Red Chicory and Candied Pecan Salad (see page 181)

Saffron Poached Pears with Chocolate Caramel Sauce (see page 256)

A BARELY-COOK SUPPER

Good Luck Salad (see page 192), with pouches of lentils, omitting the beetroot

Christmas Salad (see page 182)

A side of smoked salmon, sliced

A good loaf of bread

Some nice cheeses

AN EXTRAVAGANT SUPPER

Potted Salmon with Preserved Lemon (see page 113) with toast

Black Truffle, Mascarpone and Quail's Egg Pasta Pie (see page 150)

Red Chicory and Candied Pecan Salad (see page 181)

Christmas Salad, without feta (see page 182)

Salted Caramel Zuccotto (see page 247)

MORE PARTY THAN DINNER

Chestnut Martinis (see page 98)

Gorgonzola-Walnut Panettone Crostini (see page 92)

Roast Poussins with Crisp Prosciutto and Sage (see page 127)

Nonna's Stuffing (see page 167)

Red Cabbage, Feta, Hazelnut and Mint Salad (see page 188)

Shaved Fennel, Grapefruit and Pomegranate Salad (see page 189)

'Hedgehog' Potatoes (see page 164)

Puff Pastry Mince Pies with Boozy Amaretto Butter and Easy Peasy Hot Brandy Custard (see pages 229 and 293)

A Big Festive Buffet

For a little bit more of a to-do, this is a format that works especially well for the kind of party that bring friends and family together across generations. Put all the food out on the kitchen or dining table, or both, as you might want to consider a dinner table and a dessert table, depending on numbers, and space allowing, of course. Then pile up plates (paper if necessary), napkins and cutlery (I do like proper cutlery, so if you can borrow extra that's ideal, but otherwise disposable is fine) and encourage everyone to help themselves.

The great advantage of a buffet is that you're not restricted by the number of guests you can fit round your dining table, so you can host more friends than you typically would otherwise. It's also a delightfully cosy and relaxed way of entertaining: people can come and go as they please; children can run around; those who wish can pop in for a drink and a quick hello, while others can stay, partying on, well into the wee hours.

A HOLIDAY PARTY WITH LOTS OF FOOD

Ginger and Apricot Glazed Ham
   (see page 124)
Camembert and Cranberry Pithivier
   (see page 146)
Miniature Baked Potatoes, either
   without the crème fraîche, caviar
   or gold leaf, or just serve those on
   the side for people who want them
   (see page 110)
Shaved Brussels Sprouts with Pecorino,
   Cranberries and Pecans
   (see page 191)

Panettone Woodland Cake
   (see page 200)

MAKE-DAYS-AHEAD LUNCH OR DINNER BUFFET

Ginger and Apricot Glazed Ham, served at
   room temperature (see page 124)
Red Cabbage, Feta, Hazelnut and Mint Salad
   (see page 188)
Christmas Salad (see page 182)
Good Luck Salad (see page 192)

Flourless Chocolate Orange Cake
   (see page 212)

The Big Party with Little By Way of Food and Lots By Way of Drinks

This is a tried-and-tested way to cram in seeing lots of people, all in one go. It's also a very sensible way to host if you're the kind of person who doesn't really love to cook, or who finds catering for a larger crowd intimidating. I've given ideas for small bites – sticky sausages, mince pies, what have you – but I do so with the caveat that none of these need be homemade. You could just as well bulk-buy ready-made bits, or encourage everyone to bring along a dish; or, better still, make happily do with bowls of nuts, crisps (everyone loves crisps) and popcorn dotted around the house, alongside plenty of drinks.

For a big to-do, you'll want a playlist, be it traditional carols for everyone to sing along to, or Christmas songs (a little Sinatra, perhaps, or something more contemporary with a Christmas twist and more of a pop feel to it), or whatever you like that feels as though it will get you and your guests into a party mood.

You might also want to think about setting up a separate 'bar area'. This can be as simple as a tray with glasses, a bucket of ice and a few bottles on the kitchen table, on top of a cabinet or a console table. This way, guests can help themselves to jugs of drinks, water, wine and whatever else you lay out, without you needing to be constantly running around to fetch glasses and top up drinks.

And for my part, I quite enjoy some kind of loose theme, so perhaps encourage everyone to wear a Christmas jumper or to dress up for a 'glamorous' or 'festive' dress code. Also bear in mind that, for these sorts of events, when they're standing around, your guests typically eat much less than they do when sitting down, but drink much more, so it's worth catering quantities accordingly.

MULLED WINE AND MINCE PIES PARTY

Maxim's Mince Pies and Puff Pastry Mince Pies, with Boozy Amaretto Butter and Easy Peasy Hot Brandy Custard (see pages 228, 229 and 293)

Gingery Christmas Cake, plain with no decorative topping (see page 202), or shop-bought fruit cake for ease, served with cheese

Olga's Sticky Sausages (see page 88)

Mulled Wine (see page 89)

Spiced Hot Apple Juice (see page 96)

A HOLIDAY COCKTAIL PARTY WITH (ALMOST) NO FOOD

Christmas Mocktails (see page 97)

Amarena Amaretto Sours (see page 92)

Saffron Popcorn (see page 95)

Pistachio, Almond and Parmesan Cantucci (see page 91)

Gorgonzola-Walnut Panettone Crostini (see page 92)

COCKTAILS, CANAPÉS AND CAROLS

Amarena Amaretto Sours (see page 92)

Chestnut Martinis (see page 98)

Crisps and caviar (see page 101)

Saffron mayonnaise with red chicory leaves for dipping (see page 101)

A towering centrepiece (or two) of mozzarella minis and cherry tomatoes (see page 313)

Miniature Peppermint Meringues (see page 279)

JOLLY EGG NOG PARTY

Holiday Mood Egg Nog (see page 86)

Maxim's Mince Pies and Puff Pastry Mince Pies (see pages 228 and 229)

Gilded Gingerbread Tree Ornaments, made as cookies rather than ornaments (see page 266)

A 'BITS AND BOBS FROM THE SHOPS' HOLIDAY PARTY

Prosecco with pomegranate seeds

Sparkling pomegranate and elderflower cordial with pomegranate seeds

Bowls of crisps, nuts and olives

Gingernut biscuits with blue cheese (see page 101)

A whole panettone, sliced into smaller pieces

Christmas Eve

In Italy, the big celebration is on Christmas Eve, and growing up, Italian friends would always spoil us with feasts of seafood, buttery pasta with white truffle, whole baked sea bass and more varieties of panettone and pandoro than you could count. Now I have my own family, I treasure a cosy Christmas Eve in, all about comfort and that glorious feeling of anticipation. So here are menus for both variations on the theme, as the mood takes you.

FANCY CHRISTMAS EVE DINNER FOR A SMALL GANG

Walnut and Gorgonzola Stuffed Pears (see page 114)

Pork Tenderloin with Persimmons and Pomegranate (see page 131)
'Hedgehog' Potatoes (see page 164)
Red Chicory and Candied Pecan Salad (see page 181)

Sugar Plum Sorbet (see page 258)

MAKE-AHEAD-AND-DON'T-HAVE-TO-THINK-ABOUT-IT CHRISTMAS EVE DINNER

Mushroom Tortellini in Brodo (see page 105)
Some good crusty bread
A plate of good charcuterie

Gorgonzola, Fig and Hazelnut Terrine (see page 255) and/or Pomegranate Campari Jelly (see page 248)

A COSY CHRISTMAS EVE DINNER FOR A FEW OR FOR MANY

Gnocchi and Pumpkin Gratin (see page 154)
Wilted Kale with Marmite Butter (see page 173)
Shaved Brussels Sprouts with Pecorino, Cranberries and Pecans (see page 191)

Puff Pastry Mince Pies with Easy Peasy Hot Brandy Custard (see pages 229 and 293)

A VEGETARIAN CHRISTMAS EVE DINNER FOR A FEW

Camembert and Cranberry Pithivier (see page 146), made with vegetarian Camembert, if needed
Wilted Kale with Marmite (see page 173)
Good Luck Salad (see page 192)

Christmas Pavlova (see page 262)

A CHRISTMAS EVE PARTY

Mulled Wine (see page 89)

Spiced Hot Apple Juice (see page 96)

Gorgonzola-Walnut Panettone Crostini
(see page 92)

Ginger and Apricot Glazed Ham
(see page 124)

Camembert and Cranberry Pithivier
(see page 146)

Red Cabbage Panzanella (see page 186)

Christmas Salad (see page 182)

Red Chicory and Candied Pecan Salad
(see page 181)

Black and Gold Cake (see page 206)

Maxim's Mince Pies with Boozy Amaretto
Butter (see pages 228 and 293)

CHRISTMAS EVE SUPPER-ON-A-TRAY-WITH A HOLIDAY MOVIE

Holiday Mood Egg Nog (see page 86)

Saffron Popcorn (see page 95)

Panettone Grilled Cheese Sandwich
(see page 80)

Christmas Brownies (see page 283)

A GLAMOROUS CHRISTMAS EVE

Amarena Amaretto Sours (see page 92)

Pistachio, Almond and Parmesan Cantucci
(see page 91)

Seafood and Saffron Cocktail (see page 109)

Black Truffle, Mascarpone and Quail's Egg
Pasta Pie (see page 150)

Red Chicory and Candied Pecan Salad
(see page 181)

Shaved Brussels Sprouts with Pecorino,
Cranberries and toasted almonds,
instead of pecans (see page 191)

Pomegranate Campari Jelly (see page 248)
and/or Sugar Plum Sorbet (see page 258)

A VEGETARIAN CHRISTMAS EVE DINNER FOR A CROWD

A couple (or more) of Beetroot and
Horseradish Galettes (see page 149), served
at room temperature if that's easier

Red Cabbage Panzanella (see page 186)

Shaved Fennel, Grapefruit and Pomegranate
Salad (see page 189)

Gingerbread, Cranberry and Zabaione Trifle
(see page 250)

Christmas Day

Hosting Christmas lunch for the first time can feel intimidating, but the secret no one tells you is that it is just like cooking a Sunday roast. So, if you've done that before, then you already know what you're doing. A turkey is, in practice, just a big chicken, with cooking times and so forth that just need to be tweaked a little. (You'll find step-by-step instructions for this at pages 137–139.) The rest of the meal is easy. It's variations on a theme of potatoes, greens, perhaps some red cabbage or roasted parsnips, you might want stuffing… all simple dishes to prepare and that you can comfortably cook in advance. Don't worry: you'll find a wealth of tips in the recipes on how to tackle each and every step.

You could of course wake up on Christmas morning and set about cooking lunch from there, pottering in a leisurely fashion in the kitchen, taking your time. And on any other day of the year that would be completely fine, better then fine, even: it would be a very good day. But on Christmas Day there are a vast amount of other exciting things to be doing. I, for one, don't want to spend the whole of Christmas morning cooking (and I say this even as someone who truly loves to cook). I want to spend time with my family; I want to watch my boys open their stockings; and yes, I want to sit in my pyjamas eating soft panettone and sipping luxuriously on hot chocolate. And I can do all of that, I can relax and then enjoy a feast of a lunch; I can have my proverbial cake and eat it too, just so long as I have prepared in advance.

Do as much as far ahead of time as you can muster: lay the table the night before; prepare breakfast (or the bulk of it) the night before too; freeze things over a few weeks or even months if you can; pre-make things. Think realistically about what you are planning on cooking and when you're going to cook it and *delegate* (clearly and in advance), so that you can enjoy the day fully when it comes. I promise, you'll thank me if you do.

Cooking something for the first time is always infinitely more intimidating than cooking a recipe you know well. So, if you can, do try some of your recipes ahead of Christmas Day. To roast a full turkey for a dry run may feel excessive perhaps, but it's no great hardship to eat a few extra roast potatoes, or charred Brussels sprouts, or sticky, ruby-red cabbage with your dinner in the days and months leading up to Christmas, just to get the hang of things. And if nothing else, take the time to read the recipes well and in full beforehand, so that you know exactly what you're doing when; it will make things very much easier. Another trick is to list all your timings for when you need to put things in the oven and take them out; when you need to toss the salad, or warm the red cabbage. Whatever it is you need to do, write it all down and give it a time, even if you think you'll remember (I set alarms on my phone to remind me). I say this

because it's the accumulation of little things to think about, while fielding happy distractions from other directions, that is what so often makes Christmas cooking feel stressful. There's a page at the back of this book dedicated to your own Christmas lunch timings: use it to chart what you need to do when (ideally in pencil, so you can easily make changes) and then you can refer back to it year on year.

The biggest challenge we face on Christmas Day in the kitchen is that most often we find ourselves cooking for far more people than we're used to. The quantities can, of course, easily be scaled up or down, as you like and as you need; and within each menu, I've also tried to make life easier by striking a balance of dishes that roast in the oven and those you can warm on the hob (or even serve at room temperature), so that oven space – always at such a premium and never more so than on Christmas Day – doesn't prove a problem. Nonetheless, it's worth taking a moment to assess your kitchen: think about how much oven, fridge and surface space you have at your disposal; decide (roughly, at least) what roasting trays and serving dishes you're going to use. And do all this beforehand, if you possibly can, so there are no hiccups on the day itself.

As I write all this, I'm highly conscious that you'll have your own favourites, your own views on what Christmas lunch or dinner should look and taste like. So it is with some trepidation that I make suggestions overleaf as to what you might want to eat on Christmas Day of all days. I, by no means, would presume to challenge your traditions, but if you're looking for a tried-and-tested method, a blueprint to follow, where you don't need to think beyond following the steps outlined, then I hope you'll find something here to take your fancy. Or, at the very least, a few dishes to add to your repertoire and make your own.

Whatever you choose to cook, my one insistence is that you err on the side of excess: it is Christmas after all. I would say that, of course, being the more-is-more sort of person that I am. But I also insist upon this point for practical reasons: the leftovers are how I feed my family, with minimum effort and very much delight, in the days following Christmas. They bring festive joy beyond the day itself... And if you turn to page 294, you'll find some specific suggestions for what to do with any of that glorious excess.

Continued overleaf

CHRISTMAS LUNCH WITH ALL THE TRIMMINGS

Pomegranate-Glazed Turkey with Cranberry and Marsala Sauce (see pages 118 and 291)

Make-Ahead Gravy (see page 291)

The Best Roast Potatoes (see page 160)

Nonna's Stuffing (see page 167)

Martin's Ruby Red Cabbage (see page 170)

Sticky Roast Sprouts with Dates and Pistachios (see page 169)

Especially Good Maple-Roast Parsnips (see page 171)

Hidden Orange Christmas Pudding with Boozy Amaretto Butter and/or Easy Peasy Hot Brandy Custard (see pages 242 and 293)

CHRISTMAS LUNCH IF YOU'RE WORKING WITH A SMALL OVEN

Creamy Chestnut Soup with Pomegranate (see page 106)

Ginger and Apricot Glazed Ham, made ahead of time and served at room temperature (see page 124)

The Best Roast Potatoes (see page 160)

Panettone, Chestnut and Sage Stuffing (see page 166)

Martin's Ruby Red Cabbage (see page 170)

Shaved Brussels Sprouts with Pecorino, Cranberries and Pecans (see page 191)

Hidden Orange Christmas Pudding with Boozy Amaretto Butter and/or Easy Peasy Hot Brandy Custard (see pages 242 and 293)

CHRISTMAS LUNCH IN THE WARMER WEATHER

Seafood and Saffron Cocktail (see page 109)

Ginger and Apricot Glazed Ham, made ahead of time and served at room temperature (see page 124)

Red Cabbage Panzanella (see page 186)

Christmas Salad (see page 182)

Shaved Brussels Sprouts with Pecorino, Cranberries and Pecans (see page 191)

Salted Caramel Zuccotto (see page 247)

A VEGETARIAN CHRISTMAS FEAST

Walnut and Gorgonzola Stuffed Pears (see page 114), replacing the Gorgonzola with Dolcelatte, if needed

Camembert and Cranberry Pithivier (see page 146), made with vegetarian Camembert, if needed

Christmas Salad (see page 182), made with vegetarian feta, if needed

Wilted Kale with Marmite Butter (see page 173)

Wild Rice, Lentil, Chestnut and Pomegranate Salad (see page 178)

Gingerbread, Cranberry and Zabaione Trifle (see page 250)

AN ALTERNATIVE VEGETARIAN CHRISTMAS FEAST

Creamy Chestnut Soup with Pomegranate
(see page 106)

Stuffed Pumpkin with Wild Rice, Cranberries
and Chestnuts (see page 157)

Martin's Ruby Red Cabbage (see page 170)

Sticky Roast Sprouts with Dates and
Pistachios (see page 169)

Gingery Christmas Cake (see page 202)

A VEGAN CHRISTMAS FEAST

Chestnut Soup with Pomegranate, with no
crème fraîche (see page 106)

Nut and Cranberry Terrine (see page 142)

The Best Roast Potatoes (see page 160)

Martin's Ruby Red Cabbage (see page 170)

Sticky Roast Sprouts with Dates and
Pistachios (see page 169, use vegan butter)

Especially Good Maple-Roast Parsnips
(see page 171)

Sugar Plum Sorbet (see page 258)

CHRISTMAS LUNCH FOR A CROWD

Potted Salmon with Preserved Lemon
(see page 113)

Rolled Turkey Breast with Chestnut and Sage
Stuffing, with Cranberry and Marsala Sauce
(see pages 120 and 291)

Make-Ahead Gravy (see page 291)

The Best Roast Potatoes (see page 160)

Red Cabbage Panzanella (see page 186)

Roast Savoy Cabbage with Pancetta,
Chestnuts and Gorgonzola (see page 174)

Gingery Christmas Cake (see page 202)

A QUICK-FIX CHRISTMAS LUNCH

Seafood and Saffron Cocktail (see page 109)

Roast Poussins with Crisp Prosciutto and
Sage (see page 127)

Panettone, Chestnut and Sage Stuffing
(see page 166)

Sticky Roast Sprouts with Dates and
Pistachios (see page 169)

Martin's Ruby Red Cabbage (see page 170)

Pandoro Tower (see page 211)

CHRISTMAS LUNCH FOR THOSE WHO DON'T LIKE TURKEY OR CHRISTMAS PUDDING

Pork Tenderloin with Persimmons and
Pomegranate with Cranberry and Marsala
Sauce (see pages 131 and 291)

Make-Ahead Gravy (see page 291)

The Best Roast Potatoes (see page 160)

Roast Savoy Cabbage with Pancetta,
Chestnuts and Gorgonzola (see page 174)

Red Chicory and Candied Pecan Salad
(see page 181)

Chocolate and Chestnut Yule Log
(see page 215)

Boxing Day...

....

... AND HOSTING IN THAT BIT IN BETWEEN CHRISTMAS AND NEW YEAR

This, for me, is all about 'zhuzh-ing up' leftovers: you'll find a list on page 294 of dishes that work well for repurposing any over-catering. The formula I loosely like to follow is to serve something that I've improvised with what we have kicking around in the fridge, alongside a dish I've made well in advance and is ready to go, such as Egg Nog Cream Pie, or Maxim's Mince Pies with Easy Peasy Hot Brandy Custard (see pages 236, 228 and 293). This kind of menu both makes the host's life easier and also creates the kind of cosy atmosphere we crave in that languid stretch between Christmas and New Year.

As to decorations and so forth, I tend to keep things simpler after Christmas Day, but you still might like to add a cracker to each place setting. Or perhaps, if you would like to make it feel special without being overtly 'festive', you could give each guest a menu, either hand-written, or printed via a website such as Papier, or designed and printed yourself... just make sure to do it well in advance. Or you could give some other kind of sweet memento, such as a Polaroid photo of each guest from the lunch, or a photo from another special moment.

BOXING DAY LEFTOVERS FEAST

Leftover cold cuts

Cheesy Fondue Roast Potato Bake
   (see page 163)

Red Chicory and Candied Pecan Salad
   (see page 181)

Red Cabbage Panzanella (see page 186)

Salted Caramel Zuccotto (see page 247)

A BOXING DAY BRUNCH

Christmas Mocktails (see page 97)

Cheesy Ham and Croissant Bake (see page 83)

Turkey sandwiches (see page 294): lay all the
   bits out and everyone make their own

Red Berry Breakfast Panzanella (see page 76),
   made with leftover panettone

PICKY THINGS LIGHT BOXING DAY LUNCH OR SUPPER

Beetroot and Horseradish Galette
   (see page 149)

Shaved Fennel, Grapefruit and Pomegranate
   Salad (see page 189)

Good Luck Salad (see page 192)

Maxim's Mince Pies with Boozy Amaretto
   Butter (see pages 228 and 293)

New Year

It's a special thing to celebrate the end of the old year and the beginning of the new with people you love. You could of course go to a restaurant or a fancy gala, but, at home, you can eat what you want, be with the people you love most, stay up as long as you like, and then not worry about the logistics of getting home in the wee hours of the morning on one of the biggest public holidays of the year.

When I think New Year's Eve, I think gold and glitz. That translates to how I decorate the table: gold candles; gold ribbon to tie napkins; gold pens to write place cards; fruits to decorate the table gilded with edible gold leaf; sparklers stuck in dessert. It's quite fun to keep the Christmas decorations and add new elements: balloons, streamers, ribbons hanging from the ceiling.

You'll need a good playlist and prosecco (or Champagne) aplenty, though I'm rather partial to mixing a few Chestnut Martinis (see page 98), especially for a glamorous occasion such as this. When planning the evening, it's worth giving some thought as to how to keep people entertained until midnight, whether by making sure you have a good playlist and a corner set aside for dancing, or perhaps parlour or card games to play. A later start to dinner also helps keep the momentum going, so everyone is still in the mood to have a good time when the clock strikes midnight, rather than ready to rush home. I like a smarter dress code, because I love an excuse to dress up and it seems appropriate to send off the year in a degree of style; but a wildly fabulous evening can be had in pyjamas just as in a fancy frock. As to format, this depends on how many people you're hosting: for larger groups a buffet, where everyone can mill around, tends to work best and is certainly simpler to manage as host: all you need do is lay all the food out on a big table and encourage everyone to help themselves. For smaller groups, a more intimate sit-down dinner perhaps feels a little more celebratory: either way, you'll find menu suggestions here for both sorts of party.

All that said, there are years when I find myself shying away from the late night revelry of New Year's Eve, but still want to mark the occasion, so end up celebrating on the day itself. If the eve is all decadence and glamour, there is a sense of bright, wholesome promise to New Year's Day which I love every bit as much, perhaps more. And, forever superstitious, the one non-negotiable for me is a menu that includes at least some of those foods – lentils, pomegranates and so on – that promise health, prosperity and all good things in the year to come.

A VEGETARIAN NEW YEAR'S EVE FEAST

Creamy Chestnut Soup with Pomegranate
(see page 106)

Black Truffle, Mascarpone and Quail's Egg
Pasta Pie (see page 150), with vegetarian
cheeses, if needed

Orange, Carrot and Pistachio Salad
(see page 185)

A crisp green salad

Chocolate and Chestnut Yule Log
(see page 215)

A SPECIAL NEW YEAR'S EVE DINNER FOR A FEW

Gilded Miniature Baked Potatoes with Crème
Fraîche and Caviar (see page 110)

Cotechino and Spinach Roll (see page 132)

Good Luck Salad (see page 192)

Roast Savoy Cabbage with Pancetta,
Chestnuts and Gorgonzola (see page 174)

Black Cherry and Ricotta Cheesecake
(see page 218)

NEW YEAR'S EVE DINNER FOR A CROWD

Creamy Chestnut Soup with Pomegranate
(see page 106)

Ginger and Apricot Glazed Ham (see
page 124)

Wild Rice, Lentil, Chestnut and Pomegranate
Salad (see page 178)

Wilted Kale with Marmite Butter
(see page 173)

Red Chicory and Candied Pecan Salad
(see page 181)

Pistachio Cream and Ginger Pie
(see page 235)

A BIG NEW YEAR'S EVE BUFFET DINNER PARTY

Chestnut Martinis (see page 98)

Bowls of crisps with caviar (see page 101)

Olga's Sticky Sausages (see page 88)

A couple of Beetroot and Horseradish Galettes
(see page 149)

A big dish of Good Luck Salad (see page 192)

Gorgonzola, Fig and Hazelnut Terrine
(see page 255) with bread and crispbreads
to serve

Christmas Brownies (see page 283)

A TALISMANIC NEW YEAR'S DAY LUNCH

Pork Tenderloin with Persimmons and
Pomegranate (see page 131)

Good Luck Salad (see page 192)

Cheesy Fondue Roast Potato Bake
(see page 163)

Shaved Brussels Sprouts with Pecorino,
Cranberries and Pecans (see page 191)

Salted Caramel Zuccotto (see page 247)

Some Thoughts on Managing Dietary Requirements

It can be challenging to cater for different dietary requirements at the best of times, but at Christmas, perhaps, especially so. So much of the magic of Christmas lies in tradition and yet the classic festive menu offers little that's suitable for vegetarians, vegans or those with gluten or dairy allergies.

My strong preference is always to go with a menu that everyone can share, rather than cooking a separate dish just for the person who is restricted in what they can eat. Sometimes this means tweaking the meal for everyone: I might roast a whole pumpkin, stuffed with wild rice, cranberries and chestnuts (see page 157), for instance, instead of roasting a turkey, to make the menu vegetarian. At other times, it's just a matter of adding an alternative main course that works for everyone: I might roast a turkey, but also add a Beetroot and Horseradish Galette (see page 149), so that guests can help themselves to one or the other, or both. Then for the remaining dishes, where it's possible to tweak the recipes to accommodate everyone, that's what I do. Where things really can't be adapted, I either opt to go in a different direction, or make sure that there are plenty of other suitable dishes on the table too, so that everyone feels satisfied.

You'll have seen in this chapter plenty of lists of recipes that are suitable for (or variations of the recipes that are suitable for) vegetarians and vegans; hopefully, they will help you easily find dishes from this book to choose from when putting together your own menus.

Your
Christmas

These last few pages are for you: to make lists, to scribble notes, things to remember, lessons learned and things to do, to make your own plan for Christmas done in your way to your own timetable. I hope you'll use it this year and refer back to it in years to come. You'll find a checklist at the beginning: a gentle prompt as to what you might want to think about in the build-up to the holidays. Not everything will feel relevant, so cross out, highlight and add to it at will. Please make it yours. One you've got your list, add each task to the Festive Season Planner with a timeframe: this might be a wishful timeline, in a my-goal-is-to-get-this-done-by-this-date sort of a way, which you can correct as you go. Or you might prefer to gradually note down things as you do them; then next year you'll have your own plan and calendar to follow. Each year you can tweak it, as needed. You'll also find space to list people you want to give presents (or send cards) to, which you can update year on year, so you don't forget anyone or unintentionally give them the same gift twice. There's also a section for noting menus you've enjoyed and plan to repeat, and pages to scribble down your seating plans. You'll also find a chart for Christmas lunch timings, which you could (and should) just as well use for any other big, celebratory meals that involve careful juggling to bring all the dishes together at the right moment. This planner encourages you to break the timings down in a detailed way, in fact the more detailed the better. I find this particularly useful, as it can be a headache to work it all out, so I appreciate referring back to my notes, and if needed tweaking them, rather than starting from scratch. It's just one less thing to think about.

As with the rest of this book, I hope these pages will prove useful to you; but above all I hope that, as you scribble away on them, they come to hold many treasured memories for you, too. Happy Christmas!

Checklist of Things to Think About

ADVENT CALENDARS
☐ Buy or make calendars (see page 34)
☐ Source gifts
☐ Wrap gifts (see page 30)

CHRISTMAS CARDS
☐ Make/update list of people to send cards to
☐ Check addresses are up to date
☐ Buy or make cards
☐ Write cards
☐ Post cards

DECORATING THE HOUSE
☐ Order or buy the Christmas tree (see page 45)
☐ Make or buy (or get out of storage) any decorations
☐ Decorate the tree (and the house, if decorating beyond a tree, see page 46)
☐ Buy or make a festive wreath (see page 54)

FESTIVE BAKING
☐ Bake Christmas cakes (see page 202)
☐ Decorate Christmas cakes (see page 202)
☐ Make mincemeat (see page 286)
☐ Make cookie dough and freeze it (see pages 266 and 270)
☐ Bake Christmas biscuits

HOLIDAY HOSTING
☐ Get dates in the diary
☐ Put together guest list(s)
☐ Plan menus and make time for shopping and cooking (see pages 23–27)
☐ Put together playlist(s)

☐ Make (see page 50) or buy Christmas crackers

PRESENTS
☐ Make list of people to give presents to and ideas for what to give
☐ Shop for (or make!) presents
☐ Buy supplies for wrapping (see page 30)
☐ Make time to wrap presents

CHRISTMAS DAY
☐ Plan menu and cooking schedule
☐ Think about meals beyond Christmas lunch (Christmas Eve, Christmas morning breakfast, Christmas Day supper) and have a loose plan (even if it's takeaway), or shop for supplies and allocate time for cooking meals, or elements of meals, in advance
☐ Shop for ingredients
☐ Plan your table (any decorations, crackers and so on) and source ahead of time, as required (see pages 312–316)
☐ Lay table for lunch

BOXING DAY AND BETWEEN CHRISTMAS AND NEW YEAR
☐ Think about meals beyond Christmas and New Year, even if it's takeaway (or see pages 339–341)
☐ Plan menus (see pages 318–341)
☐ Make time for any shopping or cooking
☐ Stock up on essentials that make it easy to throw a meal together at the last minute (see page 27)

Festive Season Planner

TIME	TO DO	DONE

Christmas Gifts
(and/or Cards) Checklist

NAME	GIFT	BOUGHT (OR MADE)	WRAPPED	SENT

Menu Planner

MENU
Serves:

MENU
Serves:

MENU
Serves:

NOTES (WINES SERVED, TABLE
DECORATIONS AND SO ON)

Menu Planner

MENU

Serves:

MENU

Serves:

MENU

Serves:

NOTES (WINES SERVED, TABLE
DECORATIONS AND SO ON)

Seating Plans

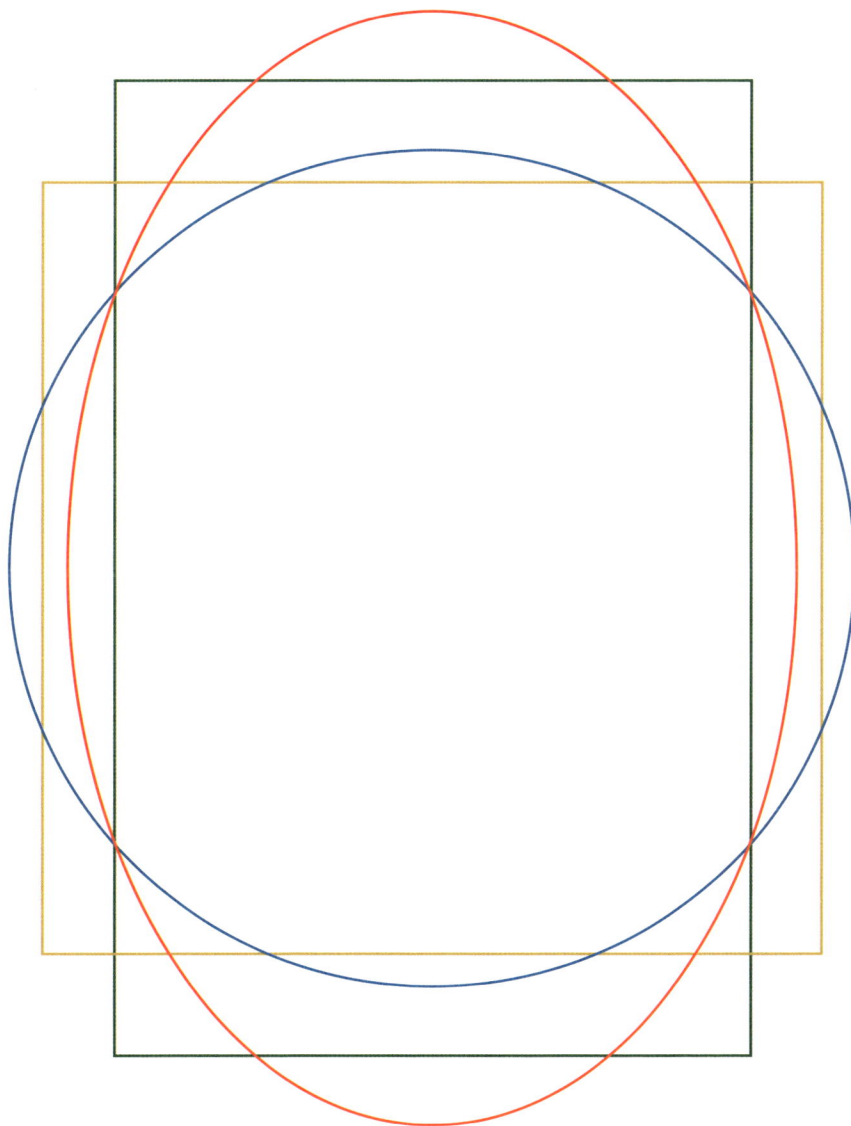

Christmas Lunch Timings

TIME	TO DO	DONE

Notes

Index

About the author

Skye McAlpine is a cookery writer who believes that food tastes best when shared with others. She is the author of three other cookbooks, *A Table in Venice*, *A Table for Friends* and *A Table Full of Love*. She writes a monthly recipe column for *The Sunday Times*, as well as the popular Substack newsletter 'The Dolce Vita Diaries'; and contributes to publications from around the world. When she's not cooking or writing, Skye works on designs for her own range of tabletop essentials, Skye McAlpine TAVOLA.

She lives between Venice, where she grew up and where her heart lies, and London, where her work most often takes her.

Acknowledgements

I'm conscious of what an extraordinary privilege it is to be given the space to write about something you love. So first and foremost, I would like to thank my editor, Rowan Yapp: *The Christmas Companion* was your idea, Rowan, and it's been my dream. I'm so very proud of how it's turned out. Thank you for taking a chance on me, and for supporting me to create the book I so strongly felt it needed to be. My profound thanks also to Lena Hall and Rose Brown for your indispensable editorial contribution, Laura Brodie for your work in production, Ellen Williams and Rob Cox in marketing, Caroline Stearns for the brilliant Americanisation of this text, Greg Heinimann, of course, for the beautiful cover, and everyone else at Bloomsbury who I know has played an important part in bringing these words and recipes to life. So very much goes into the making of a book; yet you make the process seem and feel effortless; and you're the loveliest team to work with. Thank you.

On which note, I am especially grateful to my project editor, Lucy Bannell, for so expertly pummelling the stream of consciousness that was this original manuscript into the hard-working, finished Christmas manual I'm leafing through excitedly right now. Lucy, thank you for patiently bearing with my chaos, for being so very thoughtful in your comments, for working late nights and weekends, and for genuinely caring about each little detail as much as (if not more than) I do. It has been, once again, a true privilege to work with you.

As to the design of these pages, I am so grateful to Clare Baggaley for deftly capturing the intangible, elusive magic of Christmas and translating it into this beautiful thing I can hold, see and feel: Clare, what an utterly enchanting book you have designed. Thank you also to my darling friend, Alice Edwards, for the lovingly painted illustrations which grace these pages and make them sing: they are just another example of what a creative, generous, loving and thoughtful friend you are; and of how lucky I am to have you in my life.

This book wouldn't be what it is, and wouldn't look how it looks, of course, without pictures; and for these I owe a huge debt to Ellie Mulligan for creating the most exquisite food; and to Stephie Howard and Aloha Shaw for helping me to capture its magic. I've loved working with you: and even though we've collaborated on three books together now and I really should know better by this point, I never cease to be amazed and inspired by what wonderfully talented women you are. My thanks also to Kristine Jakobsson, Eden Owen-Jones, and Talia Yilmaz for your Herculean efforts in the kitchen which made our shoot days run so very much more smoothly than I ever could have hoped.

The real foundation of any good cookbook is hard-working, solid recipes; and I wouldn't feel the absolute confidence I do in the food here, if it weren't

for Poppy Mahon's brilliant work testing each and every single recipe with the same trusty thoroughness as the recipes in all my other books and countless magazine columns. Poppy, you are a culinary genius and I don't know what I would do without you!

With every book I've worked on (and this – improbably, extraordinarily – makes four now), I am ever more grateful to my best cheerleader and literary agent, Caroline Michel. Thank you for showing such joyful enthusiasm in all my projects (even the more hare-brained ones), but in this one especially. I love that you love Christmas as much as I do. Thank you also to Laura Creyke and Mark Hutchinson for your generous encouragement, sensible advice and for the very many hours spent plotting and planning together: I always know I can count on you to tell me what I need to hear, just as I know I can count on you to steadfastly fight my corner.

Lastly, and perhaps the biggest thank you of all, I owe to my friends and family who have gamely lived 'Christmas' year-round with me for the three-plus years this book has been in the making. An extra special thank you to my mother, Romilly, for showing me how to 'do Christmas properly' and for sharing her unrivalled pudding and stuffing recipes. And to my dearest friends Bryony Sheridan, Delilah Khomo, Ashley Baker, Carolyn Asome, Richard Atkinson, and Cleo Brock Abraham: thank you for being so generous with your thoughts, sharing your recipes, testing mine, and offering me those precious words of encouragement I needed when things felt sticky. I am very lucky to call you my friends; and feel immensely proud to do so.

And last but by no means least, to my husband, Anthony, and my precious boys, Aeneas and Achille: for me, there is no such thing as a happy Christmas without you.

BLOOMSBURY PUBLISHING
Bloomsbury Publishing Plc
50 Bedford Square, London, WC1B 3DP, UK
Bloomsbury Publishing Ireland Limited,
29 Earlsfort Terrace, Dublin 2, Ireland

BLOOMSBURY, BLOOMSBURY PUBLISHING
and the Diana logo are trademarks of Bloomsbury Publishing Plc

First published in Great Britain in 2025
Text © Skye McAlpine, 2025

Photographs © Skye McAlpine, 2025

Skye McAlpine has asserted her right under the Copyright, Designs
and Patents Act, 1988, to be identified as Author and Photographer
of this work.

For legal purposes, the acknowledgements on pages 366–367
constitute an extension of this copyright page.

A catalogue record for this book is available from the British Library.
ISBN: HB: 978-1-5266-8157-7; eBook: 978-1-5266-8159-1
2 4 6 8 10 9 7 5 3 1

Project Editor: Lucy Bannell
Designer: Clare Baggaley
Photographers: Skye McAlpine, Stephie Howard and Aloha Shaw
Illustrator: Alice Edwards
Food Stylist: Eleanor Mulligan
Indexer: Vanessa Bird

Printed and bound in China by C&C Offset Printing Co., Ltd.

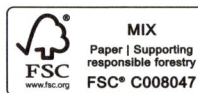

MIX
Paper | Supporting
responsible forestry
FSC® C008047

To find out more about our authors and books,
visit www.bloomsbury.com and sign up for our newsletters.

For product safety related questions contact
productsafety@bloomsbury.com